Maximalism in Conte
American Literature

This book begins a new and foundational discussion of maximalism by investigating how the treatment of detail in contemporary literature impels readers to navigate, tolerate, and enrich the cultural landscape of postindustrial America. It studies the maximalist novels of David Foster Wallace, Nicholson Baker, Thomas Pynchon, and others, considering how overly detailed writing serves the institutional, emotional, and intellectual needs of contemporary readers and writers. The book argues that maximalist novels not only exceed perceived limits of style, subject matter, and scope, but strive to remake the usefulness of books in contemporary culture, refreshing the act of reading. Levey shows that although these novels are preoccupied with detail and description, they are relatively unconcerned with the traditional goals of representation. Instead, they use detail to communicate particular values and fantasies of intelligence, enthusiasm, and ability attached to the management of complex and excessive information. Whether reinvigorating the banal and trivial in mainstream culture, or soothing anxieties of human insufficiency in the age of automation and the internet, these texts model significant abilities, rather than just objects of significance, and encourage readers to develop habits of reading that complement the demands of an increasingly detailed culture. Drawing upon a diverse range of theoretical schools and cultural texts, including Thing Theory, Marxism, New Formalism, playlists, blogs, and archival manuscripts, the book proposes a new understanding of maximalist writing and a new way of approaching the usefulness of literary objects in contemporary culture.

Nick Levey teaches in the English Department at La Trobe University, Australia. He publishes on contemporary fiction and is currently writing about post-press literature and the rise of digital self-publishing.

Routledge Studies in Contemporary Literature

For a full list of titles in this series, please visit www.routledge.com.

9 Spatial Politics in Contemporary London Literature
Writing Architecture and the Body
Laura Colombino

10 Diseases and Disorders in Contemporary Fiction
The Syndrome Syndrome
Edited by T.J. Lustig and James Peacock

11 Identity and Form in Contemporary Literature
Edited by Ana María Sánchez-Arce

12 The Vampire in Contemporary Popular Literature
Lorna Piatti-Farnell

13 Religion in Cormac McCarthy's Fiction
Apocryphal Borderlands
Manuel Broncano

14 The Ethics and Aesthetics of Vulnerability in Contemporary British
Fiction
Jean-Michel Ganteau

15 Genre Fiction in New India
Post-Millennial Receptions of "Weird" Narratives
E. Dawson Varughese

16 Rethinking Race and Identity in Contemporary British Fiction
Sara Upstone

17 A Poetics of Trauma after 9/11
Representing Trauma in a Digitized Present
Katharina Donn

18 The Cultural Politics of Chick Lit
Popular Fiction, Postfeminism and Representation
Heike Missler

19 Maximalism in Contemporary American Literature
The Uses of Detail
Nick Levey

Maximalism in Contemporary American Literature
The Uses of Detail

Nick Levey

Routledge
Taylor & Francis Group

LONDON AND NEW YORK

First published 2017 by Routledge

2 Park Square, Milton Park, Abingdon, Oxfordshire OX14 4RN
52 Vanderbilt Avenue, New York, NY 10017

Routledge is an imprint of the Taylor & Francis Group, an informa business

First issued in paperback 2019

Library of Congress Cataloging-in-Publication Data
CIP data has been applied for.

ISBN: 978-1-138-67226-0 (hbk)
ISBN: 978-0-367-87850-4 (pbk)

Typeset in Sabon
by codeMantra

This book is dedicated to the memory of my father, Peter Howard Levey.

Contents

Acknowledgments   ix

Introduction   1

1   Giants and Junk: Power-Reading Thomas Pynchon's
    Gravity's Rainbow   37

2   On Flunking: Maximalist Description in David Foster
    Wallace's *Infinite Jest*   55

3   Data-Sickle: Maximalism and White-Collar Aesthetics in
    David Foster Wallace's *The Pale King*   76

4   Just Maximalist Things: Nicholson Baker's *The Mezzanine*
    and Objects of Curiosity   97

5   Housebound: Domestic Excess in Nicholson Baker's *Room
    Temperature*   116

6   Mindless Pleasures: Playlists, Unemployment, and
    Thomas Pynchon's *Inherent Vice*   132

    Conclusion: Overflow: The Margins of American Maximalism   149

    Bibliography   165
    Index   173

Acknowledgments

Writing a book tends to be a solitary exercise, so I'm grateful for the friends, family, and colleagues who've reminded me that there are, indeed, other people out there in the world.

This project has been supported at all stages by the La Trobe University English department and the Disciplinary Research Program in English, Theatre, and Drama.

My thanks go to Sofia Ahlberg for her enthusiasm, Alison Ravenscroft for her encouragement and support, Sue Thomas for steering me in the direction of grants and other funding opportunities, Henry Veggian for feedback and advice, and to Liz Levine and the other editors at Routledge for helping turn these words into a book.

Thanks to Anthony for chats about poetry and science, to Rachel for warmth, and to mum for patience.

I want to give a special thanks to Chris Palmer for his extensive feedback, encouragement, and advice.

Introduction

Without Lamps

Upon entering the home of the Marquis d'Andervilliers, Emma Bovary cannot help but notice the vast amount of portraiture adorning the walls:

> Large gold frames hung on the dark-paneled walls, each bearing, on its lower edge, a name in black lettering. "Jean-Antoine d'Andervilliers d'Yverbonville," she read, 'Count of La Vaubyessard and Baron of La Fresnaye, killed at the Battle of Coutras, 20th October, 1587', and, on another, "Jean-Antoine-Henry-Guy d'Andervilliers de la Vaubyessard, Admiral of France and Knight of the Order of St. Michael, wounded at the Battle of Hougue-Saint-Vaast, 29th May, 1692, died at La Vaubyessard, 23rd January, 1693." The succeeding names were hard to see, because the lamps, so shaded as to throw their light on to the green cloth of the billiard-table, left the rest of the room in shadow.[1]

We can observe a battle playing out here between precision and purpose: one part of the novel wants to include the minute and detailed, to see all the portraits and read their gilded labels. But those billiard players using the room want the light for reasons more operative, for their sport and play, and so the lamp is focused on their billiard table and the novel's sight kept likewise keyed toward the functional, those aspects of narration that push a scene forward in time. The full list of paintings is too "hard to see"; eventually, Emma must move on, to look at other things, have other experiences. Janell Watson suggests that *Madame Bovary* has been "admired for [its] efficient use of description well integrated into the narrative,"[2] and such admiration is not betrayed here.

It hardly need be said that a great deal has changed about the way novels are written and read since the time of *Madame Bovary*, but one clear shift seems to be the development of an aesthetic in which the inclusion of such trivial details is desirable, rather than something to be managed, restrained, or curtailed. It at least seems that one doesn't have to halt a nagging curiosity for descriptive writing anymore, nor integrate it "into the narrative" in an "efficient" manner. Compare, for example, another description of pictures adorning a wall, this time taken from David Foster Wallace's 1996 novel *Infinite Jest*:

> Ted Schacht adjusting his wristbands and sash. Carol Spodek stretching for a volley at net, her whole body distended, face grim and full of cords. An old one of Marlon Bain at the follow-through of a big forehand, a corona of sweat shimmering around him, his bigger arm crossed across his throat. Ortho Stice doing a handstand. Yardguard gliding down through a low backhand. Wayne this summer sliding on Rome's fine clay, a red cloud hiding everything below the knees.[3]

This cataloging continues for more than three times the quoted length. The most obvious difference between this passage and *Madame Bovary*'s is the absence of the lamp controlling where attention is given. Here there is no obscuring shadow, no cautious restriction of sight to stop the endless proliferation of details, and the passage is free to continue until it has exhausted its description. But there are also no billiard players, nor a "sport" that stands against the observation of the world and interrupts the collection of its data, keeping the game on track. The passage doesn't shape itself to fit the conventional pleasures of readers. It doesn't hurry us along; it leaves us staring at the wall, hands unheld. Nor will it reward us if we attempt to make something meaningful of these images, attempting to justify their inclusion by finding in them some symbolic or narrative worth. This is simply a wall of photographs.

It does seem facile to offer up Flaubert as an example of a writer attuned to brevity rather than excess, as many of his works, and those of his peers (Zola, the Goncourt brothers), can seem just as stubbornly indulgent as Wallace's. James Wood argues that Flaubert is, to a large extent, the progenitor of just this sort of prose, responsible for the "sense that the ideal of writing is a procession of strung details, a necklace of noticings."[4] For Wood, the "post-Flaubertian tradition fetishizes ... the over-aesthetic appreciation of detail."[5] But there is a self-consciousness to Wallace's description in *Infinite Jest* that places his writing in a place of much different significance than the excited excesses of nineteenth-century naturalism. Behind Wallace's ostensible indifference and stubbornness, this feigned unawareness of what a novel might do besides describing dull objects, lies one of the most complex aspects of the poetics of contemporary literature, and one that refuses to be dismissed as simply frustrating, difficult, excessive, or encyclopedic. It forms the broad topic of this book: maximalism, which is a concept I use to describe writing that values the pursuit of detail, specificity, and comprehensiveness above other functions novels might be thought to have, and in a way that, as we shall see throughout this book, often forces us to reconsider the uses of writing and reading literature in the postwar West. This is a style of writing that certainly tries to capture a lot of the world, but not necessarily for mimetic purposes. As the often deliberately dull objects of Wallace's descriptive eye implies, it is not what is being represented that counts in the maximalist text, so much as the *activity* of representing. The maximalist novel often makes the implied process of its construction one of its strongest effects, rather than the content of its descriptions.

Instead of understanding such passages as only difficult, frustrating, or resistant to readerly desire, throughout *Maximalism in Contemporary American Literature* I consider ways in which they also indulge slightly more practical wishes that literary readers and writers might harbor, revealing fantasies and anxieties of ability, attention, and erudition that shape these works and their reception, and explain one role fiction plays in a culture where the human mind is increasingly aware of its limited ability to consider, contemplate, and master the diversity and immensity of information available to it. As this book continues, it will also become clear that as much as an author like Wallace seems openly celebratory of such stubbornly detailed, descriptive writing, his work is not at complete peace with this aesthetic either, and much of his prose negotiates the importance *and* the risks of maximalism, developing different justifications for his fondness for detail.

Off the Map

One of the early mentions of maximalism in literary criticism came in a 1984 mock editorial for a spoof academic journal named *Guest Editor*. In it, Steve Katz gave an account of "Post-Hoc Maximalists"—artists who having chosen an impossible degree of specificity, now faced the difficulty of their chosen enterprise:

> I had hoped this could be the occasion to present the work of Istvan Kottki, once known as the Charlie Parker of maximalist writing. The visual maximalism of his sister, Muriel, is better known than his verbal contribution; particularly her piece from the mid-sixties called Broadway and Houston, which was composed of that busy intersection and all its traffic. ... Little known is that in '72 she transferred her piece to the center of the Verrazano Narrows bridge, causing its collapse.[6]

For artists like the fictional Kottki, the pressure to include everything, and to represent the world in such high definition, was so keen that it resulted in her taking the real intersection as her representation of it.[7] Any lesser degree of specificity would have been unsatisfactory. The question implied for literary writers was that if a real intersection could not be moved to another real location without disastrous results, then what hope did one have of containing it in the pages of a book? The further dilemma for the critic was how to actually find and appraise these works. As the title of the editorial—"Post Hoc Maximalism"—connotes, because they are indistinguishable from the real, one can only happen upon these works after the fact, something Katz realized when appraising one of Kottki's "most spontaneous and ambitious works," the 1970 shooting of students at Kent State University.[8] The maximalist's work asks impossible feats of its readers just as it seems impossibly ambitious itself.

Although Wallace's description of the wall of photographs seems to aim for a similar one-to-one mapping of its imagined object, and thus threatens to overrun his novel with the same disastrousness as Muriel Kottki's work, there is more to Wallace's fascination with representation than a now familiar discourse on the diminishing difference between the "real" and its copy in postmodern culture.[9] Katz's "editorial" obviously parodies contemporary art pretensions and invites a discussion about simulation, reality, and the idea of the frame that would fit neatly with the work of Jean Baudrillard. The primary object of Katz's parody, however, is the place of excess in representation: no one needs a representation of an intersection to be so specific that the real intersection is used instead. But what's interesting in the works of the writers studied in *Maximalism in Contemporary American Literature* is that what might otherwise be seen as excess or redundancy is redirected by readers back into the aesthetic experience as a form of value—redundancy becomes *necessity* if these texts are to be experienced as enjoyable. The nature of this enjoyment is different in each of the writers studied here, but at the core of all examples exists a set of ideas about what writing and reading maximalist works allows a person to "do." To be organized, expansive, attentive, and polymathic to unusual degrees—these are some of the possibilities offered by maximalism.

It should be made clear at the beginning that *Maximalism in Contemporary American Literature* is not an exhaustive account of maximalist literature and the aesthetics of detailedness it describes in contemporary fiction. For starters, I am knowingly approaching the topic in a very unmaximalist way, considering at length the work of only three American, male authors, Thomas Pynchon, David Foster Wallace, and Nicholson Baker, at the exclusion of many of their peers and literary predecessors, some of whom go unmentioned, others afforded only passing reference (Flaubert, Whitman, Proust, Woolf, Joyce, Gaddis, Perec). There are reasons for this narrow focus, which will become clearer later. Because of the lack of other studies on maximalism (something also to be discussed later), this book might initially seem designed to offer a form of genre criticism, but I am relatively uninterested in defining or defending a model that might be used to infallibly label texts as maximalist or not, or in arguing why maximalism is a style more suited to representing Western society in the late twentieth and early twenty-first centuries than, say, its nominal opposite minimalism. My work throughout does, by necessity at least, orbit a proposed definition of the style, and theorizes connections between these texts and place, race, and gender, but I will be more interested in what the maximalist elements of novels are *used* for, what relations, conflicts, and fantasies they inspire within particular segments of reading culture, than in cataloguing the style itself. What I am trying to assert is that I'm interested in issues other than the topographical and taxonomical.

Although it has been described as several things, many of which I will cover in this introduction, the maximalist novel is here positioned as a literary work keen to demonstrate its ability to see and record the world in great detail, as well as manage the resultant text, which might be tumescent in size, troublingly dense in complexity, or tedious in its obsession with particulars. As John Kuehl puts it, maximalists are "putter-inners" rather than "leaver-outers,"[10] and I would add that their works tell stories about the importance of specificity and detailed "noticing" in the literary arts and wider culture, commenting upon our ability to describe the world beyond what we feel is relevant for the needs of verisimilitude, or usable in literary interpretations. On this point, maximalist works often illuminate and critique the activities involved in literary reading and writing by exceeding the possibility of their performance. That is, they present so much material so stubbornly that they bring into focus either the staleness of many of our expectations of novels or the weakness of our methods of making them meaningful. Tom LeClair suggests that excessive writing is especially important in the current literary environment—one plagued by fears of the marginalization and obsolescence of written texts—because "excess is a strategy that first meets and then transforms conventional, even popularly engineered expectations to have an impact on the reader."[11] The too-many details included in a maximalist text unsettle the sediments of literary reading, and thus stand to speak to a reader in a way they might be unprepared for. In Wallace's *The Pale King*, for example, boredom is offered to readers as the goal of their reading, whereas it is normally the sign of a book's failure.

A style nominally engaged with limits, maximalism's most recognizable traits involve the transgression of what is usually considered the acceptable amount of detail able to be included in a novel,[12] as well as challenging what *kinds* of details are considered to be of novelistic interest (hence, as I will argue later, the overall unsuitability of the "encyclopedic" label for books like Wallace's *Infinite Jest* or Baker's *The Mezzanine*, which are often written against the privileged facts of the world collected in an encyclopedia). So, the maximalist is here a writer who refuses to overlook, and as a result is one who tends to *over*-look, becoming obsessed with the importance of an unwavering attention to detail. This approach to writing is often labeled indulgent, but more accurately might be called confident or ambitious. Nicholson Baker's work even exhibits a "dorky" epistemological optimism.

Maximalism also offers many things to a reader—indeed, by its nature, it offers more than many things. *Infinite Jest* and *Gravity's Rainbow*, for example, offer a wellspring of "employment" opportunities to readers by providing more text to use than a less maximalist novel. An exhaustive catalog of paintings like the one we encounter in *Infinite Jest* is also a demonstration of an inexhaustible focus, an ability to "see" beyond the shadows of weariness and boredom. And readers who can make meaning of this hard work participate vicariously and so make similar claims of their own hardiness. Such considerations will be particularly important in my discussion of Thomas Pynchon, but they become something of a straw man against which my reading of Wallace's *Infinite Jest* will be set, a novel that, I argue, uses maximalism as a way of refusing some of the greatness expected of the author of "big" books. In all cases, however, contemporary maximalist novels ask us to consider why this style of writing is increasingly valued in the contemporary age, particularly considering the vexed history of other detailed writing, which we'll cover in some detail below.

Stefano Ercolino recently claimed that it is "difficult, if not impossible, to imagine a maximalist novel that is not long."[13] But here, in this book, maximalism isn't exclusively attached to a certain *kind* of novel such as the "encyclopedic" or "mega" novel, which is often taken as the most obvious result of a maximalist approach to writing. Instead, I see maximalism as a mindset and approach to novelistic poetics that finds the lure of detailedness irresistible, despite its often troublesome nature. There's no necessary relationship between length and maximalism, at the very least. Wallace, for example, was also a writer of short stories, and it seems limiting to suggest his writing is not maximalist simply when it appears in shorter forms. To borrow a phrase from Arthur Saltzman's study of minimalism, I aim to view maximalism as a "mode of inquiry," a "set of ways of asking questions about the contemporary world," rather than a particular kind of text.[14] To restrict discussion of maximalism only to those works that appear ostentatiously excessive is to overlook many of its most interesting manifestations. It's probably even more accurate to say that some of the books we study here (those of Nicholson Baker and Pynchon's later work, *Inherent Vice*) might only have maximalist *aspects*, rather than being entirely maximalist objects. All good maximalist novels seem also to reflect on maximalist writing, therefore it's important to recognize that these writers' relationship to the style often changes or is revised over the course of their careers. My discussion of all three authors seeks to show that their works are involved in a continuing evaluation of the maximalist mode of inquiry, and that these writers revise its usefulness to their work as their careers evolve. This does mean that this book takes on the somewhat tricky task of offering a portrait of a largely undefined object of study, as well as critiquing that object, showing how writers practice *and* critique maximalism, never letting it be simply one thing.

Against Encyclopedism

My assertion that literary maximalism engages primarily with detail, description, and specificity is slightly different to the standard employment of the term within literary analysis and other aesthetic fields, and I feel it needs a little bit of justification before we begin. Indeed, many of the qualities I will offer up as maximalist have previously been considered *minimalist*—the focus on small and trivial details and the preference for detached description over narration, in particular. This confusion is particularly relevant in

Nicholson Baker's miniaturist maximalism, as we will see in Chapters 4 and 5, which has often been labeled a minimalist body of work.[15]

The potential overlap raises a key issue of definition that we should tackle here at the beginning: despite the popularity of the concept of minimalism in the arts and criticism, its nominal counterpart maximalism has strangely garnered far less critical attention—and in the field of literature especially. As Michel Delville and Andrew Norris claim in one of only a few dedicated studies of it (and even theirs is focused on the music of Frank Zappa and Captain Beefheart rather than the form of the novel), "the term is systematically absent from all lexicons of literary terms."[16] Even when a clear opportunity arises to use it, such as when Saltzman states that Baker's prose "has a vigor and sinuousness that contradicts, or at least offers an alternative to, the parched last resort complained of by detractors of minimalist fiction,"[17] critics seem wary of—if not just unconfident—employing the more unfamiliar term. Saltzman never once considers that Baker actually might be a *maximalist*, rather than a minimalist, which is surely the conclusion his argument implies.

This does not mean, however, that maximalism hasn't been discussed with more serious intentions outside of the literary arts, in other disciplines, or simply using a different vocabulary. It is a far more familiar and well-defined concept in art history and musicology, for example, and it is from the world of music that a firm grasp of the style can be gleaned. For Richard Taruskin, much early twentieth-century Western music in the Wagnerian tradition should be considered more properly maximalist than modernist, in that it evidences "a radical intensification of means toward accepted or traditional ends," rather than an outright rejection of them.[18] Here maximalism is understood as the amplification and exaggeration of the contours and boundaries of traditional forms, which in the process produces somewhat non-traditional results (excessive dissonance due to increased compositional complexity, for example). There are various methods by which composers might achieve this maximalism:

> Turning musical works into awe-inspiring mountains—by extending their length, amplifying their volume, and complicating their texture—became an obsession. Another way of amplifying the sense of musical space … was to increase the range and maneuverability of "tonal navigation," that is, the range of key relationships. Yet another area … was the sheer level of tolerable (or at least tolerated) dissonance, and even more important, the postponement of its resolution. The former maximized the representation of emotional tension, the latter maximized the listener's participation in it.[19]

Understanding qualities of amplification and inflation as maximalist, we can see how such an analysis easily crosses over into the literary arts. But while Taruskin's description of turning "works into awe-inspiring mountains" certainly seems to be the *modus operandi* of the maximalist artist, it gives the slightly incorrect impression that their works are only interested in an expansion outwards toward something of epic range, grandeur and loftiness, or a melding together of incongruent textures and tones. What I wish to refocus our account on is that the expansions that occur, at least in the work of the three authors studied here, are generally the result of a desire for specificity, for not excluding the middle, so to speak. Again, viewing maximalism first and foremost as a "mode of inquiry" is key. While the "increase [in] the range and maneuverability of 'tonal navigation' [and] the sheer level of tolerable (or at least tolerated) dissonance" certainly speaks to a desire to enlarge traditional forms, it is also the consequence of a compositional desire to include the overlooked harmonies that pre-Wagnerian composers had largely struggled to find a place for in Western music, just as Wallace's account of all the trivial photos on an office wall is an attempt to gather together the overlooked "tonal" possibilities of the novel. A novel in the key of beige is a possibility his maximalism explores with (ironically) a great deal of excitement. So while many of the texts studied here can certainly be seen as exaggerations of "ordinary" novels, offering something along the lines of what Charles McGrath has called a "souped-up, knockout, total fiction experience,"[20] the intensification is frequently in relation to an amplification of the unappealing aspects of fiction, and the magnification of those aspects of life that generally preclude novelistic interest, rather than those of epic grandeur.

Taruskin's useful account of maximalist aesthetics does make it clear that various appellations have been used to describe styles of writing similar to the musical maximalism he outlines. Literary maximalism is probably not such an overlooked thing after all—its supposed neglect might just be due to the use of different vocabularies. Edward Mendelson's "encyclopedic narratives," Tom LeClair's "systems novels" of excess and mastery, Frederick R. Karl's "mega novels," and, most recently, James Wood's genre of "hysterical realism," all discuss aspects of novelistic discourse that seem broadly maximalist.[21] Yet none are entirely suitable for our present purposes either. To take the most influential of these examples, Mendelson's proposed genre of encyclopedic narrative appears to discuss what I'm calling maximalism, placing a suitable focus on texts' relationship to detail and the collection of specifics. For Mendelson, encyclopedic novels are those works, such as Dante's *Inferno*, Joyce's *Ulysses*, and Pynchon's *Gravity's Rainbow*, that attempt to "render the full range of knowledge and beliefs of a national culture, while identifying the ideological perspectives from which that culture shapes and interprets its knowledge."[22] A necessary part of this attempt to evoke the episteme of a culture is the reliance on descriptive detail as a kind of short-hand for signifying the imagined totality of the world, which seems to be now beyond the grasp of relatively simple acts such as narrating and plotting: "because they are products of an era in which the world's knowledge is vastly greater than any one person can encompass, they necessarily make extensive use of synecdoche."[23] So if not capturing their objects entirely (as if that were at all possible) then these books at least give the impression that they conceivably could.[24] To return to the example of Wallace once more, the maximalist writer's ability to exhaustively catalog all the photos on a wall is taken as proof of his ability to catalog the rest of the world in similar detail, if only he could be bothered.

In Mendelson's account, the "sight" of the novel is certainly amplified, but this fails to account for the imbalance in the amplification we can observe in the three authors studied here. That is, I find that the encyclopedic label is not wholly suitable for describing many of these texts because their fixations are often on information and knowledge that resist the conferred significance that any fact included in an encyclopedia—being precisely the collection of privileged facts of the world—necessarily undergoes. *Gravity's Rainbow* certainly seems to be interested in providing an account of the social, technological, and economic developments of the postwar West, but it and other texts studied here are full of details that would be considered trivial, banal, and useless. What encyclopedia captures the implications of the transition from paper to plastic drinking straws, for example, as Baker's *The Mezzanine* does? And what value would a collection of amateur tennis photos hanging on a waiting-room wall, as we read in *Infinite Jest*, add to a compendium of knowledge? These are details largely designed to disrupt what we might otherwise want to get out of an encyclopedia. Indeed, in an inversion of T.S. Eliot's idea of "relevant intensity," James Wood claims that in Wallace's writing *irrelevant* intensity "becomes a motor of the prose."[25] Maximalism, at least as practiced by Wallace, Baker, and Pynchon, seems to love the forgotten or overlooked knowledge of the world just as much as the established facts.

To some extent, this is to be viewed as a consequence of these texts' historical moment—that is, they might very well demonstrate an encyclopedic breadth, but one filtered by the politics of postmodernism and poststructuralism. According to Mendelson, the encyclopedic novel is particularly beloved of modernism and speaks to this period's indelible ambitiousness, something of the Wagnerian *Gesamtkunstwerk*. But its postmodern form would presumably be affected by the poststructuralist preference for "local knowledge" and excluded voices, and hence mark a shift toward the overlooked particulars we notice in these later works. Another reason the encyclopedic label seems unsuitable, and another point *Maximalism in Contemporary American Literature* will try to argue when we reach our discussion of Nicholson Baker, is that maximalism is in no way exclusive to big books. If anything, it is more of a phenomenological and epistemological standpoint—Saltzman's "mode of inquiry" again—than a claim to physical dimension. All of the works of Baker are strong examples, as is Pynchon's *The Crying of Lot 49* and many of Wallace's short stories.

As suggested above, there has been some direct engagement with the concept of literary maximalism in recent years. McGurl's *The Program Era* is one example and will be brought into play in several chapters here, including the present one. Ercolino's 2012 article "The Maximalist Novel" and his 2014 book of the same name are obviously further instances,[26] but Ercolino's approach to maximalism is so different to mine as not to be of much useful comparison. Ercolino is interested in defining ten aspects particular to maximalist novels: "length, encyclopedic mode, dissonant chorality, diegetic exuberance, completeness, narratorial omniscience, paranoid imagination, inter-semiocity, ethical commitment, and hybrid realism."[27] From such an account we gain the impression that maximalist literature attempts to present a wide range of literary effects available to modern writers, what Ercolino terms a "multiform maximizing,"[28] a sort of formal devouring that produces the somewhat contradictory effects of chaos and completion. My approach differs to Ercolino's in several ways, and I find that viewing a maximalist work through a topographical framework will produce only the sense that it contains a lot of different aspects, which is something we can probably just infer from its generic label. This sort of account is, in general, of the kind I wish to avoid, as it tends to describe these works as objects with hardened traits, rather than understanding the complexities of the mode of inquiry that produces them and the role readers play in creating their effects. Ercolino's approach also precludes contemplation of examples of maximalist writing that differ from the norm, such as Baker's novels that would certainly not meet his maximalist criteria.

Bad Details

There is a second aspect of maximalism's alleged absence from critical accounts that Delville and Norris touch upon in their essay on Captain Beefheart and Zappa—that of a cultural bias against the style, a stubbornly persistent distaste for the long-winded and over-particular. As John Barth puts it with inimitable wit:

> the oracle at Delphi did not say, "Exhaustive analysis and comprehension of one's own psyche may be prerequisite to an understanding of one's behavior and of the world at large"; it said, "Know thyself."[29]

Such concerns—the distaste for excess and superfluous specificity—subtly shape the way many of us attend to our intellectual and artistic work, and can result in a dismissal of maximalist detailedness as redundant, absurd, or only interesting to the pedant or bore.[30] As Francis Bacon once asked in a complaint about scholastic over-specificity, "were it not better for a man in a fair room to set up one great light, or branching candlestick of lights, than to go about with a small watch candle into every corner?"[31] The quote's resonance with my opening example from Flaubert should be clear. To offer a more recent example of this bias (and the influence of Bacon's preference), here is Martin Jay's *Marxism and Totality*:

> The literature on Sartre is too lengthy to list here.[32]

> How successful he was in this endeavor, how completely he overcame the antinomian terms of his early position instead of merely reformulating them, has been the source of spirited debate. To follow all of its ramifications is impossible.[33]

> Without going into its intricacies, it seems fair to say that Sartre extends alienation beyond the realm of labor.[34]

While entirely reasonable for any writer not compiling a database, Jay's omissions nevertheless imply that to provide a complete account of even a relatively small subject like the criticism on Jean-Paul Sartre is a tiresome, laborious, and intellectually thankless exercise. Even more importantly, it is assumed to be virtually impossible to fit it within the pages of a book without significant disruption to argument, coherency and readability (not to mention publication budgets and binding limitations). While Jay's book, peppered with detailed footnotes, actually displays a relatively maximalist ethos, there is still a clear limit to what its author feels is necessary. To claim to name everything is not just intellectually dangerous—who knows what Jay might miss if he attempted to do so—it marks the death of style. We don't gain enough from the specifics to warrant their inclusion.

As McGurl has examined, if there is a bias against maximalism in the contemporary literary field it can be understood in relation to the institutionalization of creative writing in the postwar West—or, more properly, the establishment of minimalism as the standard production of the creative writing program. McGurl argues that maximalism is a style of writing that conflicts with many practical realities of tertiary writing programs, and so tends to be frowned upon in institutional environments in favor of the more suitable form of the minimalist short story. This occurs for several reasons: the understatement and self-concealment of minimalism suits students nervous about the workshopping environment; the brevity of the style suits professors having to grade students' writing assignments; and the tightly hewn edges of minimalist prose provide evidence of craft, signifying that the student has worked on their writing and learned the trade:

> The excisions and understatements that are the hallmarks of minimalism ... can be understood as analogous to the self-protective concealments, like shielding the eyes, triggered before, during, and after the fact of shameful exposure. The very shortness of the short forms associated with minimalism (and with creative writing instruction in general) puts "mastery of form," a solid sense of completion, within

visible reach of the student. ... If the modern world is a world of risk, a "Risk Society," then minimalism is an aesthetic of risk management, a way of being beautifully careful.[35]

Maximalism, on the other hand, tends toward over-exposure and pride; excessive length; and gives the impression of unedited unruliness—all values that conflict with the needs and realities of the "program." It is thus natural that most universities have a much higher output of minimalist writers than maximalists, as, to a large extent, the maximalist will struggle to exist within the creative writing program's boundaries. Wallace claimed, for instance, that one of his undergraduate workshop teachers thought the writing he was producing at college was "pretentious, and wordy," and that he felt surrounded by writers who wanted "to write *New Yorker* stories."[36]

It should be made clear, however, that if there is any bias against maximalism in the literary arts, then it is mostly owing to readers rather than writers. For despite the strictures of the creative writing institution, we've always had maximalist writing of one sort or another; it's just that our willingness to engage with it has been intermittent at best. To study maximalist writing, then, is also to study what has sometimes made readers resistant to it, as well as what makes many ready to celebrate it today.

But what is so troubling about detailedness? In the Tudor aesthetics of George Puttenham, too much detail could lead to the "vice of surplusage" in which "the Poet or makers of speech become vicious," harming readers with not only "a word or two more than ordinary, but in whole clauses, and peradventure large sentences impertinently spoken, or with more labor and curiosity than is requisite."[37] For Francis Wey, the over-detailed writing of nineteenth-century French authors was the symptom of a decadent society, and for him excessive detail could likewise become "vicious."[38] An early reader of *Great Expectations* remarked that Dickens' stories were "always interesting," but "would be more so if they were less encumbered by minute details."[39] So if not being vicious, excessive detail was simply boring. Although James Wood suggests that "nineteenth-century realism, from Balzac on, creates such an abundance of detail that the modern reader has come to expect of narrative that it will always contain a certain superfluity, a built-in redundancy, that it will *carry more detail than it needs*,"[40] such redundancy seems to worry readers whose job is felt to be the unveiling of what Richard House calls "purposiveness" in the literary object, the assumption that each component of a text is "related to the whole as a means to an end."[41] As House puts it, the judgment that a novel contained unreadable "noise" was in earlier generations taken as "the sign of defective reading,"[42] signifying only that the reader hadn't worked with enough rigor to connect all the dots. The problem primarily seemed to be a hermeneutic one: although all novels are made up of details of one kind or another, when the focus seemed to be as much on those details as what greater purpose they were serving, readers weren't quite sure how to understand them. The potentially excessive detail thus beckoned anxiety: it was never stable, never trustworthy, always liable to become significant at some later moment and make one look foolish for not having noticed its importance in the first place.

As Naomi Schor shows, excessive details have also tended to be equated with the equally problematic category of the feminine, and thus many readers' resistance to detailed prose has historically been intermingled with a certain quality of misogyny. Schor quotes from Lord Kames who argues that excessive ornament has "no better effect than to confound the eye, and to prevent the object from making an impression as one entire whole."[43] The weakness of the over-detailed artwork is, for Kames, equated to a tasteless woman who is "apt to overcharge every part of her dress with ornament."[44] In the classical aesthetics of Kames and others, detailism threatens "to hasten the slide of art into femininity" by drawing attention away from the sublime in favor of trivial particularism.[45] As we'll see in my reading of Nicholson Baker's work, the category of the "trivial" is something the maximalist writer seeks to deconstruct, challenging the notion that information can be labeled as significant or insignificant.

Writers who enjoy detail have most commonly been dismissed as cheap show-offs, however. The leader of this mode of critique, at least in modern literary criticism, is Georg Lukács, who in a series of influential readings of naturalist and modernist literature, saw excessively detailed description as a corruption of the revolutionary potential of the novel, or at least a symptom of the hardening of capitalist ideology in Western society. As Pauline Johnson suggests, Lukács saw literary detailedness as part of "the emergence of a defensive ideology which strove to naturalize the existence of capitalism."[46] For a Marxist like Lukács, the effort of conceiving of reality—what is sometimes called totalization—was the first and most necessary form of literary praxis. At the heart of this ambition was, by implication, a necessary ethics of mimesis, of how one went about representing reality, giving it parsable shape and form. If it was essential to grasp the whole, then one needed a proper way of transcribing it; not just any old mimesis would do. Lukács frequently railed against what he saw as the wrong sort of representation, that which, rather than enabling the world to be apprehended and "defetishized," fell into collusion with its mode of production. He initially called this type of writing naturalism, a style that he opposed to realism proper, what he eventually called critical realism. One of the most important criteria for failed or successful mimesis—for complicit or resistant representation—was the handling of descriptive detail. The naturalist (and later the modernist) failed to observe the crucial division between the "significant and irrelevant detail,"[47] the separation that for Lukács constituted the core of the ethics of artistic practice: art was "the selection of the essential and subtraction of the inessential," after all.[48] The critical realist, on the other hand, "with his critical detachment, places what is a significant, specifically modern experience in a wider context, giving it only the emphasis it deserves as part of a greater, objective whole."[49] The naturalist, the prime example of which he took to be Émile Zola, was essentially "uncritical towards many aspects of the modern world,"[50] guided by a complacency that manifested in a desire to catalog its contents to exhaustion without any attempt at synthesis or critique—to describe for virtuosity's sake, rather than to create or further the totalizing movements of narrative. While in naturalism and certain types of modernism there was expressed a defensible need to represent the world, to include as much of it as possible within literature, descriptive detail stood to negate the purpose of representation if it was valued only as description, as a kind of baroque decoration or index of artistic skill. Reading a particularly detailed description of a horse race in *Nana*, for example, Lukács contended that the "description of the race [was] a brilliant example of Zola's virtuosity," with "every phase from the saddling of the horses to the finish … investigated meticulously." But for all of its virtuosity the description was "mere filler in the novel." It had no vitality; it "could be easily eliminated."[51] Detailed descriptions were to be explained away as a form of novelistic showing off, the demonstration of skill rather than vitality.[52]

It can be taken as a given that Lukács would have had nothing but distaste for many of the authors under analysis in this book, and more will be made of his critique of description in our later discussion of Wallace's *Infinite Jest* in Chapter 2 and Baker's *The Mezzanine* in Chapter 4. His criticism of the maximalist use of detail in naturalist novels, however, is influential and perhaps goes some way toward accounting for the difficulty in appreciating the intricacies of this style or the lack of attempts that try to do so. Where Lukács' account is most influential, perhaps, is in its suggestion that the prose of the maximalist author has a key relationship with capitalism. Janell Watson all but confirms this aspect of Lukács' influence for us: "Though I do not share [Lukács'] modernist aesthetic, I do share his conviction that heavily descriptive novels are produced by the conditions of capitalism. … The logic of modern material culture under consumer capitalism permeates, indeed generates, the heavily descriptive novel."[53] For Watson, the descriptive excesses of the writers Lukács groups under the heading of naturalism can be explained by "the logic of the marketplace"[54] that invades their novels, leaving behind lists, catalog-like descriptions, detailed inventories, and ornamental excesses as it passes through their pages.[55] But Lukács' work suggests a conclusion that isn't quite borne out by the literary industry, or at least shows that words are not, after all, the same as "things." In modern capitalism, excessive detail and overproductivity has become synonymous with cheapness and tackiness and is at the core of a complex class-based aesthetic distinction. In the field of marketing and product design, excessive ornamental detail is often used to signify "added" value to the naive consumer at the same time as it signifies poorness of craft and tackiness to the knowledgeable. We can see this in the way the busy maximalism of an advertisement for a discount rug store's "fire sale"[56] contrasts to the minimalist quietude of an advertisement for Scandinavian designer furniture, or the manner in which a modified car "tricked out" with lots of visible "extras" compares to the sleek, self-contained elegance of a Mercedes-Benz. Consumers with less economic power confuse a maximalist approach to detail with signs of craftsmanship and bonus value, whereas "sophisticated" consumers recognize the cheapness of excess (both in terms of excessive details and the excessive production of objects) and its relationship to junk. If the detailed novel is to be seen as "permeated" by "modern material culture," it would then risk cheapening itself, which is certainly not what we see in the excessive value placed on authors of contemporary maximalism like Wallace and Pynchon. A simple homology between capitalism and maximalism has limitations, or at least needs to be nuanced enough to account for the complexities of the contemporary consumer world.

American Excess

My claim that the maximalist works studied here are unified by something akin to what, reading Walt Whitman, Franco Moretti calls a "rhetoric of inclusivity,"[57] begs to be connected to the cultural landscape my selected maximalist authors occupy (namely, post-1970s America). We should at least be curious about taking the somewhat formalist account of maximalism offered previously a step further, in search of a cultural explanation. So, what makes these contemporary American authors obsessed with seeing in exhaustive detail, and what makes this writing interesting to contemporary readers? What relevance can an excessive description of bland photographs have for today's readers? And what is American about the maximalist writing of Pynchon, Wallace, and Baker?

From its beginnings, American writing has always dealt with the problem of excessive detail. The American Puritans believed that the founding of a new world should have a writing uncluttered by the complexity and chaos of the land from which they'd exiled themselves, so early authors like William Bradford were determined to write "in the plain style, with singular regard unto the simple truth in all things."[58] The "spare utility" of expression championed by Bradford in *Of Plymouth Plantation* expounded, as Ruland and Bradbury put it, "a metaphysic of writing which endlessly sought meaning by separating the word from ornate and ceremonial usage."[59] This is a style that would seemingly account for the genesis of, say, Ernest Hemmingway and Raymond Carver hundreds of years later, but not Djuna Barnes or Thomas Pynchon.

What's important for the study of maximalism is that this aim of clear disclosure embodied in the "plain style" ironically seems generative of an equally Puritanical obsession with the overanalysis and scrutiny of the world—what in *Gravity's Rainbow* Thomas Pynchon calls the "Puritan reflex of seeking other orders behind the visible, also known as paranoia."[60] In the writings of Bradford and other early Puritan settlers, "the movement of history, the detail of daily event, demands scrupulous attention because these things partake of an allegorical mystery."[61] If one is always watching for signs of God and deceptions of Satan, then a scrupulous attention to detail is a necessity, a defense against straying into sin. A certain thoroughness is needed to keep the life of the "plain style" on track. So although a utility and plainness of language is to be emphasized, one still needs to pour over everything lest they leave unexamined corners of the world in which unseemly forces might be hiding. The excessive interrogation of events, objects, and thoughts typical of contemporary maximalist prose perhaps owes just a little to this Puritanical search for significance and certainty in every atom of the world, even if the "plain style" is otherwise decidedly unmaximalist.

Michelle Burnham argues that Bradford's "plain style" is not just an expression of concerns central to the Puritans' theology, however, but also of their dissatisfaction with the mercantile culture taking shape in the New World, an economy increasingly driven by the exchange and circulation of abstracted values rather than the "simple" production of goods. Burnham argues that the plain style "appeared to offer a kind of antidote to the linguistic and economic confusion associated with merchants and their profits,"[62] expressing distaste for the prolix language of mercantile professionals who were seen as "a distinct social group characterized by interconnected economic and linguistic qualities, including excessiveness, mysteriousness, secret-keeping, and deception."[63] Describing the world in simple and direct terms, without adding unnecessary words, was essential for grounding a market quickly becoming incomprehensible to anyone but sophisticated bankers and merchants, holding too many opportunities for deception and confusion. *Of Plymouth Plantation* was, Burnham suggests, "an attempt at the very level of style to avert the economic, social, and linguistic dangers associated with merchant capitalism."[64] Maximalism, with its celebration of abstruseness, excess, and redundancy, would initially seem to be a style *of* the overcomplicated market, rather than one positioned against it, but as we'll see in my discussion of Wallace's *The Pale King* in Chapter 3, it can also take a corrective standpoint toward the exclusions from political and economic power that occur because of deliberate prolixity. Rather than attempting to avoid any overcomplicated language by using a plain aesthetic, however, Wallace encourages readers to embrace the complex nature of much political and economic legislation by developing a stubbornly maximalist attention to detail. An unwillingness to understand or engage with complex taxation laws and processes (aspects of culture the Puritans would, according to Burnham's account, have held in some contempt), results in a powerlessness Wallace wants to teach readers to counter.

Other homologies between the American economic system and maximalist writing are common and intuitive. The reception of the poetry of Walt Whitman, for instance, offers us an example in which the spread of consumer culture is seen to result in texts bloated with details. Franco Moretti suggests that the listing form responsible for much of Whitman's maximalist inclusivity was a response to the polyphony of nineteenth-century American society and its developing consumerism, with the poem being analogous to something like a store catalog.[65] Allen Grossman takes a different tack in claiming that the "subject of liberation" drives Whitman's inclusivity, and that the "sorting index" of representation—that process which decides what is worthy of inclusion in a literary object or not—is driven simply by "mere being-at-all."[66] Like my chosen maximalists, Whitman looks upon the objects of the world without discrimination. Anything his eye touches is included in his poems in something like a poetics of democracy (or the free market). But both critics assert a caution, too. As Moretti suggests, for all of its inclusivity, Whitman's style is also one of monologism, an attempt to restrictively contain the multitude of the busy world under a single gaze:

> Whitman's list is not a neutral container, but an organizing module: a "symbolic" form ... which subordinates the variety of America to an omnipresent and invariant poetic voice. A voice, or more precisely a grid—a *gaze*.[67]

For Grossman, the maximalist inclusivity of Whitman's poetry overcomes the "difference of the social body" at the expense of the individual, becoming "a servant of persons, but not itself personal."[68] Inclusivity comes at the cost of intimacy; totalization is achieved at the cost of the individual. We can then say that Whitman's maximalist lines express both the liberating sense of the new, collecting all of its shiny and heterogeneous colors and textures together, and the anxieties of a society becoming overpopulated by a mass of diffuse and endlessly proliferating "things" and sensations. The poet wants to capture the multitude of modern experience to defend the troubled human subject of modernity against it, or, on the other hand, capture the experience at the cost of that same subject.

Despite its apparent engagement with the American economic "spirit," maximalist writing has not always had an unproblematic reception in American culture. Indeed, what best distinguishes contemporary American maximalist writers like Pynchon and Wallace from those of earlier generations is their relatively unproblematic success and the accompanying assurance (obtained in Wallace's case by the instant celebrity that followed the publication of *Infinite Jest*) that the overdetailed novel is not just a difficult and unwieldy aberrance, but a valuable artistic commodity that is as carefully structured as it is "wild."

Ulysses is obviously an important landmark for all contemporary maximalist writing, filled with lists, copious details, and the description of acts thought scandalous and obscene enough to have the book banned. Joyce's work also had a particularly strong influence in the American literary scene, and it might be argued that Pynchon and Wallace are Joyce's proper heirs, more so than any Irish or British authors.[69] Despite this, Ellsworth Mason, a collaborator of Joyce's biographer Richard Ellmann, suggests that during the first half of the twentieth century, "nobody really read it. ... Nobody knew how to read it."[70] It could be argued that *Ulysses*' appeal in America was primarily symbolic, its difficulty and experimentation congruent with the ambitiousness of an American culture bent on modernization and technological innovation, and a way for literary readers to feel involved with the other industries of progress. John McCourt argues that American academic institutions also saw in Joyce a chance to appropriate a progressive and important author whom the British establishment was treating unfavorably at the time,[71] involving Joyce in what Julie Sloan Brannon calls "a tradition of American revolution against British insularity."[72] The celebration of *Ulysses* in America became a way for the United States to reassert its revolutionary spirit.

Although the influence of Joyce in America is notable, America had its own maximalist novelists, too. The stylistic influence of these "native" predecessors on contemporary writers is important, but so too is the fact that, like Joyce, they often struggled to find a positive reception in their original publishing climate. Herman Melville's *Moby-Dick* is an obvious starting point for a historical investigation of American maximalism because Melville's interest in information and baroque expression often interrupts the novel's more traditional narrative interests (it has become commonplace for many readers to skip the chapters on cetology to get to the "real" story, for instance). Like Joyce's work, *Moby-Dick* also required a hard sell. In the years leading up to its publication, Melville admitted an "earnest desire to write those sort of books that are said to 'fail,'" sensing the critical mood of the times and preparing the ground for the lack of success his novel would garner in the economic and critical marketplace.[73] It was not until the 1920s that a "Melville revival" of sorts would occur.

Even with the increased interest in excessive novels that *Ulysses* and the Melville revival marked, the reception of William Gaddis' *The Recognitions*, published in 1955 and commonly cited as an influence on both Wallace and Pynchon, was lukewarm at best. Even after the novel gained fame in later years, Gaddis remarked that fans must have been passing around a single copy of the book, for its renown was definitely not reflected in its sales.[74] Like Joyce's and Melville's works, it took the American reading public some time to judge Gaddis' works as valuable, which if nothing else suggests that readers needed considerable time in order to process the proper worth of these dense and complicated texts.

The existence of these literary forebears is certainly important for preparing readers for the arrival of works by Pynchon and other recent maximalists, and so one might propose that the relatively unproblematic success of these contemporary authors owes a lot to the fact that writers and readers have taught themselves to tolerate maximalism through prior exposure. I don't want to focus too much on narratives of artistic influence, however, because what gives the maximalism of writers from Pynchon onwards its unique resonance is the manner in which readers and writers appreciate it as sublimely skillful rather than simply chaotic, erratic, or overindulgent. What I argue in this book is that the contemporary embrace of maximalist novels is less difficult because of the rise into public consciousness of the putative "information economy," and the manner in which it allows the notation and management of detail in novels to become visible as a "valuable" activity, rather than a problematic aesthetic choice. In the work of Lukács, we've seen that the maximalist habits of nineteenth-century novelists were thought to express an unhealthy fascination with the overproduction and over-consumption of physical "things." But for writers from (at least) Pynchon onwards, details are not necessarily attached to things, and nor do they necessarily communicate an engagement with material culture (perhaps this is why so many of the objects that feature in *Gravity's Rainbow*s descriptions are discarded and broken, items that have lost their value as objects of consumption. They are postconsumption). The details in contemporary maximalist novels do not necessarily reflect outwards onto the world, but inward toward the inferred character of the author who through them performs his ability to operate skillfully (and perhaps then also to intervene) within the economy of information. Lukács could only see Zola's descriptive "virtuosity" as contemptible, signifying that author's abandonment to the superficialities of capitalist production. But it's clear that writers from Pynchon onwards have been more easily able to capitalize on a different value of excess, and I would argue that this is largely due to the nature of a culture in which labor has moved progressively away from the production of goods to the management of data and its conversion into information. The contemporary maximalist isn't hypnotized by the details of proliferating "things" in the manner of Zola and Flaubert, but is engaged instead by problems of notation, collation, and management.

I agree with David Golumbia's skepticism of the extent to which the so-called information age marks a new development in human society, "as if past generations had not been involved deeply in the exchange, storage, preservation, and use of information."[75] But when many of the most profitable corporations today collect and sell information rather than physical objects, there is at least a popular consensus that information is more dominant today than in previous periods of history, even if it is not the radical shift that the term "information age" imagines. As the former head of Citibank once put it, "the rules and customs, skills and talents, necessary to uncover, capture, produce, preserve, and exploit information are now mankind's most important rules, customs, skills, and talents."[76] And the maximalist novel's ability to manage large amounts of complex (often banal) data, and to be endlessly scrupulous about specifics, could then be seen as having increasing cultural capital *because* our society also values these skills and techniques of information management above other abilities. The relatively recent fascination with maximalist authors, and the awe with which readers sometimes regard their texts, is then at least a partial effect of maximalism's alignment and congruity with the current mode of production, one in which, supposedly, the most valuable work is the collection, exchange, and management of data and its turning into information.[77] As suggested previously, the important push of Wallace's writing is that rather than trying to shun the world of complexity, readers should develop the patience, attention, and information-management skills necessary to navigate this world successfully. Might we then also say that he is training readers for their arrival as workers in postindustrial capitalism?

Whatever else they might be, contemporary maximalist novels like *Infinite Jest*, *Gravity's Rainbow*, and *The Mezzanine* do seem to function as answers to Alan Liu's concern about "the future of literature and literary study when all culture is increasingly the culture of information."[78] I don't think that we can say the economy of information has produced maximalist novels in any particular respect, or it that it factors into our overt enjoyment of them, but it is at least one reason why they are increasingly visible and held in high regard, their polymath authors often viewed as geniuses, workers above the common lot. Although in the past excessive texts have often been criticized, as Naomi Schor puts it, for a "poor management of linguistic capital,"[79] many excessive novels of the contemporary world are seen as efficient, operating skillfully within a naturally overloaded landscape and existing as the record of valuable work.

Maximalism feeds off the information economy in another, more oppositional manner. Whatever impression a maximalist author gives of their ability to collect and assemble data is infused with a certain quantity of nostalgia when we consider that novel writing is still thought to be a largely human kind of labor (even if researched or written on a computer, there's still the fundamental idea that each word is manually entered by a writer) and most other information work today is done either wholly by or with the aid of digital technologies. The sense of powerfulness attached to contemporary maximalist writers tends to be appreciated as the result of human patience, record-keeping, and organization, abilities that are today better performed by computers (few today would trust a person to copy a legal document by hand like Melville's scriveners when a photocopier or Ctrl+C function on a computer leaves minimal risk of error), or at least readers seem to focus on what these novels suggest of the abilities of their authors without considering the ease of information management that digital tools allow. The maximalist novel, in this way, becomes the vehicle for fantasies of human ability. Particularly in the case of *Gravity's Rainbow*, maximalism appears valuable because it is the performance of "heroically" human feats of information wrangling, the record of the "analog" agent's mastery of data from all corners of the contemporary world, and (in the case of *Gravity's Rainbow* at least) without the aid of Google and digitally searchable archives.[80] Wallace's commitment to writing the first draft of *Infinite Jest* by hand can perhaps be understood as partaking of something similar—a feeling that this is one man working to make sense of the complexity and chaos of contemporary culture armed with only a notebook and pen. As much as the maximalism of Wallace, Baker, and Pynchon is fascinated by technology and enriched by the information economy, their novels are also perhaps the nostalgic records of human labor potential in a world where the post-human digital worker is increasingly dominant. It's easy for a computer to generate 400,000 words of text, or a person with a computer to copy and paste a million-word document. That the maximalist author seems to have the ability to do this manually and in a manner that is not yet able to be recreated by machine algorithms suggests that the fascination with maximalist writing, if not all novels, is partly explainable by the cultural redundancy of this very activity. A marathon runner could travel 42 kilometers a lot faster in a car, but we're excited by the unassisted quality of their endeavor, and so too with the "unassisted" nature of information management supposedly performed by the maximalist author.

Beyond Context

There are, of course, many factors that influence the reception of novels,[81] and a growing consensus that the proliferation of information and its technology is a significant development in everyday life—and, relatedly, that readers feel that managing complex information is a worthwhile activity that has returns outside of reading literature—surely contributes to the confidence with which novelists of the past few decades have embraced a maximalist mode of inquiry and have been able to achieve relatively immediate success. It also helps explain why a writer like Gaddis had to wait until later in his career to achieve renown. It is not that maximalism is unique in literary history, but that it has perhaps needed to wait until the rise of the information society to be appreciated as an *obviously* valuable mode of literary production. That the most prominent maximalist authors—or at least those whose works most immediately come to mind when discussing detailed writing—are American, is perhaps also explainable by the fact that America is the symbolic homeland for the excesses of material and informational consumption that typify standard accounts of the postwar world.

Although it is certainly fruitful to read contemporary maximalism as expressive of a mode of production or as a style that mirrors the excesses and anxieties of contemporary consumer culture, we have to be careful not to neglect that these writers often seem thrilled by detailedness in a manner that might be irreducible to this or that mimetic function, having just as much to do with how the craft of novel writing is positioned in the contemporary cultural field. There are strong connections between academic institutions and the reception of Joyce, Melville, Pynchon, and Wallace (and to a lesser extent, Baker), and so one could argue that the difficult amount and kind of detail that fills these writers' works is related to an academic preference for difficulty, a way for institutionalized readers in English departments to demonstrate that they are performing "hard" work (if not also a way to soothe the anxiety that reading is a "soft" form of labor). These are novels that appeal to a professional class of readers because they appeal to qualities that appease insecurities of being an English department academic in the twentieth and twenty-first centuries. But we can see excessive description as one performance of an author's avowed professionalism, too—a demonstration of skill and virtuosity not dissimilar to a violin cadenza or a guitar solo, as well as a defense against the possible insecurities of working as a writer in the contemporary world, a laborer bound mostly to a desk, stuck inside rather than engaging "productively" with other people and the outside world. McGurl has shown that minimalism is the style of writing that most obviously promotes a "professional" engagement with craft in the postwar American literary scene,[82] but the difficult compositional acts of maximalist authors similarly expresses an intensive professionalism—an exaggerated claim to creativity, productivity, and project management.

Focusing on ideas bound up with the craft of writing allows one to suggest that the choice of subject matter of many maximalist works even appears to be influenced by the preference for writing in a detailed, excessive manner, rather than content dictating form. The experiences of manic drug addicts in *Infinite Jest* and overwhelmed Internal Revenue Service (IRS) employees in *The Pale King* lend themselves well to maximalist treatment, and the consistency of Wallace's choice of such "naturally" maximalist subject matter should make us aware that it is sometimes the needs of form and style that motivate the selection of content. Wallace's career almost appears as a search for a topic that would best suit his love of maximalist prose, one he arguably fulfilled with *The Pale King*'s interest in boredom and attention. In examples such as Wallace's, we perhaps need to focus our analysis away from what shapes of culture these texts appear to mime in their detailedness and comprehensiveness, and toward what encourages their authors to write in this particular manner in the first place, what practical needs—fantasized or actual—are sated by writing a maximalist novel. In general, I wish to avoid viewing these novels as symptomatic of broader social issues and troubles, in favor of something like Nicholas D. Paige's understanding of fiction as a "nebula of writing practices and ideas about writing-techniques invented and modified ... through a difficult-to-specify dialectical relationship with what people think literature can and should do."[83]

Although it seems somewhat tautological to propose that detailed novels exist because some writers like to write detailed novels, what we do receive in maximalist writing is an encouragement for us to focus on the practice of writing, rather than only what areas of culture it serves. I take this partly to be a reaction to what William Paulson describes as the reduction of literature to an "ever more circumscribed role" in contemporary culture.[84] For Paulson, much of the knowledge literature was once thought to provide—the understanding of humans and their culture, for example—is now covered by more rigorously "scientific" disciplines, such as psychology, economics, neuroscience, and biology, a development that threatens the legitimacy and prestige of literary knowledge. As a result, literature is increasingly marginalized in culture, its purpose unclear and even esoteric. In light of this sense of the object's marginalization (which only increases in the age of cinema, the internet, video games, and other rival media[85]), a lot of literary criticism can be viewed as the attempt to rediscover the ailing purpose of the literary, to make claims for its vitality, to theorize a critical cultural function it might once again possess. But this frequently occurs by piggybacking other discourses, by making claims for the literary that might also just be translations of its content into the terms of psychology, neuroscience, and economics, or by moving the effect of a book very far away from what many of us actually experience as the activity and value of reading and writing. Although often valid, the focus on what wider social, cultural, and political issues literature reflects can stand to take focus away from what writing *is* as a form of work or leisure, what activities are involved in its production and reception, and what readers use it for in their lives outside critical professions. Rather than augmenting literature's importance, then, such accounts might risk obscuring it. As we will see in each of the following chapters, maximalist literature constantly wants to draw our attention back to activities and intellectual processes involved in the creation of literary texts, and to show us how these activities and processes are often meaningful enough already, without having to be laden with other, "deeper" significances. To steal some words from Terry Eagleton's study of Samuel Richardson, I am less interested in what the maximalist novel mirrors, "than in what it *does*."[86] For all of the complexity (or banality) that Wallace's description of a wall of unremarkable photos seems to imply, it is perhaps also just a vision of writing as a material practice, a reminder of what it is and isn't in its simplest form.

The Uses of Detail

A step in the direction of addressing this alleged shortcoming is to understand the maximalist novel not as a mimetic object, but as a text in which the presentation of specificity gains meaning and effect as an *activity*—as the demonstration of various abilities assumed to be necessary to create the text and which might be used by readers to claim similar things for themselves in their critical productions and reading experiences. The maximalist novel certainly captures a great deal, but the fact of having provided such a large amount of detail is meaningful over and above the significance of whatever is represented. For example, one might recognize the importance of the ambitiousness performed by all maximalist instances of description and "noticing," and consider that readers encounter these texts as a record of ambition and skill, equally as much as a narrative about particular subjects, characters, or settings. Tom LeClair suggests that *Gravity's Rainbow* "is about forms of mastery and employs excess for ... three kinds of mastery— over the contemporary world, artistic methods, and the reader."[87] Similarly, David Cowart says of Pynchon's ability to present details from a wide spectrum of erudite disciplines, that "if he does not, in the end, master it all, he sets a formidable example of dauntlessness before the awesome modern diversity."[88] Just as important as the thematic content of *Gravity's Rainbow*, then, is the example of mastery its maximalist management of detail sets. Pynchon's ability to create a vast assemblage of information from diverse areas of study—history, philosophy, economics, mathematics, and engineering, to name a few—makes a claim for the author's ability to reconcile, often within his own figure, the complexity of the contemporary intellectual landscape. Despite the care *Gravity's Rainbow* takes to confound almost all hermeneutic avenues that would end in a point of textual unification, and despite Pynchon's care to remain absent from the public eye, ultimately the *fantasy* of Pynchon the Author still rests at the core of his novel as a supreme, maximalist intellect able, if not to resolve, then certainly stand above many of the felt epistemological uncertainties of the postmodern world. As we will see in Chapter 1, Pynchon—or at least our imagined, polymathic version of him—is one of the shadowy giants that haunts the landscape of his novel, and is a figure readers of the text often aspire to sit alongside.

Although Brian McHale has argued that no consistent voice in the text can be plausibly labeled as Pynchon's own and that the text defeats any attribution of its voice to a stable origin,[89] there is nevertheless felt to be something of a meta-agent that is seen as being at least responsible for the assemblage of the work, if nothing else. It is a voice perhaps never present in the text—for to label it as such would be to subject it to the novel's undermining of stable points of origin—but that is nevertheless seen as responsible for organizing all of its content. It might be a fantasized projection, of course, but it is a necessary one. As Delville and Norris claim, "to accept the death of the author as implicitly true of maximalism would, we suggest, imply an inconceivable mastery of such art on the part of its audience."[90] Henry James put it similarly when he bemoaned that with "large loose baggy monsters" of books, we tend to find ourselves looking "in vain for the artist, the divine explanatory genius who will come to our aid."[91] The ironic comfort that the difficulty of Pynchon's maximalism presents us with lies in the prospect of becoming someone who will no longer require such authorial aid, and will be able to substitute the text's "explanatory genius," offering assistance to other readers less able.

Such ambitiousness enables us to supplement mimetic understandings of maximalist prose by shifting attention to what values are implied by the act of representation, rather than its content. For a reader, what's important isn't necessarily what is being represented, but that so much *is*, that so much "difficult" looking has been achieved. Viewing a work like *Gravity's Rainbow* in this manner enables us to understand that despite its difficulties, maximalism is almost by necessity reassuring, if not pleasurable, for a readership painfully conscious that the possibility of intellectual mastery and control of the "modern diversity," as Cowart puts it, is a fantasy only the most naive mind clings to. The function of these texts is to be comforting (especially apparent in the work of Baker, as we will see), but also to operate out of a fantasy of intelligence attached to their authors who, despite this difficulty, have constructed these works (especially relevant in the work of Pynchon). The author is not, in these maximalist texts, the "dregs of his work, the human shambles that follows it around," as William Gaddis once put it.[92] Nor is he necessarily the figure in which all questions must find their answer. The author is the fantasized figure within whom many of the contradictions, tensions, and ambivalences of the book and the world it depicts seem resolved, not because he can provide all the secret meaning of the text, but because he is responsible for the seemingly superhuman task of its construction. As Mark Greif puts it:

> [in the big, ambitious novel] all knowing is accomplished through countless limited and idiosyncratic characters who together prove a kind of encyclopedic or superhuman range that must belong to the author but is never acknowledged as an authorial possession. This paradoxical position of the author, too, seems central to the form and its conditions for existence: as if the continuing vitality of the novel were partly proven in the enigma of a single mind containing and activating the dispersed knowledge that should only belong to aggregate or collectively authored "forms" (the newspaper, the radio, the historical atlas, or the census).[93]

Among other things, maximalist works then offer us a chance to critique the now conventional dismissal of the figure of the author from the field of literary analysis. By and large, they do so by returning to the textual object, and its reception, an appreciation of literary labor. As Henry Veggian suggests, theories that justified the demise of authorship in favor of ideals of autonomous textualism were "not so much the avant-garde of literary studies but a circus act whose penultimate trick was making the labor of book production vanish into a puff of smoke."[94] The result, as Veggian writes elsewhere, is that a literary work is often regarded "as a sort of passive commodity that suddenly appears as the result of predetermined social pressures,"[95] rather than through the toil of an author making relatively autonomous decisions. A book written with a maximalist mode of inquiry, however, implies an almost "superhuman" exertion of labor, and thus demands we appreciate the effort required to produce it. The tedious descriptions of banal settings we find in Wallace's *The Pale King*, descriptions that persist long after any mimetic or semantic purpose has disappeared, seem determined to have readers appreciate what the majority of an author's work consists of—sitting down, typing away in an often tedious, dull, and repetitive employment. Maximalist novels exaggerate the labor of writing and encourage readers to appreciate the work of writing (and reading) the text as part of its aesthetic effect.

A novelist who has a handle on the management of complex information is also likely to provide reassurance for those of us worried by the flood of information typifying our present age and the general epistemological powerlessness of the individual subject figured in theories of postmodern culture.

We could even go so far as to suggest that many of the novels studied here aim to teach readers coping mechanisms for life in the information society (especially apparent when one considers Wallace's fascination with the "self-help" genre[96]). The maximalist love for specificity and detail sets an ideal of dauntlessness that readers might be inspired to follow, an idea we'll explore further later. As will become apparent in Baker's work in particular, max-imalism also encourages us to turn abilities of data management back to areas of personal and material life that we might have thought uninteresting or trivial, making them "re-experiencable."[97] *The Mezzanine's* enthusiasm for drinking straws and shoelaces is pursued with the same intense focus on detail as would be expected of a financial document, but with far more enriching results for those of us outside the stock market.

But there are of course values other than comfort implied by maximalist texts when we view them as objects with a function exceeding mimesis (and, as we will consider in our discussion of *Gravity's Rainbow*, this comforting function of the novel initially depends on the reader feeling the *opposite* of comfort—the experience of insufficiency). David Foster Wallace's *Infinite Jest*, one of the key works of contemporary maximalism, certainly flirts with many fantasies of ambition and indeed claims similar qualities of ability as Baker's and Pynchon's works. But it also complicates whatever powerful-ness is attached to its status as a "big" novel. By and large, the maximalist descriptions used in *Infinite Jest* encourage a focus on behaviors and activi-ties that "flunk" whatever purposes we might want to see in texts. The con-fident and ambitious scope of the novel is balanced by a certain amount of fatigue with what is expected of the author of such a large work. As such, it becomes clear that as much as it wants to dazzle us with its power, *Infinite Jest* also wants to evade or even sabotage fantasies of literary value and greatness by being dysfunctional. This novel looks with maximalist specific-ity because it wants to create a text that will fail—and so resist—whatever grading processes we might approach it with, forcing us to revise our expec-tations of the literary object.

Wallace's fascination in *Infinite Jest* with blank details also pushes us toward recognition of the writer as a figure with a somewhat strained rela-tionship to ideals of social usefulness. *Infinite Jest* is marked throughout by a tension between its desire to offer fiction as something of a social panacea, and the author's wish to have his working life—sitting still for long periods, putting words to a page—validated as a worthwhile and significant activity in itself. The wraith haunting the world of *Infinite Jest* is at times an author stand-in for Wallace, and Wallace uses it to speak directly to us about the process of constructing this work:

> it took incredible discipline and fortitude and patient effort to stay stock-still in one place for long enough for an animate man actually to see and be in any way affected by a wraith, and very few wraiths had anything important enough to interface about to be willing to stand still for this kind of time, preferring ordinarily to whizz around.[98]

It seems an obvious cry for appreciation beyond whatever literary values a novel promotes. The maximalist descriptions that celebrate what I call flunking also encourage us to view the activity of writing in something of an objective appraisal. In a sense, this is to appreciate the life of the fiction writer in a more direct manner than when we load him with literary virtues, and is perhaps to recognize the violence of judging the worthiness of objects—and, by extension, lives—at all. Again, it is also to view the significance of the written object not for what it mirrors, but, as Wallace's wraith points out, for the concentration, patience, and commitment necessary to construct it. As Wallace well knew, the modern world is certainly buzzing with distractions; besides the many ways *Infinite Jest*'s narrative registers the busyness of contemporary experience, that such a long and tightly organized work exists affirms that it's still possible to work in a "slower" manner that resists the imperative of speediness underpinning so much of modern culture.

Even though we've again arrived at a somewhat comforting function, I don't want to give the impression that maximalist writing is *only* comforting. I at least need to make it clear that this comfort isn't simply that which comes through knowing lots of things in great detail. Pynchon's *Inherent Vice*, for example, takes aim at the cultures of maximalist reading that have risen up around works like *Gravity's Rainbow*, playing with and ultimately resisting the fantasies of intelligence and identification this and other of Pynchon's novels elicit. *Inherent Vice* aims to provide an immersive experience of maximalism that doesn't allow the methods of "escape" Pynchon's earlier works afforded, and instead embraces the benefit of withered mental powers. Motivating Nicholson Baker's stunning uses of insight are rebukes of those aspects of culture that deem some things worthy of study, whereas others only suitable for the background matter of descriptions. His commitment to seeing and describing the particulars of an object or a feeling is an attempt to counter the romanticization of ineffability and evocations of the sublime that dominate many literary descriptions, as well as much postmodernist and poststructuralist writing that fetishizes the interminable and incomplete.

So, alongside whatever fantastically comforting or optimistic function these effusive works might achieve, the maximalism of all three authors also rests upon an attempt to *discomfort* the often stale situation of literary evaluation at the turn of the millennium, asking us to reevaluate how, and why, we read novels in the late twentieth and early twenty-first centuries, and what it means that we do so. An over-long description of a wall of banal photos forces us not just to question how we might employ its excess data, but why we should feel compelled to employ things at all.

White Noise

This book has always carried an open sense of direction, but some of the order it has found has come from exclusions, and there are other areas of study and a long list of authors that are largely bracketed here, pursued in the conclusion in relative brevity. I wanted to focus closely on the maximalism of a limited group of writers whose works are closely connected to develop a sense of the complexity of the maximalist mode of inquiry, rather than make broad claims from the vantage point of "distant reading." This has resulted in what might be taken as a limited focus, but I would reassure the reader anxious to point out all I've overlooked that I offer this as just one example of how maximalist poetics are used in contemporary literary culture.

That said, there are exclusions that need some mention as they bring to light areas in need of further study. The gender of the chosen writers is perhaps the factor that is hardest to ignore, and that which presents itself as the most difficult to account for because the focus on male writers extends beyond my own study. The three authors on whom the majority of this book focusses are, of course, white men. If we were to add other obvious maximalist authors to the study—William Gaddis, Joseph McElroy, John Barth, Roberto Bolaño, James Joyce, Herman Melville—the exclusively male (and mostly white focus) would still remain (although maximalist texts from popular nonwhite authors, including Samuel Delany's *Dhalgren* and, recently, Marlon James' *A Brief History of Seven Killings*, would initially suggest the style is skewed even more along gender than racial lines). Do only male authors write maximalist novels? No, not exclusively, but it does seem that the genre is dominated by this demographic. This seems ironic when, as Schor points out, overdetailed writing has historically been associated with female authors. Schor quotes William L. Courtney's 1904 remark, for instance, that "a passion for detail is the distinguishing mark of nearly every female novelist."[99] A male maximalism becomes more understandable when we consider that many maximalist novels also demonstrate a fascination with the display of technical know-how (an aspect of what McGurl calls technomodernism[100]), evidenced both in the ability to grapple with technical disciplines and complex approaches to the structuring of information in the novel. Whatever complex socialization influences the gender divide in Science, Technology, Engineering, and Mathematics fields of work finds another expression in maximalist writing.

There are, of course, female authors of long, expansive, contemporary novels that can be considered maximalist. Leslie Marmon Silko's *Almanac of the Dead* and Karen Tei Yamashita's *I Hotel* are works that find value in specificity, using detail to assert the density and reality of the overlooked experience of marginalized identities—in Silko's case, that of Native Americans, and in Yamashita's, of Asian Americans. The multiform nature of Yamashita's novel, drawing upon a range of writing styles and modes including reportage, illustration, and film script, harkens back to Joyce's *Ulysses* and indicates the extensive and varied research behind the work. In the Afterword, Yamashita speaks of the wide range of materials consulted for *I Hotel* (including more than 150 interviews), as well the challenge of balancing the endlessness of historical information with the needs of a novel: "At some point, I realized that I was supposed to be writing a novel, and the research had to stop."[101] This is a text assembled from a variety of sources, and Yamashita reminds us of the complexity of her subject matter through the varied nature of the novel's form, most forcefully in the fact that it is divided into ten relatively distinct novellas. In the end, the density of her historical subject matter was presumably too great to organize into a more conventional narrative. Instead of narrative unity, the novel takes a geographical landmark as its anchoring point—the International Hotel of its title. Although on the level of its prose, the novel isn't as outwardly maximalist as Wallace's or Pynchon's, its form implies a maximalist engagement with history, research, and information nonetheless.

That women (and nonwhite) authors such as Yamashita exist largely in the margins of the maximalist "canon" (Yamashita was a finalist for the National Book Award but has not achieved the mainstream success of Pynchon, Baker, or Wallace) suggests that what many readers want from maximalist novels is not always present in texts that articulate a non-mainstream, marginalized experience, or at least that the readers of maximalist novels tend to be primarily interested in the maximalist expression of relatively mainstream cultural positions. Wallace once stated that the readers who seemed most excited about *Infinite Jest* were "young men,"[102] and elsewhere imagined them to be "people more or less like me, in their twenties and thirties, maybe, with enough experience or good education to have realized that the hard work serious fiction requires of a reader sometimes has a payoff."[103] Although this is, of course, only a heuristic judgment, it does nevertheless express a feeling that books like *Infinite Jest* and *Gravity's Rainbow* are representations of a specific cultural position in the same manner that Yamashita's maximalism can be seen as her attempt to place Asian-Americanness in the literary spotlight. When employed by writers like Yamashita, maximalism involves the effusive expression of a set of cultural experiences kept out of a nation's dominant narrative. The implied point of Yamashita's claim that she was nearly overwhelmed by the research she undertook for *I Hotel* is that there is enough material in the "margins" of any culture to constitute a parallel and equally rich narrative alongside the mainstream. My point is that when in the hands of white, male, educated Americans (and whiteness is the unnamed quality of Wallace's "people like me"), we can perhaps view maximalism as an attempt to express the complexity of mainstream elements of American culture with the enthusiasm and energy (and perhaps even pride) other kinds of "white" American writing seem reluctant to admit. McGurl suggests that minimalism, for instance, is "despite a few exceptions, quite white," but it is also mostly apolitical, promoting a "politics of silence" in which lower-middle-class white characters experience their lives as disconnected from larger "issues of the day," practicing "self-concealment" rather than the obsessive self-reflection typical of Wallace's fiction.[104] The popularity of minimalist writers such as Carver in the postwar environment is perhaps then in a dialectical relationship with the success of writers like Pynchon and Wallace, the max-imalists complementing the minimalists and allowing Wallace's "people like me" to engage with their cultural position in a way that minimalism doesn't quite allow. Amid the expansive discussions of offices, shopping malls, the role of Britain and America in WWII, 1960s hippie movements, the cultures of consumption, institutions of education, and so forth that are the settings and subject matter of the maximalist novels studied here, we find something like the shared landmarks of postwar American society as seen through the eyes of those middle-class, educated Americans who have the luxury of being relatively free from racial and economic concerns. That these novels are difficult to read and fetishize ideals of "hard work" allows readers to avoid some of the discomfort otherwise present in the authors' mainstream interests because the effort of reading them makes this focus feel carefully considered rather than cheap or lazily "white." These ideas will be returned to in the concluding chapter of this book.

The shape of the remainder of *Maximalism in Contemporary Literature* is as follows (much of this has been discussed in bits and pieces here, but it's probably helpful to lay it out here in a more straightforward fashion). I begin with a discussion of Pynchon's *Gravity's Rainbow* that aims to estab-lish the basic nexus between the reader and writer of maximalist novels as one of insufficiency. When encountering Pynchon's work, a reader is asked to tackle an impossible multitude of signs that are all charged with poten-tially significant meaning, and thus stands to become lost in a "swirling fog" of details. But because of its difficulty, reading *Gravity's Rainbow* can, ironically, become a very comforting experience, with the maximalism of the text used as a means of clawing one's way above whatever insufficiency it otherwise provokes. What *Gravity's Rainbow* becomes for many readers is a document that both expresses the epistemological anxieties of its historical moment *and* provides a means for their escape.

My discussion of Wallace's *Infinite Jest* in Chapter 2 views maximalism as a style used to express uncertainty about the intersections between literary writing and institutions. Although *Infinite Jest* is an encompassing and eru-dite work that discusses philosophy, aesthetics, tennis, pharmacology, and calculus with Pynchonian confidence, the text's maximalist "intrusions"—long and resistant descriptions such as the enumeration of photographs offered at the start of this introduction—appear designed to refuse any easy use or "grading" of the text. Like several of the novel's protagonists, these descriptions express fatigue with being made to perform in a valuable manner.

In Wallace's *The Pale King*, the subject of Chapter 3, the "flunking" of *Infinite Jest* is developed into a deliberate aesthetic of dullness and boredom, but one intended to have a more positive effect than was possible in *Infinite Jest*'s maximalism. This work aims to move beyond the weary stubbornness of the earlier novel and take the possibilities of its unappealing maximalist prose very seriously, erasing the conflict between descriptive dysfunction and literary value, by, as it were, connecting the two. The novel is set in the largely dull offices of the IRS, and filled with deliberately tedious characters, ruminations on tax law, and a narrative that, either by design or as a result of the work's unfinished nature, fails to offer much diversion. But *The Pale King* sees such dullness as possessing great importance, both politically and personally. By learning to enjoy boredom and tedium, we stand to be able to engage with those aspects of life that flow beneath the threshold of the interesting and yet contain so much we need to be aware of. By embracing dullness we also, it is implied, stand to negate the need for constant stimulation that derailed so many of *Infinite Jest*'s addicts. The most interesting aspect of *The Pale King* for our purposes is that Wallace's approach to this novel theorizes a way in which writing maximalist prose is seen as a socially useful act in itself. By overloading his novel with particulars, Wallace aims to teach lessons in patience and attention, and suggests that the importance of this writing does not lie what it represents, so much as what practical challenges it puts upon its readers.

In Chapters 4 and 5 we look at two brief but intellectually expansive works by Nicholson Baker, *The Mezzanine* and *Room Temperature*, which are here deemed maximalist miniatures. In Baker's work the somewhat anxious status of detail and specificity in Wallace's and Pynchon's writing is resolved through the development of a casually ambitious maximalist relationship to everyday life. Baker works hard to develop the comforting functions of a high-definition attention to detail, and it is through his microscopic attention to specificity that he is able to create works of an epistemological optimism rarely found anywhere else in the largely anguished body of contemporary literature. The point of including Baker with more obviously maximalist authors is also to suggest that a maximalist mode of inquiry need not result in a long novel.

The last chapter of this book returns to Pynchon and one of his most recent novels, *Inherent Vice*. This work, I argue, is interested in resisting many of the effects and fantasies that have attached themselves to the reading of maximalist novels in the past—fantasies touched upon in my discussion of *Gravity's Rainbow*. If anything, *Inherent Vice* isn't so much a maximalist novel as one written *about* maximalism, and the insufficiency encountered in this work is approached in a very different manner than it was in *Gravity's Rainbow*. By the time of *Inherent Vice*, it is probably fair to say that Pynchon seems far less excited about the potential of the novel to be a socially disruptive object. But what he gains from the waning of ambition is a sense of quiet comfort that doesn't necessarily mark a retreat from the grandness and seriousness of his earlier works, so much as an admission that novels are perhaps much more effective at giving readers experiences to help them deal with daily life, rather than escape or shatter it. The mode of this novel's maximalism is ultimately immersive, and I feel it wants to teach us to "surf" the buzzing circuits of contemporary life, rather than escape them through the mastery promoted in some of Pynchon's earlier works.

Notes

1. Gustave Flaubert, *Madame Bovary*, tr. Gerard Hopkins (Oxford: Oxford University Press, 1981), 44.
2. Janell Watson, *Literature and Material Culture from Balzac to Proust: The Collection and Consumption of Curiosities* (Cambridge: Cambridge University Press, 1999), 115.
3. David Foster Wallace, *Infinite Jest: A Novel* (New York: Back Bay Books, 1996), 1034n209.
4. James Wood, *How Fiction Works* (London: Vintage, 2009), 61.
5. Ibid., 58.
6. Steve Katz, "Post Hoc Maximalism," *Guest Editor* 1 (1984): 3.
7. This is somewhat similar to the filmmaker James O. Incandenza's "found drama" in Wallace's *Infinite Jest*. Wallace, *Infinite Jest*, 1027–1028n145.
8. Katz, "Post Hoc Maximalism," 3.
9. Throughout this book, I am primarily referring to writing produced in America from the 1970s to the 2010s. There are various terms used to describe the social, economic, and artistic tenor of this period, such as postindustrial, postmodernist, and late-capitalist. My intention here is not to weigh in on any debate for which is the most suitable appellation, or for arguing the compatibility between the different conditions they delineate. I use the terms with the recognition that each has its descriptive strengths and weaknesses. In general, I employ the term postindustrial for the shift toward "knowledge work" that it describes, but much of the work I aim to do here discusses a cultural situation better described as postmodern, or at least Fredric Jameson's writing of the postmodern as the product of "late" or globalized capitalism. Much maximalist writing seems to discover the way supposedly bygone relations of material production—or at least the fantasy of them—are present in the writing and reading of "difficult" and excessive texts. Maximalism, as an aesthetic practice, could be seen as an attempt to ground the knowledge economy of postindustrialism in a material relationship to texts that almost mimics the labor of older modes of production, and would thus not completely fit within the domain of a society geared toward a service economy (to invoke the main aspect of Daniel Bell's vision of the postindustrial society). The focus on work is perhaps also presented as a way to fend off the anxiety that literary reading is a "soft" form of labor. Daniel Bell, *The Coming of Post-Industrial Society: A Venture in Social Forecasting* (London: Heinemann Educational, 1974).
10. John Kuehl, *Alternate Worlds: A Study of Postmodern Antirealistic American Fiction* (New York: New York University Press, 1989), 104.
11. Tom LeClair, *The Art of Excess: Mastery in Contemporary American Fiction* (Urbana: University of Illinois Press, 1989), 26.
12. What is "usually" considered the acceptable amount of anything is obviously impossible to define in any proper way, as it is a constantly changing and subjective judgment. Nevertheless, we can suggest that an acceptable amount of detail is that which readers can find a "use" for. As we will discuss later, when felt to go beyond the needs of verisimilitude, or exceeding the means of interpretation, detail is often felt to be superfluous, and can bring to the aesthetic object an impression of unruliness or lack of care in relation to craft. See, for example, the discussions of the equation of detailed art with decadence in Naomi Schor,

Reading in Detail: Aesthetics and the Feminine (New York: Methuen, 1987). A maximalist text, however, is interested in the uses of detail beyond what appears useful in relation to the cultures of reading contemporary to it.

13. Stefano Ercolino, "The Maximalist Novel," *Comparative Literature* 64, no. 3 (2012): 244.

14. Arthur M. Saltzman, "To See a World in a Grain of Sand: Expanding Literary Minimalism," *Contemporary Literature* 31, no. 4 (1990): 424. Interestingly, Saltzman includes David Foster Wallace in his discussion of minimalist writers, although this was the pre-*Infinite Jest* Wallace.

15. See, for example, Saltzman, "To See a World," 425–29.

16. Michel Delville and Andrew Norris, "Frank Zappa, Captain Beefheart, and the Secret History of Maximalism," in *Contemporary Poetics*, ed. Louis Armand (Evanston, IL: Northwestern University Press, 2007), 126. As we will see, their claim is a little hyperbolic—there are several studies that make mention of it—but seems to hold true in general, at least at the time they were writing. Since then, Mark McGurl and Stefano Ercolino have both written about maximalism in a sustained manner. Nevertheless, in comparison to studies of minimalism, maximalism does still seem underutilized as a critical concept. Mark McGurl, *The Program Era: Postwar Fiction and the Rise of Creative Writing* (Cambridge, MA: Harvard University Press, 2009); Stefano Ercolino, *The Maximalist Novel: From Thomas Pynchon's Gravity's Rainbow to Roberto Bolaño's 2666* (London: Bloomsbury Publishing, 2014).

17. Saltzman, "To See a World," 428.

18. Richard Taruskin, *The Oxford History of Western Music*, volume 4, *Music in the Early Twentieth Century* (Oxford: Oxford University Press, 2005), 5.

19. Ibid.

20. Charles McGrath, "The Souped-Up, Knock-Out, Total Fiction Experience," *New York Times*, April 17, 2005, C16.

21. Edward Mendelson, "Encyclopedic Narrative: From Dante to Pynchon," *MLN* 91, no. 6 (1976); LeClair, *The Art of Excess*; Frederick R. Karl, *American Fictions: 1980–2000: Whose America is it Anyway?* (Bloomington: Xlibris, 2001); James Wood, "Human, All Too Inhuman: The Smallness of the 'Big' Novel," *The New Republic*, July 24, 2000.

22. Mendelson, "Encyclopedic Narrative," 1269.

23. Ibid.

24. Ibid.

25. James Wood, "The Digressionist," *The New Republic*, August 9, 2004, 30.

26. Ercolino, "The Maximalist Novel,"; Ercolino, *The Maximalist Novel*.

27. Ercolino, "The Maximalist Novel," 242.

28. Ibid., 241.

29. John Barth, "A Few Words About Minimalism," *The New York Times*, December 28, 1986, BR2.

30. Indeed, James Wood once bemoaned that David Foster Wallace's writing was marred by a "numbing pedantry" of style. Wood, "The Digressionist," 29.

31. Francis Bacon, *The Advancement of Learning* (New York: Modern Library, 2010), 28.

32. Martin Jay, *Marxism and Totality: The Adventures of a Concept from Lukács to Habermas* (Cambridge: Polity Press, 1984), 336n18.

33. Ibid., 344.

34. Ibid., 351.

35. McGurl, *The Program Era*, 294.

36. David Foster Wallace, interview by Larry McCaffery, "An Expanded Interview with David Foster Wallace," in *Conversations with David Foster Wallace*, ed. Stephen J. Burn (Jackson: University Press of Mississippi, 2012), 37.

37. George Puttenham, *The Art of English Poesy: A Critical Edition*, ed. Frank Whigham and Wayne A. Rebhorn (Ithaca: Cornell University Press, [1589] 2007), 343.

38. See Schor's commentary on Francis Wey. Schor, *Reading in Detail*, 43–46.

39. William Spalding, *The History of English Literature: With an Outline of the Origin and Growth of the English Language. Illustrated by Extracts. For the Use of Schools and of Private Students* (Edinburgh: Oliver and Boyd, 1853), 400.

40. Wood, *How Fiction Works*, 64. Emphasis is Wood's own.

41. Richard House, "The Encyclopedia Complex: Contemporary Narratives of Information," *Substance* 29, no. 2 (2000): 40.

42. Ibid., 35.

43. Lord Kames, *Elements of Criticism* (New York: Johnson Reprint Corporation, 1967), 3: 300, quoted in Schor, *Reading in Detail*, 19.

44. Ibid.

45. Schor, *Reading in Detail*, 18.

46. Pauline Johnson, *Marxist Aesthetics* (Hoboken: Taylor and Francis, 2013), 29.

47. Georg Lukács, *The Meaning of Contemporary Realism*, tr. John and Necke Mander (London: Merlin Press, 1963), 51.

48. Ibid., 53.

49. Ibid., 51.

50. Ibid.

51. Georg Lukács, *Writer and Critic, and Other Essays*, tr. and ed. Arthur Kahn (London: Merlin Press, 1978), 110.

52. Today, it seems, the opposite is true, or at least the situation is more complicated. Although "literary maximalism can be thought of as a form of verbal pride," as Mark McGurl puts it, there is also a "prideful attention to craft" that typifies *minimalist* work, with the maximalist, in contrast, being seen as unruly, impulsive, and careless. McGurl, *The Program Era*, 296–301.

53. Watson, *Literature and Material Culture*, 110.

54. Ibid., 114.

55. Ibid., 109.

56. The Australian satirical television show *The Chaser's War on Everything* produced a useful parody of such advertisements: ChaserChannel, "The Chaser's War on Everything—Persian Rug Fire Sale," YouTube video, 0:46, posted November 18, 2007, from *The Chaser's War on Everything*, season 1, episode 3, https://youtu.be/jayAGGoU2Oc.

57. Franco Moretti, *Modern Epic: The World System from Goethe to Garcia Marquez*, tr. Quintin Hoare (London: Verso, 1996), 64. Moretti is actually citing Allen Grossman here, but there seems to have been a slight alteration when Moretti's work was translated into English. The phrase Grossman uses is "trope of inclusion," but I find the (mis)translated Moretti's "rhetoric of inclusivity" more useful. Allen Grossman, "The Poetics of Union in Whitman and Lincoln: An Inquiry toward the Relationship of Art and Policy," in *The American Renaissance Reconsidered: Selected Papers from the English*

Institute, 1982–83, ed. Walter Benn Michaels and Donald E. Pease (Baltimore: The Johns Hopkins University Press, 1985), 195.

58. William Bradford, *Of Plymouth Plantation 1620–1647* (New York: Random House, [1856] 1981), 1.
59. Richard Ruland and Malcolm Bradbury, *From Puritanism to Postmodernism: A History of American Literature* (New York: Routledge, 1991), 22.
60. Thomas Pynchon, *Gravity's Rainbow* (New York: The Viking Press, 1973), 223.
61. Ruland and Bradbury, *From Puritanism to Postmodernism*, 19.
62. Michelle Burnham, "Merchants, Money, and the Economics of 'Plain Style' in William Bradford's *Of Plymouth Plantation*," *American Literature* 72, no. 4 (2000): 706.
63. Ibid., 701.
64. Ibid., 702.
65. Moretti, *Modern Epic*, 64–65.
66. Grossman, "Poetics of Union," 192, 188.
67. Moretti, *Modern Epic*, 66.
68. Grossman, "Poetics of Union," 195–96.
69. In 1950, the Irish poet Oliver Gogarty disparagingly labeled America "the chief infirmary for Joyceans," with *Ulysses*' difficulty appealing to a "unique class" of Americans—fans of crossword puzzles and detective stories—who think that "the unravelling of an enigma or a puzzle is the height of poetry." Oliver Gogarty, "They Think They Know Joyce," in *James Joyce: The Critical Heritage*, ed. Robert H. Deming, vol. 2, *1928–1941* (London: Routledge, 1970), 765.
70. John McCourt, *James Joyce in Context* (Cambridge: Cambridge University Press, 2009), 55.
71. Ibid.
72. Julie Sloan Brannon, *Who Reads Ulysses? The Common Reader and the Rhetoric of the Joyce Wars* (New York: Routledge, 2003), 24.
73. Herman Melville to Lemuel Shaw, October 6, 1849, in *Correspondence: The Writings of Herman Melville*, ed. Lynn Horth (Evanston: Northwestern University and The Newberry Library, 1993), 139.
74. John Beer, "William Gaddis," *Review of Contemporary Fiction* 21, no. 3 (2001): 72.
75. David Golumbia, *The Cultural Logic of Computation* (Cambridge, MA: Harvard University Press, 2009), 215.
76. Walter Wriston, quoted in Richard A. Lanham, *The Economics of Attention: Style and Substance in the Age of Information* (Chicago: The University of Chicago Press, 2006), 4.
77. But only, that is, if one is a member of the "knowledge work" class. As André Gorz suggests, the information age is supported by a mass of service sector employees who pick up the slack of those whose economic success allows them to neglect the physical labors that constitute the rest of life—cooking, cleaning, etc. André Gorz, *Critique of Economic Reason*, tr. Gillian Handyside and Chris Turner (London: Verso, 1989), 5–6.
78. Alan Liu, *The Laws of Cool: Knowledge Work and the Culture of Information* (Chicago: University of Chicago Press, 2004), 1.
79. Schor, *Reading in Detail*, 85.
80. Pynchon's *Inherent Vice* seems designed to deflate these fantasies, however. See Chapter 6.

81. See, for instance, James Barker-Nunn's and Gary Alan Fine's discussion of the manner in which Melville's interactions with the Young American group of critics shaped both the form and reception of his novels. Jeanne Barker-Nunn and Gary Alan Fine, "The Vortex of Creation: Literary Politics and The Demise of Herman Melville's Reputation," *Poetics* 26 (1998): 81–98.

82. McGurl, *The Program Era*, 294.

83. Nicholas D. Paige, *Before Fiction: The Ancient Régime of the Novel* (Philadelphia: University of Pennsylvania Press, 2011), 205.

84. William R. Paulson, *The Noise of Culture: Literary Texts in a World of Information* (Ithaca: Cornell University Press, 1988), 17.

85. See Kathleen Fitzpatrick, *The Anxiety of Obsolescence: The American Novel in the Age of Television* (Nashville: Vanderbilt University Press, 2006), and Jeremy Green, *Late Postmodernism: American Fiction at the Millennium* (New York: Palgrave Macmillan, 2005), for discussions of the anxiety of obsolescence that plagues the novel.

86. Terry Eagleton, *The Rape of Clarissa: Writing, Sexuality and Class Struggle in Samuel Richardson* (Minneapolis: University of Minnesota Press, 1982), 4.

87. LeClair, *Art of Excess*, 36.

88. David Cowart, *Thomas Pynchon: The Art of Allusion* (Carbondale: Southern Illinois University Press, 1980), 4.

89. Brian McHale, *Constructing Postmodernism* (London: Routledge, 1992), 95–96.

90. Delville and Norris, "Secret History of Maximalism," 136.

91. Henry James, *The Art of the Novel: Critical Prefaces* (Chicago: University of Chicago Press, [1934] 2011), 84.

92. William Gaddis, *The Recognitions* (London: Atlantic Books, [1955] 2003), 96.

93. Mark Greif, "'The Death of the Novel' and Its Afterlives: Toward a History of the 'Big, Ambitious Novel,'" *Boundary 2* 36, no. 2 (2009), 28.

94. Henry Veggian, "Anachronisms of Authority: Authorship, Exchange Value, and David Foster Wallace's *The Pale King*," *Boundary 2* 39, no. 3 (2012), 116n39.

95. Henry Veggian, *Understanding Don DeLillo* (Columbia, SC: University of South Carolina Press, 2015), 2.

96. See, for example, Maria Bustillos, "Inside David Foster Wallace's Private Self-Help Library," *The Awl*, April 5, 2011, http://www.theawl.com/2011/04/inside-david-foster-wallaces-private-self-help-library.

97. This is a term used by Georg Lukács to describe one of the effects of realist totalization. As we will discuss at the end of Chapter 5, Baker's *The Mezzanine* offers something of a retake on Lukácsian realism. Georg Lukács, *Writer and Critic, and Other Essays*, 38.

98. Wallace, *Infinite Jest*, 831.

99. Schor, *Reading in Detail*, 20.

100. McGurl, *The Program Era*, 42.

101. Karen Tei Yamashita, *I Hotel* (Minneapolis: Coffee House Press, 2010), 610.

102. David Lipsky, *Although of Course You End Up Becoming Yourself: A Road Trip with David Foster Wallace* (New York: Broadway Books, 2010), 273.

103. Larry McCaffery, "An Interview with David Foster Wallace," *Review of Contemporary Fiction* 13, no. 2 (1993): 128.

104. McGurl, *The Program Era*, 314–15.

1   Giants and Junk

Power-Reading Thomas Pynchon's
Gravity's Rainbow

Clash of the Titans

I have a friend who's trying to read *Gravity's Rainbow* for the third time, having been unsuccessful on her previous two attempts. What is it about this book that, despite having not enjoyed it on two other occasions, makes her willing to persist with it yet again? What makes it worthwhile? What pressures her to read it "successfully" when there are so many other books on which to spend one's limited time?

She's certainly not lacking in company though. Of the most "liked" reviews of *Gravity's Rainbow* on the online community Goodreads, many foreground the concept of reading, reflecting on the activity's challenges and benefits as they relate to Pynchon's novel. One user helpfully lists "advice for a first time reader" struggling to make it through.[1] Another employs the metaphor of wrestling to declare that after three months she "pinned this sucker down for the count of ten."[2] The novel also prompts a reviewer to investigate the reasons why he reads at all.[3] As if responding to this intro-spection, one user worries "that someone would read books like this purely in order to show off or impress people."[4] For a user whose reflections seem the most typical, it took "a couple of tries to make it through Pynchon's Great Thing; the first time I began it eagerly enough, only to smash head-first into an impenetrable wall of thick, viscous prose that so entangled and bewildered me that—after some seventy-odd pages—I said Enough!" But, like my persistent friend, they found themselves drawn back to "give it another try. Determined to see it through."[5]

Professional critics approve the feelings of these readers when they con-firm that the most common relation to the poetics of this novel is indeed one of insufficiency—a felt lacking of power, size, perspective, or erudi-tion required to "successfully" encounter or account for the work. To feel dwarfed or at least partly overwhelmed by the gigantic text is something akin to its proper reading. As Tony Tanner put it:

> I think it is important to stress that the novel provides an exemplary experience in modern reading. The reader does not move comfortably from some ideal "emptiness" of meaning to a satisfying fullness, but instead becomes involved in a process in which any perception can

precipitate a new confusion, and an apparent clarification turn into a prelude to further difficulties. So far from this being an obstacle to appreciating the book, it is part of its essence.[6]

Brian McHale echoes these thoughts: "Pynchon's readers have every right to feel conned, bullied, betrayed. Indeed, these responses are the essence of the aesthetic effect of *Gravity's Rainbow*."[7]

It's one thing for a book to be difficult, but it also needs to offer readers the right amount of motivation to persevere if reading is to seem more than just hard labor. And if a book is difficult in the manner *Gravity's Rainbow* can be, the force of attraction pulling readers through needs to be especially strong. We can infer that something must be distilled by *Gravity's Rainbow* that, more than most other books, makes people keen to persist with it beyond what they might otherwise feel is reasonable.

Looking at the experiences recorded on Goodreads and elsewhere, it's clear that *Gravity's Rainbow* encourages readers to reflect on the activity of reading—question its purpose, theorize its strategies, and relate it to personal narratives of achievement and growth—often before matters related to its narrative interests. If the novel tells a story about anything, then, an investigation into how and why some of us read books today surely forms a large part of its plot, as it seems to ask readers to engage in some degree of self-reflection. The "impenetrable wall[s] of thick, viscous prose" that fill *Gravity's Rainbow* force many readers to articulate—either in the positive or negative—the value they attach to the time spent sitting down in their homes, on public transport, or in cafes with their eyes attached to (and often attacked by) Pynchon's prose.

But the primary reason *Gravity's Rainbow* maintains its status as something of a literary litmus test is because of its maximalism—that commitment to prose "thick" with detail. These details tend to be drawn from a wide range of cultural discourses—music, economics, politics, philosophy, mathematics, engineering, pop culture—so that the novel's author seems like a team of experts rather than a lone individual typing away in a beachside shack in California. Pynchon is arguably the most "taught" postmodernist author in university English programs, and so the reading of his work is perhaps motivated by the sense there is some tangible educational benefit to be had from it, the author's polymathy describing him as an ideal academic model, fluent in the full range of educational disciplines. As I'll argue in this chapter, one possible explanation for why readers feel moved to persist with this strange and dense novel is that Pynchon's maximalism draws them into fantasies of intellectual and critical ability enmeshed with the postwar American landscape. Although the novel's subject matter—the complex social, psychological, and political aftermath of World War II—is important for the insights it provides into the shaping of the contemporary world, there are other texts from the disciplines of history, economics, and politics that would do just as good a job. What's most useful about *Gravity's*

Rainbow today is that it has become a tool that helps articulate how some readers go about using literary novels in the contemporary landscape, as well as what value they put in the very human qualities of perseverance, patience, learning, erudition, and intelligence that the novel seems to throw into relief, and that have an increasingly uncertain value in an age where we are often asked to consider the limitations of human intellectual power.

But this is all to come. First, we need to jump into the midst of the novel and look at its sometimes-protagonist Tyrone Slothrop as he stands with Geli Tripping atop the Brocken, a mythically charged mountain in northern Germany. The Brocken has featured in other literary works before Pynchon's, but what makes it especially useful in *Gravity's Rainbow* is the peculiar illusion it is known for producing: the *Brockengespenstphänomen*.[8] If you stand in the right place atop the mountain at the right time of morning, when the sun rises and crests the mountain's peak it will cast your shadow far across the landscape below, as if you were a giant. As the troubled characters Slothrop and Geli look down from the mountain across the war-ravaged landscape of Germany, the sun hits their backs and throws their immense shadows before them, and they experience this illusory gigantism not just as a trick of the light, but as a fantasy that they are small individuals no longer—that they have a giant reach, covering a wide landscape, able to hold the complexity of postwar Europe in their fists, unfettered by the usual constraints of human perspective and dimension. They have "God-shadows."[9] Slothrop indulges the fantasy by raising his arm and letting his fingers play over the towns below, finding in this action a salve for what has been the progressive loss of his identity throughout the novel. In this moment of play, he sees himself as a relative of the mythical Titans thought to inhabit the mountains, those beings "impossibly out of scale," untroubled by the constraints of human size and strength (330). To corrupt the words of Oedipa Maas, an earlier Pynchon character, these characters don't "project a world" so much as project themselves over one.

Edward Mendelson has suggested that the titans and giants roaming the pages of *Gravity's Rainbow* provide an image of the novel's own scale.[10] But I would add that they are involved in a more complex dynamic of projection and identification that is representative of readers' experiences of the novel. The paranoid strain of *Gravity's Rainbow* would have it that Slothrop actually is something of a giant, that his body effectively extends over the landscape of war-torn Europe in the manner of this enlarged shadow, influencing and influenced by a multitude of others. With his supposed control (or at least precognizance) of the V2 rocket strikes in London, where his penis is akin to a missile-guiding beacon, his body overlays and affects a whole city of other matters and beings. The responsibility of this gigantic influence is something he could probably do without, but to be such a giant or titan is also surely a pleasing fantasy, for small moments of abandon at least. As another character, Oberst Enzian, worries just a few pages before Slothrop appears on the mountain, the "thousands of details" that flood the text and its world, swirling "like fog, each particle with its own array and forces and directions," threaten to overwhelm anyone of average dimensions, leaving them desperate to become titanized:

> Enzian would like to be more out of the process than he is—to be able to see where it's going, to know, in real time, at each splitting of the pathway of decision, which would have been right and which wrong. [...] he can't handle them all at the same time, if he stays too much with any he's in danger of losing others ... (326–27)[11]

To solve the difficulty, Enzian resorts to fantasies of gigantism—of being "more out of the process than he is," of *not* being an individual restricted to a singular perspective, a defined location in time and space. He wants to occupy a position above the events that are above him—the perspective of the giant, the titan, the Slothrop-atop-the-Brocken. And, as we will attempt to study here, the text's maximalism, its commitment to searching out and including those "thousands of details," has often left readers contemplating similar methods of escape.

What I hope to show here is that pursuant to the insufficiency enforced by the novel's maximalism is a felt pressure to grow oneself to gigantic dimensions to contain or at least glimpse the full range of its landscape, as Slothrop does atop the Broken. Goodreads shows that some readers get there, others do not. But the effect of the novel's maximalism—its inclusion of enough detail to develop strategies to manage it all—is always to be considered in relation to certain pressures of dimension and ability it places on the comparatively small subjects who enter the text, and those readers who let it loose in their lives. In this chapter, I'll engage the novel and the work of readers particularly invested in its explication in order to show that what *Gravity's Rainbow* continues to offer is a way to test what claims of identity and power are able to attached to the act of reading a novel—an outwardly passive activity that is pursued with patience and perseverance that outweighs any objective gain to be had through its performance. There is no prize awaiting those who finish the novel; no guaranteed revelations that occur after its final page. But there's something that pulls readers through nonetheless.

Evensong

Before we get to any of this, we need to work harder to set the basic scene of *Gravity's Rainbow*'s maximalism to get a sense of exactly what makes Slothrop so ready to enjoy his projected gigantism and readers so keen to persist with the novel. There are examples of Pynchon's maximalist approach to writing on every page, but a particularly illustrative passage occurs early on in the novel when Jessica Swanlake is with her wartime lover Roger Mexico at a church, and she soon becomes swept up in the nostalgic mood of caroling performed by a roughly assembled choir (129–36). In this scene, Pynchon demonstrates the theme of this novel's maximalism in both form and content. The passage begins conventionally enough, describing the temperature and smell of the church and initially focalized through Jessica, but it soon opens out into a rhapsodic and vertiginous accumulation of details, at first briefly, as if being fought, before becoming completely overrun. As in Yeats' widening gyre, the center cannot hold and the grounded consciousness from which the experience begins falls away, is left below, soon unable to be heard. What starts out as nostalgic reflection for Jessica, the original focalizer of the passage, is soon overtaken by a cacophony of other minds clamoring to speak, "voices overlapping three- and fourfold, up, echoing, filling the entire hollow of the church" (136), desperate to force themselves into the scene.

The accumulation of details and other voices carries the passage away from Jessica's control—it is too much for any one mind to synthesize, so the novel adopts a more distanced, but also more chaotic, perspective. Soon enough, the novel is listening to the scene from a perspective that either dwarfs the characters in it—a giant's view—or else is no stable perspective at all, is perspective's collapse. Jessica's point of view becomes crowded by the presence of surrounding voices, if not overtaken by them. The uncertain focalization of the passage responds to what Alan Clinton describes as the fear, typical in encyclopedic novels, that "the individual may literally be crowded out" by the proliferation of rival objects in the text.[12] Clinton is specifically speaking of commodities, but the presence of other voices evokes much the same anxiety. Jessica is crowded out of her own passage by rival voices and objects.

The resulting cacophony of competing voices tends to be difficult for the prose to extricate itself from—indeed, it seems addictive for the novel, which is constantly pulled toward a sort of rhapsodizing that threatens endlessness. The only way these riffing passages seem able to resolve is to reach either, as in Yeats' "centerless" poem, the moment of a question, a crossroads, or else some vision of death or stillness, a pause in which an individual consciousness is able to be recast, allowing the ordinary mode of narrative presentation to resume. The pauses in the present passage are as follows. First, a mind chasing voices is returned to briefly before being left behind, unable to keep up and hear everything, reminded only of its insufficiency:

> the fear that she was beginning to lose them, that one winter she would go running to look, out to the gate to find them, run as far as the trees but in vain, their voices fading ... (128)

Roger's image is here beyond Jessica's descriptive power:

> he wasn't looking nihilistic, not even cheaply so. He was ... (129)

Here an intractable ambiguity dominates:

> Is the baby smiling, or is it just gas? Which do you want it to be? (131)

A final image of isolation:

> for you to take back to your war-address, your war-identity, across the
> snow's footprints and tire tracks finally to the path you must create by
> yourself, alone in the dark. Whether you want it or not, whatever seas
> you have crossed, the way home … (136)

The effect of these pauses and their elliptic questions is to bring the immense,
roaring weight of the passages, often overfull with matter, back to bear on
the individual—and it's always a lonely, paralyzed person, beleaguered by
intimations of insufficiency, doubt, impotence, feeling "alone in the dark."
A teetering tower of accumulated meanings, references, and signs likewise
balances in front of the reader. And it is to these points that the novel, both
on the micro-level of these rhapsodic passages and as a whole, constantly
returns: not to a plenitude of understanding, but a feeling of insufficiency
that floods the individual yearning for a such a gigantic, bird's-eye view, and
who must hopelessly scramble to weave the text's "thousands of details"
into a meaningful tapestry through the patient effort of close reading.

This is to look at the passage in a largely formal manner, however. We
begin to get a sense of the different directions in which the novel points
readers when we consider the form of this description in relation to its content. So, alongside the insufficiency caused by the maximalist density and
drift of the prose, this passage tells a story about the transfiguring mechanisms of the war, its ability to turn inert, everyday rubbish (toothpaste tubes
and other discarded junk) into objects of value. And although this might
seem like a slightly terrifying process—our discarded toiletries coming back
to haunt us as bombs—it's eventually one of comfort, allowing the reader
who can recognize it a feeling which is something of the opposite of insufficiency. That is, *insight*:

> one by one these old toothpaste tubes are emptied and returned to the
> War, heaps of dimly fragrant metal, phantoms of peppermint in the
> winter shacks, each tube wrinkled or embossed by the unconscious
> hands of London, written over in interference-patterns, hand against
> hand, waiting now—it is true return—to be melted for solder, for plate,
> alloyed for castings, bearings, gasketry, hidden smokeshriek linings the
> children of that other domestic incarnation will never see. (130)

The toothpaste is a complex object. It interferes with words, mumbling
the speech of those who try to talk with a mouth full of it, "among the
chalky bubbles." It also records an "unconscious" language, written in the

"interference-patterns" left by hands that squeeze the tubes. But as the tubes are reincarnated into material for the War, these idle conversations and unthinking movements are swept up and overrun by a larger purpose.

This method of "reincarnation" describes a hermeneutic process most novels and types of literary criticism encourage, and one particularly important to the reading and writing of *Gravity's Rainbow*. Namely, *paranoia*, the notion that "everything is connected" (703), that every object, utterance, and sign has a secret, undisclosed relationship to a "holy Center." As McHale discusses, following the work of Thomas Siegel, most critical reading can be safely described as paranoid in one sense or another: "*everything is connected* would make an apposite epigraph for a good many books of literary criticism written since 1925 or so."[13] The paranoid hermeneutic that pervades *Gravity's Rainbow*, and for which Pynchon's work is well-known, is one that ensures its details, no matter how trivial, can tremble with terrifying significance. In a paranoid world, every toothpaste tube will find a significance belying its humble exterior. And, for a reader, this habit of connecting part to whole is one that bestows power and perspective that the maximalist density and drift of the novel otherwise denies. The propaganda of the War "will always stress unity, alliance, pulling together" (130), and so do the critical habits of the reader. The many small parts of the text are pulled magnetically toward a center, able to be viewed in relation to something much larger. The paranoid worldview offers relief from the mess of details that flood the text and threaten to drown the reader. Paranoia is seeing giants at the center of everything, giant hands controlling the small movements of the world. But it is also the fantasy of possessing "giant" insight oneself, being high enough above a situation that one can see what all of life's toothpaste tubes end up becoming.

The "agency panic" that Timothy Melley argues is endemic to postwar American culture is here both stimulated and soothed by the maximalist novel. For Melley, when faced with a political and social world that seems increasingly chaotic, individuals tend to fantasize about larger, overarching systems of control and agency that "they suspect have been depleted from themselves or others around them."[14] Most of Pynchon's characters seem hopelessly trapped within such panic and paranoia, but readers are allowed here to feel some satisfaction that an order persists beyond the viewpoint of any one individual.

Paranoia functions, then, in a manner not terribly dissimilar to Lukácsian totalization, the effect of fiction that places a character meaningfully within a world governed by purposefulness. The feeling of insight that, for the reader at least, overlays the otherwise scattered passage certainly erases "the separation between the particular and the general," suspending the "fragmentary, heterogeneous attitude of everyday life" under advanced capitalism by revealing the relation of part to whole (the larger purpose of the toothpaste tubes, etc.).[15] In the novel, all details become part of the War, linked to the mysterious powers behind its events. Outside the novel (if we can be so schematic as to suggest such a division), all of these details are united by another power: the partly absent, partly omnipresent, partly imagined, partly real figure of Thomas Pynchon.

Sublime Reductions

A brief but necessary detour: in Neil Hertz's reading of Kant's mathematical sublime, an experience is described that maps neatly over the kind of insufficiency stimulated by *Gravity's Rainbow*'s maximalism:

> There is, according to Kant, a sense of the sublime—he calls it the mathematical sublime—arising out of sheer cognitive exhaustion, the mind blocked not by the threat of an overwhelming force, but by the fear of losing count or of being reduced to nothing but counting—this and this and this—with no hope of bringing a long series or a vast scattering under some sort of conceptual unity.[16]

Hertz calls this impasse of counting "blockage"—the feeling that one cannot both keep track of the thousands of details and understand them at the same time. As the quotes from Enzian and Tony Tanner cited previously describe, to follow one detail of *Gravity's Rainbow* is to potentially miss out on a myriad of others. But while this blockage leaves the trembling subject overwhelmed, in Hertz's account the admission of defeat, which is also an acknowledgment of the sublime, is *tactical*, marked by careful maneuvers designed to claw back some of the lost control. For Hertz, "the scholar's *wish* is for the moment of blockage," because this admittance of defeat is actually the moment "when an indefinite and disarrayed sequence is resolved ... into a one-to-one confrontation."[17]

That an immense and overwhelming situation, object, or experience is able to be viewed as a conflict between subjects—one impossibly immense and powerful, one small and powerless—is preferable to the other option: the defocalization and dissolution that Jessica Swanlake experiences at the church, or the "scattering" that is Slothrop's ultimate fate in the novel (712). The troubling excess that caused the impasse of "counting" is able to be "converted into [a] supererogatory identification with the blocking agent that is the guarantor of the self's own integrity as an agent."[18] In this process, excess is recognized as the controlled output of a sublimely powerful agent, rather than simple chaos; the trembling subject maintains a stable identity (albeit an initially powerless one) defined reflexively against the first; and whatever dangers the sublime threatened one with are, if not reduced, than at least objectified, restrained, located in a figure that one can set oneself against. As Jonathan Culler states, misrecognizing an epistemological threat as this "structured conflict *between* subjects" allows the mind to reduce whatever dangers or fears of dissolution the sublime evokes.[19] Such is the function of the paranoid toothpaste insight that flows alongside Jessica's defocalization, pushing details toward a structuring center at the same moment it lists more and more defocalizing matter. In this manner, proclaiming the sublime is actually the defense against—or reduction of—sublimity.

Hertz's treatment of the sublime helps describe the importance of the figure of the author in maximalist texts like Pynchon's, as well as the figure of the polymath genius in the postindustrial "information age" in general. In a time when we are constantly encountering the blockage of the mathematical sublime—the eponymous immensity of "Big Data" and the difficulty any one human mind faces analyzing even a small portion of it—it is pleasurable for us to believe that some minds can rise above the landscape, enclosing it all within a gigantic novel. And, in many ways, this is what the maximalist novel is: the controlled (and contrived) performance of a mind able to *simulate* mastery of the endless array of information that is the contemporary world. As Joseph Tabbi suggests, "in the absence of former certainties that might sustain a collective reality, many of Pynchon's characters project worlds of their own."[20] Pynchon's readers—if not readers of all maximalist novels—might be described as doing something similar, turning novels into spaces where superseded domains of human capability can be experienced as continually vital. Here, reading literature becomes a "safe space" for human ability and productivity.

But although the giants and the anxious minds that desire them certainly dominate the text's epistemology, the novel occasionally teases us with the experience of a maximalism unshaped by such projections. Some of the text's most forceful moments occur when it denies the easy fantasies that giants and paranoia offer, and when it instead lets the world roam unattended, free from the shadow of voluminous masters. It is in these moments that the novel also offers us an image of a self momentarily free from anxieties of insufficiency, as I'll explain.

In an oft-quoted passage, Slothrop begins to lose the will to center all the mass of detail and information the novel contains, and instead drifts into "anti-paranoia, where nothing is connected to anything, a condition not many of us can bear for long" (434). In this state, Slothrop feels vulnerable and decentered, the "Listening Enemy" no longer there to spy on him, revealed to be merely "pasteboard images" rather than actual agents (or readers). What immediately follows, as Slothrop makes his way through the streets of Berlin, are suitably "decentered" descriptions:

> Shattered Biedermeier chair, mateless boot, steel eyeglass frame, dog collar (eyes at the edges of the twisting tail watching for sign, for blazing), wine cork, splintered broom, bicycle with one wheel missing, discarded copies of *Tägliche Rundschau,* chalcedony doorknob dyed blue long ago with ferrous ferrocyanide, scattered piano keys (all white, an octave on B to be exact—or H, in the German nomenclature—the notes of the rejected Locrian mode), the black and amber eye from some stuffed animal ... The strewn night. (434)

This world here is "strewn" rather than centered. Slothrop's decentering—his "anti-paranoia"—is registered in the dispersed matter littering the streets. The stuff is all junk of one kind or another, all broken objects. The mess of production litters the landscape and is simply listed, not swept up by the rhapsodizing voice of other dense descriptions (see Jessica Swanlake's scene earlier in this chapter). It also constitutes, at least for a moment, signs of a becalming peace. This junk turns the giants haunting this world—here the "Listening Enemy," an obvious nod toward us readers—into mere posters, "only pasteboard images" of a controlling power.

While the discarded toothpaste tubes that crowded Jessica Swanlake's mind were "returned to the War," "melted for solder, for plate, alloyed for castings, bearings, gasketry" (130), there is a sense here, for a moment at least, that this won't happen. In Slothrop's anti-paranoia these objects and their corresponding presence as details in the novel will remain only unusable junk—or at least this is the hope of anti-paranoia, that details will be merely what they seem, won't slide off into other orders of significance. These signs will only be signs, will not offer themselves up as weapons against us, "returned to the War," and the novel can simply feel justified presenting detail without having to control it or make it mean anything other than what it states. Although there is a lot about anti-paranoia that makes it "a condition not many of us can bear for long" (434), it also offers a peace, an assurance that things are only what they seem. This brief moment of anti-paranoia enables a kind of quietude to descend upon Slothrop's mind, a calm in which he is powerless to act and yet unaffected by other powers. It's a comforting insufficiency that comes through leaving detail alone, not trying to manage it with hermeneutics. Slothrop refuses insight here, and although he thus fails to achieve the totalizing comforts that accompany the Lukácsian relation of part to whole, he avoids the panic that comes with the price of knowledge in this overloaded and over-determined world.

It is perhaps predictable, however, that this anti-paranoid description of Slothrop's path through the Berlin streets has been viewed as not completely anti-paranoid after all. While a certain amount of these details seem designed to resist what can be easily recuperated, some readers have nevertheless been able to point anti-paranoia back in the direction of a totalizing meaning. As with the supposedly destroyed factory Enzian encounters toward the end of the novel, this rubble is perhaps only pretending to be inert: it is "not a ruin at all. It is in perfect working order. Only waiting for the right connections to be set up, to be switched on" (520).

Steven Weisenburger's *A "Gravity's Rainbow" Companion*, an extensive collection of notes that expands upon many of the opaque historical and cultural references embedded in Pynchon's prose, attempts to provide such a supplement to the passage, and, as such, is as much a book about encountering maximalist poetics as it is one about Pynchon's novel. Weisenburger offers four notes for this relatively short description of Slothrop in the streets of Berlin:

> **Biedermeier chair** ... The Biedermeier style of furniture was a nineteenth-century German imitation of French Empire style ... but plainer and less ostentatious that its predecessor. The emphasis was on *Gemütlichkeit* (comfort, coziness). The name was a portmanteau word, from Biedermann and Bummelmeier, comical characters in a Berlin journal who were meant to satirize bourgeois values.
>
> **Tägliche Rundschau** A Berlin newspaper nearly as old as the *Times* of London, whose title translates as The Daily Review.
>
> **chalcedony doorknob** ... **ferrocyanide** A doorknob made from this milky-gray quartz with its ferro-cyanide compounds could, under the right circumstances, react with sodium or potassium salts and produce a deadly white powder, sodium or potassium cyanide (NaCN or KCN).
>
> **B...or H...the rejected Locrian mode** A vexed business, but the general idea is that in German musical notation the "hard" or "square" "B" is written as an H, and only the "soft" or "rounded "B" (the flat) is designated by the "B" itself. This detail plays a key role in Thomas Mann's *Doktor Faustus*, which many be on Pynchon's mind here. In *Faustus* the "H" allows composer Adrian Leverkuhn to devise a "note-cipher," his "haetera esmeralds," in honor of his beloved, the woman who is also the source of his disease. Yet this bit of musical nomenclature has no essential relation to the "Locrian" or "Hyperphrygian" mode of music handed down from Hellenic culture. In that mode, which has only a theoretical existence, the interval between the first and the fifth is a diminished rather than a true fifth.[21]

So a hundred-word passage is supplemented by some 300 of Weisenburger's own, increasing the complexity of the text at the same time as it reels it in, restrains it. Pynchon's descriptive details are indexes for more words, more details, more stories—but a *more* that aims to reassure rather than confound. These are stories that push the details back toward the giants haunting this world, giving flesh to the "Listening Enemy" (us readers) once again, and reaffirming the penetration and insight of our gaze. The Biedermeier chair becomes a symbol for the overturning of bourgeois comforts. It is thrown out in the street because its owners and their way of life have met the same fate. The chalcedony doorknob is revealed to be a latently deadly object: like the Jamf Ölfabriken Werke that Enzian encounters, it is only "waiting for the right connections to be set up, to be switched on" for its other purpose. The mention of the "rejected Locrian mode" reveals that Pynchon himself is perhaps a little sketchy on the details, but

German musical notation's suggested relationship to cryptography is certainly pertinent for a reader wanting to "giganticize" these bits of data. It seems clear that we can still read this rubble and reassert our place as readers above it.

But Weisenburger's sleuthing does give off a few whiffs of desperation, an anxious reaching for the sort of hermeneutic comfort this passage is supposed to force us to relinquish. To some extent, the challenge assumed and taken up by Weisenburger—to find the hidden meaning of these details—is the wrong one to be gleaned from this scene. The test of the anti-paranoid passage's maximalism is not whether we can make its details significant, but whether we can tolerate it being *insignificant*, truly disconnected. Scanning the text for its allusions and facts is a last gasp effort to maintain control, to describe the landscape as humanly relevant, to cast a giant shadow (of history, research, science, intellect) across it. As in Hertz's reading of the sublime, it sees the passage as a conflict between subjects: an author who fills a text with opaque details and a reader whose job it is to elucidate them through patient scholarship. So what is interesting here, greater than whatever results such micro-reading produces, is that we feel compelled to read in this manner at all. Weisenburger's reader's guide almost presents a vision of literary criticism dissembled into its constituent parts. In some ways, Pynchon's novel exists to give validation to the literary critic's ability to patiently sort through cultural archives looking for the sources of references. For most readers, it doesn't really matter if they know the significance of the Locrian mode or not. It does matter that Weisenburger has been able to uncover it, however.

I'm being just a little unfair to Weisenburger, however, by calling his unpacking of this passage desperate. It is almost taboo to speak directly about the author of *Gravity's Rainbow*, both because of his reclusiveness and the era of literary theory in which his novels were written, but this novel's oscillations between the anti-paranoid and paranoid also reveal that Pynchon himself is perhaps slightly wary of letting the maximalist elements of his writing become dominant to a point where they force a reader to give up all promises of larger meaning, all the critical habits they are accustomed to. When, earlier in the novel, the young mathematician Roger Mexico argues with Ned Pointsman over the significance of Slothrop's map of conquests/rocket strikes, he suggests that "no matter how many [V2 rockets] have fallen inside a particular square, the odds remain the same as they always were. Each hit is independent of all the others" (56). It's the anti-paranoid pole of the novel again. Pointsman, a stubborn Pavlovian, is aghast at such a proposition, seeing in it the destruction of the "elegant rooms of history:" "What if Mexico's whole generation have turned out like this? Will Postwar be nothing but 'events,' newly created one moment to the next? No links? Is it the end of history?" (56).

We can assume that Pynchon himself feels that novels can no longer continue to organize the complexity of the world into "elegant rooms" of meaning, but it doesn't mean that he is certain how to move it entirely into what Pointsman calls this "postwar" generation. This text can only flirt with it for brief moments; there is still a lot of Pointsman guiding its construction, as much as he is painted as its villain. Pynchon at least appears hesitant to create a novel in which walls of detail completely refuse the operations of interpretations that, as much as he problematizes and parodies them, he still enjoys. Like Leni Pökler, he wants to map "onto different co-ordinate systems" (159), but is still conscious, as is her engineer husband Franz, of making something that will "work" (159). What I'm trying to suggest is that what makes the anti-paranoid moments of this text brief and fleeting is perhaps Pynchon's own fear of the insufficiency with which maximalist writing can threaten reader and author alike. These walls of inert detail ultimately come to express uncertainty about how novels are to be written and read, if they are not to be used to express maximal greatness or giant ability. If we replace Pointsman's worry about the end of history with the end of the novel as a form able to represent the contemporary world, we get a firmer sense of this equivocation at the heart of the novel.

As if responding to this unsettledness, Weisenburger's textual explications work in two appeasing directions at once, and in a manner not wholly uninvited by the text. On the one hand, they convince us of the partly real, partly imagined Thomas Pynchon's polymathic brilliance and the immense amount of erudition needed to author *Gravity's Rainbow*. With Weisenburger's aid, the text becomes a testament to learning, to the powers of the modern intellect as expressed by the maximalist novel. On the other hand, Weisenburger makes the novel itself seem less difficult, more approachable for the everyday reader by explaining what a Biedermeier chair is and translating *Tägliche Rundschau*. The novel's complexity and magnitude are increased, but so too the reader's ability to deal with the specificity of the details—as long as they have the *Companion* within reach, of course. In *The Crying of Lot 49*, Oedipa Maas struggled with the many "crowding in" details of Pierce Inverarity's will, wishing that "so much didn't stand in her way: her deep ignorance of law, of investment, of real estate."[22] A text like Weisenburger's *Companion* would be this supplement to Oedipa's intelligence, enabling her to bring the complexity of her world into "pulsing stelliferous Meaning, all in a soaring dome around her."[23] By describing the text as one that engages with "real" history, and supplementing our limitations as individual readers, the *Companion* allows us to close the gap between the limited capacity of individual knowledge and the "strewn night" of errata that fills Pynchon's text. The giant, this time figured as Pynchon himself *and* the newly enlightened reader, closes over the perceived gap in understanding, moving us away from insufficiency. We tolerate Pynchon's maximalism by parsing his references, but in the process move away from the threat posed by its detailedness. Once again, however, it's a somewhat unsettled resolution, accepting the achievement of insight by admitting our inability to tolerate the text's maximalist specificity.

Heavy Mettle

If modern technology and science have helped create a reality that no longer responds to the scale and powers of unassisted human sensory ability let alone the representational powers of novelists—a reality of the CPU, the molecular microscope, Big Data, and High Frequency Trading—then humans are naturally anxious about their ability to remain epistemologically potent. We build technological devices and still control how and if they function, but the reason we desire computers, radio telescopes, and the internet is because these things do what we can't—if not just what we can't be bothered.

The novel exists as a strange technology amidst these other ones. It helps us record the world and provides stimulation for the empathic, moral, and imaginative faculties of the mind. But it also exists, like most artworks, as a technology that we value because in it we see a record of certain kinds of labor that aren't necessarily valued—by the economy or other people— elsewhere. Joseph Tabbi suggests that readers have used "terms of aggrandizement" in describing the work of Pynchon and similar writers so that novels like *Gravity's Rainbow* would seem to "match the sheer productive power of the larger culture" of which they are part.[24] A literary field that exists within a wider maximalist culture and economy (one that produces and consumes excessively) needs maximalist novels to feel commensurately productive. Tabbi's statement implies that our relation to a novel such as *Gravity's Rainbow* is an index of our relationship to the wider landscape of late-capitalism, but one in which readers can play at achieving mastery while the real sublime of postmodern capitalism—the market mediated by technological processes and collective forces too complex to figure—extends always further beyond the powers of the individual mind to grasp. But these "terms of aggrandizement" with which we describe maximalist novels also register that the technology of the novel allows, justifies, and gives value to kinds of work that are, at least in the twenty-first century, no longer necessary for humans to perform.

Many of the readings *Gravity's Rainbow* inspires are to be considered a set of reactions caught between Slothrop's fantasized titanism—strategies of enlargement that "threatened" or dwarfed beings are likely to make in the face of maximalist immensity and complexity—and Jessica Swanlake's defocalization. The maximalism of the book throws down an intellectual gambit of a sort. One part of it seems to demand that readers become equally maximalist if they are to meet its task, become equally gigantic and full of as much knowledge as the text in order to successfully encounter it. A maximalist novel births maximalist readers. As a letter to Peter C. Tamony reveals, Pynchon was confused about "the point of being historically accurate [when] no one's going to notice one way or another."[25] Although he might have been perplexed, for readers like Weisenburger, accuracy has become one of the central values of the text. As McHale suggests, Pynchon's critics "have seemed particularly irritable in their reaching after fact and reason."[26] They *do* notice the accuracy; it's what they want from the text; it's what they *need*.

But it's a desire that can soon grow stale, a fate Weisenburger has witnessed. After the publication of his *Companion*, several readers in the Pynchon community were moved (or enraged) enough to supplement the guidebook with a list of corrections and improvements—a reaction that presumably led Weisenburger (or his publisher) to release a second, "revised and expanded" edition in 2006, which incorporated many of the suggested changes. Two of Weisenburger's strongest critics were Ben Teague and Donald Larsson, each of whom authored their own companion in response to Weisenburger's.[27] Teague summarizes his corrections, and his evaluation of Weisenburger's work, in the concluding section of his "Notes and Rebuttals:"

> In the end, what we have is a vast conversation starter: 300-odd pages of W's sweat that have incited a yarnball of web authors to dish out their own answers. I can't admire the execution as a whole, but the devotion fills me with awe. What I regret is that W's book is the only such collection of references and has led a generation of young readers astray in some important respects.[28]

In the Acknowledgments for the second edition of his *Companion*, Weisenburger speaks openly about these criticisms, and the debt he is in to those like Teague who pointed out his errors (as well as several of Pynchon's own previously overlooked):

> Readers of *Gravity's Rainbow* and of my *Companion* have demanded that one be "historically accurate" even in treating the most minor details, such as the precise spelling of idiomatic foreign expressions. With great good humor they have trounced my work for its errors and needled Pynchon's (many fewer) errors too, despite all that he clearly did to get things right in *Gravity's Rainbow*—even down to his characters' Argentine Spanish slang. I trust that this revised second edition of the *Companion* better lives up to that shared faith and joy in fact and fiction.[29]

Although Weisenburger certainly accepts these criticisms with humility, there is no small amount of weariness in his recognition of readers' demands for "historically accurate" explication of "the most minor," and, we are to presume, tedious details. Here, Weisenburger—as thoroughly convinced as anyone of the importance of reading Pynchon closely—tacitly admits of the tedium of such exercises. Perhaps in no other book does an author's spelling of idiomatic foreign expressions, or his reader's spelling of the same phrases, seem to matter so much.

The merit of these quibbles and their critical applicability is certainly debatable, but they do tell us that reading *Gravity's Rainbow* has become about more than simply reading the book. Or, to put it another way, *Gravity's Rainbow*'s maximalism makes sure its story is more than a fictional narrative. It's clear that readers' battles with the detailedness of the text have turned it into something of a warring ground for ideas about intellectual ability. What the novel becomes for many of us is not simply a story, a portrait of a historical moment, or a rich example of postmodernist aesthetics, but a testing ground of mental mettle. If this novel represents the complexities of the postwar world, it is as much through the desire readers feel to manage its maximalist presentation of detail as anything these details represent. To limn the importance of *Gravity's Rainbow*, then, it's not just that it teaches readers about the various industrial-military cartels pulling the strings of the postwar world, or the dangers of a deterministic view of the human subject. The novel also shows that in this period of human history readers can be left feeling so helplessly insufficient that they need to argue over the details of a textual object, making themselves feel powerful through the performance of acts of sustained patience and attentiveness. The results of much of the reading that Weisenburger and others perform are less important than the ideals of "slow" human labor that they imply. For readers, the focus arguably becomes not what the details represent but what it means that someone else has been able to assemble them for us through patient, detailed, and attentive scholarship. Within the "modern diversity" of postwar America it is exciting that there is someone out there who appears to be expert enough in so many fields that they can write a novel like *Gravity's Rainbow* and a guide like *A "Gravity's Rainbow" Companion*.

The other part of the intellectual gambit proposed by the text, of course, is the challenge to embrace the anti-paranoid relationship that Slothrop occupies for brief moments, and that we might too if we resist the desire to annotate its descriptions. This approach encourages us to remain in the thick of insufficiency, to read the novel's maximalism without hope of insight. For *Gravity's Rainbow*, this latter position is more attractive in theory, but less tolerable in practice. The novel certainly looks upon the anti-paranoid with a fascination, but can't quite figure how to reside in it for very long. It ultimately leaves the task of embracing this maximalism to the "future" generation Pointsman dreads so much. It can't yet predict what we might do with a work that will do nothing itself, that will refuse its reader a fetishized practice of insight. In the next two chapters we'll encounter texts that can.

Notes

1. User 1, review of *Gravity's Rainbow*, Goodreads, May 16, 2007, https://www.goodreads.com/book/show/415.Gravity_s_Rainbow.
2. User 2, review of *Gravity's Rainbow*, Goodreads, October 1, 2012, https://www.goodreads.com/book/show/415.Gravity_s_Rainbow.
3. User 3, review of *Gravity's Rainbow*, Goodreads, December 18, 2015, https://www.goodreads.com/book/show/415.Gravity_s_Rainbow.

4. User 4, review of *Gravity's Rainbow*, Goodreads, May 7, 2015, https://www.goodreads.com/book/show/415.Gravity_s_Rainbow.

5. User 5, review of *Gravity's Rainbow*, Goodreads, February 22, 2011, https://www.goodreads.com/book/show/415.Gravity_s_Rainbow.

6. Tony Tanner, *Thomas Pynchon* (London: Methuen, 1982), 75.

7. McHale, *Constructing Postmodernism*, 81.

8. A similar phenomenon also occurs in David Foster Wallace's *Infinite Jest*, during the long conversation between Hugh Steeply and Remi Marathe on a hilltop outside Arizona. Wallace, *Infinite Jest*, 88.

9. Thomas Pynchon, *Gravity's Rainbow* (New York: The Viking Press, 1973), 330. Subsequent references to this text in this chapter are given in parentheses. Pynchon uses frequent ellipses, especially at the end of sentences, which I've preserved. All of my own omissions will be signified by the use of editorial brackets.

10. Mendelson, "Encyclopedic Narrative," 1271.

11. Pynchon is here alluding to Kant's "mathematical" sublime, which will become important in our discussion of Neil Hertz later: "with the advance of apprehension comprehension becomes more difficult at every step and soon attains its maximum. ... For if the apprehension has reached a point beyond which the representations of sensuous intuition in the case of the parts first apprehended begin to disappear from the imagination as this advances to the apprehension of yet others, as much, then, is lost at one end as is gained at the other, and for comprehension we get a maximum which the imagination cannot exceed." Immanuel Kant, *Critique of Judgment*, tr. James Creed Meredith, ed. and rev. Nicholas Walker (Oxford: Oxford University Press, 2007), 82.

12. Alan Clinton, "Conspiracy of Commodities: Postmodern Encyclopedic Narrative and Crowdedness," *Rhizomes* 5 (2002): para. 4, http://www.rhizomes.net/issue5/clinton.html.

13. McHale, *Constructing Postmodernism*, 88. See also 81–82.

14. Timothy Melley, *Empire of Conspiracy: The Culture of Paranoia in Postwar America* (Ithaca: Cornell University Press, 1999), 13.

15. This is Pauline Johnson's description of Lukács' understanding of the importance of the totalizing outlook provided by realist fiction. Johnson, *Marxist Aesthetics*, 41–42.

16. Neil Hertz, *The End of the Line: Essays on Psychoanalysis and the Sublime* (New York: Columbia University Press, 1985), 40.

17. Ibid., 53. Emphasis is Hertz's.

18. Ibid.

19. Jonathan Culler, "The Hertzian Sublime," *MLN* 120, no. 5 (2005), 977.

20. Joseph Tabbi, *Postmodern Sublime: Technology and American Writing from Mailer to Cyberpunk* (Ithaca: Cornell University Press, 1995), 76.

21. Stephen Weisenburger, *A "Gravity's Rainbow" Companion: Sources and Context's for Pynchon's Novel*, 2nd ed. (Athens, GA: The University of Georgia Press, 2006), 245. It should be noted that in the reference to Biedermeier on this page, Weisenburger cross-references an earlier definition he gave on page 111, from which the explanation quoted here is taken.

22. Thomas Pynchon, *The Crying of Lot 49* (London: Vintage Books, [1965] 2000), 56.

23. Ibid., 56.

24. Tabbi, *Postmodern Sublime*, 12.
25. Weisenburger, *Companion*, xii.
26. McHale, *Constructing Postmodernism*, 88.
27. Ben Teague, "*A 'Gravity's Rainbow' Companion* Companion: Notes and Rebuttals to *A Gravity's Rainbow Companion*," accessed June 1, 2011, http://www.benteague.com/books/titles/gravitys.html; Don Larsson, "A *Companion's* Companion: Illustrated Additions and Corrections to Steven Weisenburger's *A 'Gravity's Rainbow' Companion*," accessed June 2, 2011, http://english2.mnsu.edu/larsson/grnotes.html.
28. Teague, "*A Gravity's Rainbow Companion* Companion."
29. Weisenburger, *Companion*, xii. See Simon Peter Rowberry's excellent discussion of the different *Gravity's Rainbow* reader's guides for a more detailed discussion of the reaction to Weisenburger's work. Simon Peter Rowberry, "Reassessing the *Gravity's Rainbow* Pynchon Wiki: A New Research Paradigm?," *Orbit: Writing Around Pynchon* 1, no. 1 (2012), DOI: http://doi.org/10.7766/orbit.v1.1.24.

2 On Flunking

Maximalist Description in David Foster Wallace's *Infinite Jest*

A Bad Student

The challenge that reading David Foster Wallace's *Infinite Jest* poses is that there are so many words for which to find a use. Dave Eggers complained in his early 1996 review that the novel's "sentences run as long as 800 words. Paragraph breaks are rare. ... Things like tennis matches and math problems are described in excruciating detail."[1] As with *Gravity's Rainbow*, books like this aren't just big, they also demand we expand our abilities as readers. Ed Finn's analysis of the habits of Wallace's readers suggests that many tackle the novel to achieve a "workout for the brain,"[2] and the novel's original marketing campaign exploited a sense of competitiveness, taunting readers with a dare: "are you reader enough for this book?"[3]

As in Pynchon's works, matters of endurance filter down through the novel and are shared by many of Wallace's characters, who can seem beleaguered by the density of the textual world they inhabit. We note this in the confusion Don Gately feels, for example, when late in the novel he finds himself in conversation with a ghost who, like the genie in John Barth's *Chimera*, seems to be a stand-in for the author himself. While Gately is lying semiconscious in a hospital bed, the ghost sends bursts of obscure words like "lordosis," "sinistral," and "chronaxy" rushing into his thoughts, making him want to scream with frustration.[4] The unrelenting intensity of the maximalist novelist wears out Gately's mind, and Wallace is here nodding toward his readers who have probably felt similar things while reading the book.

It's the beginning of the novel that most forcefully expresses a sense of weariness, however—a feeling that stands not only for any exhaustion readers of maximalist texts likely face, but also the burdens of the maximalist author. The scene unfolds as Hal Incandenza interviews for a tennis scholarship at the University of Arizona and is asked to quell suspicions that the essays he has submitted with his college application are written by nepotistic helping-hands. The thing at stake in the interview is his ability as a writer, as there are few doubts about his tennis prowess. But, recalling Kafka's Gregor Samsa, when Hal opens his mouth to defend his value the only sounds that come out are "*sub*animalistic noises" (14). This promptly terrifies all those in attendance who presume he is having some kind of seizure and take him to a bathroom where he is made to lie down on the floor. Hal, however, feels more-or-less fine and is focused on simply lying still, remaining calm and passive. He is far more preoccupied with the "leonine roar" of the toilets and his restricted field of view, describing the small details of the space with writerly enthusiasm. Eventually he is wheeled off to hospital, the sun blaring through his closed eyelids—an experience the novel will return to at key points in several other characters' narratives.[5] Even with his eyes closed, Hal cannot escape from the world (or cannot stop recording it).

After we read the rest of the novel, it won't seem surprising that Hal acts so strangely in this opening scene. We will see him in various states of decline, none more pertinent than a progressive loss of enthusiasm for tennis, the sport he's been training for most of his life. He will lose a match against Ortho Stice that he shouldn't; toward the end of the novel he will realize for the first time that he doesn't want to play tennis at all and will consider committing self-harm to avoid it (954). It's tempting to see Hal's collapse as some sort of metaphysical disintegration of the self, the result of watching his father's infamous film cartridge, the depersonalizing effects of marijuana withdrawal, or even an accidental ingestion of the drug DMZ. But what we can easily overlook is that perhaps all that has occurred in this opening scene is an expression of exhaustion. Hal's inability to speak is perhaps also a strangely expressed desire—whether his own or that of his author's—to *flunk*.

Wallace is, Mark McGurl suggests, a writer whose career is inseparable from institutions. He was "a superstar student" at various elite colleges and later a teacher of creative writing, and he "could not have asked more from an educational institution in officially recognizing his worth, including his worth as a fiction writer."[6] But in scenes such as the above that open *Infinite Jest* (or even open *and* close it, being both the first in terms of *syuzhet* and last in terms of its *fabula*), this overinstitutionalization seems to generate within Wallace's writing a fantasy of failure, uselessness, and collapse that shows some degree of ambivalence about his reliance on the institutions that support fiction writers. As much as Wallace relied on universities for work and learning throughout his life, Hal's collapse at the beginning/end of the novel might rightly be seen as Wallace's fantasized expression of a desire to fall out of a "system," to escape from a life figured as an endless tennis match, and to opt out of a career involving the constant play against other people, interests, and institutional processes. If, as D.T. Max suggests, Wallace dreaded interviews,[7] here at the beginning of his biggest novel is a chance to safely fail one, or at least express weariness about the prospect of literary fame at the same moment he courts it. For if it is not that Hal outwardly chooses to flunk in this opening scene, then it is at least Wallace who forces this failure, who puts him on this path to institutional implosion. When we consider that, as Max reveals, Hal's failed interview was one of the last sections that Wallace wrote before the novel was published,[8] and that the original opening scene had Hal in another more successful interview of sorts (the section that now appears as his consultation with the "professional conversationalist"),[9] the opening scene at the University of Arizona garners the sense of being a *closing* interview of the text's author in which he is asked to defend the legitimacy of the writing he has prepared to submit for examination.

The failed interview is also, in one way or another, Wallace signaling a change in how his central character will value himself, one that will presumably force Hal to separate ideas of self-worth from the processes of evaluation, examination, and controlled competition upon which Wallace himself so heavily relied. Regardless of everything else that might come together in this moment—the raft of questions we can read back into it after the end of the novel, charging every detail with immense narrative significance—the one thing that is most likely to happen is that Hal will not gain smooth entry into this world of professional tournaments and celebrity, where life is defined by the neat rules and demarcations of the sporting field and the university tennis scholarship. The curious thing is that he seems quite content with this. The opposite end of the novel, in the period leading up to this scene, finds Hal lying down on the floor of Viewing Room 5 at the Enfield Tennis Academy (ETA), in much the same position as he is at the start of the novel when being restrained in the bathroom. When supine in the video room refusing to do anything but watch films, he feels "awakened to a basic dimension" he had neglected during "years of upright movement, of standing and running and stopping and jumping, of walking endlessly upright from one side of the court to the other." He feels "denser now ... impossible to knock down" (902). There's almost something of Herman Melville's Bartleby in Hal, "preferring" to be stationary and letting stubborn passivity be the assertion of the rights of the individual over the needs of the institution.

Writer as Critic

Before we understand how Wallace's maximalism relates to a sense of weariness pervading *Infinite Jest*, we first need to set the scene of the literary culture in which this novel appeared. Synoptic remarks about a varied and large cultural field are difficult and often facile, but one thing we can safely say about American writers of Wallace's generation is that they are aware of what words "do." The last hundred years or so of critical work, philosophy, and psychology have taught anyone who's cared to listen that words are the royal road to the unconscious, the medium of all thought, the oppressor, liberator or creator of the self. Words are sometimes devious and repressive, but if used correctly can be transcendent of just about anything that tries to hold them or you in place. Demarcations of race, geography, reality, sexuality, the mind, the body—words can have some part in both creating and undoing all of these things. When we read them they tend to be simultaneously understood and misunderstood, when we write them they partly do what we want but mostly disobey us. They come in and out of usage, change over time, and while we can learn to wield them without any great effort, they will always escape our mastery, do more by themselves than we are ever able to do with them.

That we can say with almost unswerving confidence that recent American writers know these things is testament to the important influence the tertiary institutionalization of literary criticism and creative writing has had on the last fifty years or so of fiction, a subject that has been studied at length in McGurl's *The Program Era*. Almost all American novelists now spend time at a university learning to read and write books, either studying creative writing directly, or at one step's remove in the form of literary criticism, cultural studies, philosophy and the like. The result is that "postwar American literature can profitably be described as the product of a system," and that "the creative writing program produces programmatically, but also in rich and various profusion, a literature aptly suited to a programmatic society."[10] For McGurl, many developments in twentieth century fiction are to be seen either as responses to ambivalences about creative institutionalization, or symptoms of it in some broader sense. While commonly viewed as an expression of the recursivity celebrated in various strands of postmodernist thought, for example, metafiction can also be understood as a consequence of the dual relationship many writers found themselves having to the literary object, being both its producers and analysts. As McGurl explains, "we could read the reflexive prose experiments of academic creative writers ... not as radically 'deconstructive,' as they sometimes are, but as radically conventional, as testaments to the continuing interest of literary forms as objects of a certain kind of professional research."[11]

What we witness here is the closing of any assumed gap between creative and critical practice, and a dismissal of the popular notion that critics are only parasitically attached to the work of authors. Surely, to a large extent, the knowledge about words and fiction that literary critics provide bolsters a writer's sense of cultural importance (and most fiction authors have also played at being critics themselves in university English departments, reassuring themselves of the value of their craft). When it is said by Wallace, for example, that fiction "locates and applies CPR to those elements of what's human and magical that still live and glow despite the times' darkness,"[12] then other budding authors can feel okay about telling their relatives at Christmas time that they are quitting their day-jobs to become novelists or are choosing to pursue an English degree rather than follow the more financially-secure paths of law, medicine or IT. The sculptor of words is here, in Wallace's conception, almost a doctor anyway. Most other utterances taken from the annals of criticism have, either deliberately or by implication, the similar function of bestowing upon the written word and its scribe a job of some importance.

Wallace is probably the archetypal knowledgeable novelist we are describing here. He is highly educated, having studied creative writing, philosophy, and mathematics at various stages of his life. He also spent a lot of time—considerably more than novelists like Pynchon and Don DeLillo, who might otherwise seem his literary predecessors—making attractive statements about the value of writing in the cultural economy of the 1990s. As a result, when *Infinite Jest* was published in 1996, readers were not necessarily unprepared for its arrival, as the long, difficult, and blazingly excessive work came with a supplemental framework of literary value that Wallace had laid down for it in preceding years. A 1993 edition of the *Review of Contemporary Fiction* featured both an essay by and interview with Wallace that more or less provided readers with a solid way of understanding the book. For Wallace, "irony and ridicule [were] entertaining and effective," but at the same time were "agents of a great despair and stasis in U.S. culture" that it was fiction's job to try and heal.[13] Much has already been written of the impact that "E Unibus Pluram: Television and U.S. Fiction" had on the reception of Wallace's work, encouraging readers to view *Infinite Jest* as a novel that could teach them to be sincere in their interactions with others, so I won't repeat its thesis in any great detail here.[14] What I will say is this essay and the accompanying interview support Wallace's admission that he was anxious that *Infinite Jest* was "just not going to make *any* sense," that his readers were not, for example, "going to see *significant* relationships between ... my relationship to television, and some of these people in the halfway house's relation to, say, heroin."[15] There was a use for this book, and he wanted to help us realize it.

It's difficult—if not impossible—to judge whether Wallace's fiction has achieved any of its stated goals, but his declarations of literary purpose have noticeably emboldened the reading public to make similar pronouncements about the value of fiction in an age where its status as a commodity and a dominant form of media is arguably in decline.[16] Where Wallace's writing has been particularly effective is in reinvigorating many readers' beliefs that literature can change lives, if not the world, and in demonstrating that difficult, high-literary fiction can find a receptive audience (and purpose) outside of the academy (although Wallace himself admits that his readers are most likely to have a "good education"[17]). In Kathleen Fitzpatrick's account of *Infinite Summer*, an online community dedicated to a collective reading of Wallace's novel, she quotes from the blog entries of one user who supposedly found in Wallace's book a reason to stop taking drugs. In their words, the novel "*made me want to be a better person.*"[18] Fitzpatrick notes that such accounts are struck through with "a certain naïveté about the novel's power," and are just a little dubious, giving the impression of "having mistaken a text about the struggle with addiction for the struggle itself."[19] In this account, overcoming drug addiction is as easy as reading a novel. But the point is that in the post-Wallace environment, a relatively wide range of readers find a clear and easily comprehendible "point" to writing and reading—whether it be overcoming the addictive irony of television, using anti-escapist "mindfulness" to tolerate the dull realities of everyday

American life, promoting sincerity in interpersonal relationships, or using empathy as a way to overcome loneliness and detachment. This is almost literature envisioned as a math equation: reader + book = a better person.

Wallace's ideas about the uses of literature are attractive, but an essay by Mary K. Holland describes how they often struggle to be borne out by his fiction. Holland contends that "we cannot help but read [*Infinite Jest*] only in the context of the agenda that Wallace so clearly and passionately articulated shortly before its publication and by considering its success in implementing that agenda."[20] Holland attempts to subvert the voice of Wallace, showing that his authorial remarks often pull the proverbial wool over our eyes: "We come to David Foster Wallace's fiction through the lens of irony, a tricky, risky, even at times useless lens. We refract our reading in this way because Wallace instructs us to, which puts us and his fiction in a precarious position."[21] But the most important argument Holland makes is that Wallace's novel fails to break out of the system it critiques, becoming victim to the same malaise of narcissism and irony it describes. *Infinite Jest*, rather than being a text that actualizes its author's goals, is a great example of words breaking free of authorial grip, practicing their own textual autonomy. Despite the careful and persuasive description of literary value that Wallace attaches to his work, *Infinite Jest* proves recalcitrant, disruptive, even contradictory.

Holland's point not only suggests that Wallace was overeager to write a great and very long novel that came neatly packaged with a guide to the form's usefulness in contemporary American culture. It also helps explain, as I will show, why this novel is so interested in describing those moments of collapse, flunking, and failure typified by Hal's failed interview. For although Wallace's eagerness to ensure readers understand his work frequently results in attractive proclamations about the usefulness of fiction, it also generates a contradictory interest in those parts of a novel that fail to offer any clear sense of usefulness and in which Wallace gets to be a "bad student," perhaps tired of having to be a writer who has taken on the task of "healing" a culture. There is a constant and largely overlooked tension in Wallace's fiction between its desire to function valuably—in terms of a conception of literature in which words and authors of novels are given an almost magical ability to do many impressive things to us—and its desire to resist this pressure and promotion of literary value, wishing to be something more reflective of what writing is as an activity, process, and form of work. Such tension is articulated in several areas—the weariness of characters, Hal Incandenza's flunked college interview—but none more important than the maximalist nature of Wallace's prose and what details he is motivated to record within it.

Blue Things

In what follows, I'll move through several possible approaches to Wallace's passion for "excruciating detail," with the help of Barthes, Lukács, Jameson, and other readers of description who put focus on the expectation to have fiction provide a "service" of some sort. But what we'll find particularly interesting about *Infinite Jest* is that, be it in an intense increase of detail that accompanies a character's drug-induced seizure or an affectless description of the blue items in a headmaster's waiting room, Wallace evidences an increased fascination for the writing and cataloguing of the world at the same time that his characters fall out of its conventional systems of valuation and achievement, losing competitions, flunking university interviews, and becoming locked into various form of antisocial stasis that fail to offer a clearly graspable purpose. While on one hand this is a text that laments that so many of the world's citizens are flunking out of life, and one that encourages us to repair ourselves, it is seems energized by the fact that this dysfunction allows such an enthusiastic practice of maximalist writing.

As discussed in the previous chapter, the difficulty and detailedness of maximalist writing is often found to be edifying for readers, but the construction of such a large and complex novel should also be understood as having put a significant amount of strain on its writer, requiring an exercise of literary labor beyond the norm.[22] All of Wallace's other novels and story collections feature explicit engagements with the often tiresome realities of the professional writer's life. His first novel, *The Broom of the System*, has editor-in-chief Rick Vigorous struggling with the arduous task of evaluating story submissions from college students: "I'm starting to think something is just deeply wrong with the youth of America. First of all, a truly disturbing number of them are interested in writing fiction. Truly disturbing."[23] "Westward the Course of Empire Takes its Way," the novella-length story that closes *Girl with Curious Hair*, has a group of creative writing students engaged with overcoming the influence of their professor's work (the "Course" of the title is perhaps a reference to the creative writing degree as an institution).[24] "Octet" in *Brief Interviews with Hideous Men* is a metafictional conversation between author and reader that deals with the "unfortunate" reality of being a fiction writer, and the collection's opening story, "Death is Not the End," tells of the emptiness of a writer who has won all the awards there are to win, and whom "two separate American generations have hailed as the voice of their generation."[25] *Oblivion*'s "The Suffering Channel" features a writer from a magazine called *Style*, writing a portrait of an artist who works with excrement.[26] *The Pale King* is framed as "David Wallace's" memoir, a text that has been forced into masquerading as fiction due to legal reasons regarding its discussion of the Internal Revenue Service. These are just a few examples.

This consistent engagement with the pragmatics of fiction writing makes it strange that such considerations are largely absent from *Infinite Jest*, but it should also make us ready to look for them in less obvious places. Of the few direct reflections on writing we receive in *Infinite Jest*, nearly all come in the form of student essays and related anxieties about grading as a form of evaluation. Indeed, the treatment of writing in this novel is largely inseparable from the notion of testing and examination.[27] Two of the essays we get to read in the novel, one written by Hal, the other by fellow student

Jim Struck, are both presented with an accompanying anxiety of institutional evaluation. Hal's essay on heroism in cinema is criticized for a lack of formal coherency (140). Jim Struck's essay, which we see him writing in a long footnote, is haunted by the specter of plagiarism, as Struck is copying out whole paragraphs from academic articles he hopes none of his teachers will have read (1055n304). Similarly, Hal's essays discussed in the opening scene of the novel are suspected of being written by other family members.[28]

Writing thus seems curiously bound within the school environment in *Infinite Jest*, and it's plausible to see in Hal and the other student writers a commentary on broader areas of unease in Wallace's own literary practice, if not just a simple confirmation of the central thesis of McGurl's *The Program Era*. The most interesting manner in which this expectation to "meet the grade" is expressed, however, can be found in the novel's form, and, in particular, the way it seems designed to respond to readers' demands that textual details "perform" in a particular manner. And here is where Wallace's maximalist approach to writing comes into its own.

It will benefit us to note that there is often a clear and important instability in *Infinite Jest*, as in all of Wallace's writing, between what Roland Barthes once termed the cardinal functions and catalyses of narrative art:

> Referring back to the class of functions, its units are not equally "important": some constitute actual hinges of the narrative (of a fragment thereof); others do no more than "fill in" the narrative space separating the hinge-type functions. Let us call the former cardinal functions (or nuclei), and the latter, in view of their complementary nature, catalyses. In order to classify a function as cardinal, all we need verify is that the action to which it refers opens (or maintains or closes) an alternative directly affecting the continuation of the story, in other words, that it either initiates or resolves an uncertainty. ... On the other hand, between two cardinal functions, it is always possible to bring in subsidiary notations, which cluster around one nucleus or another, without modifying its alternative nature[29]

While even in Barthes' essay the terms are openly unstable, there being no way for a narrative "to acknowledge the existence of noise" without conferring meaning upon it,[30] the terms are still useful heuristic devices able to help us elucidate the operations of a maximalist narrative aesthetic like Wallace's. Indeed, *Infinite Jest* is obsessed with description that resists "functional" modes of novelistic presentation, and this can be seen as a style of writing that thematically matches and formally accompanies Hal's flunking. Consider, for example, the long description, focalized by Hal, of all the instances of blue found in a waiting room:

> The following things in the room were blue. The blue checks in the blue-and-black checked shag carpet. Two of the room's six

institutional-plush chairs, whose legs were steel tubes bent into big ellipses, which wobbled, so that while the chairs couldn't really be rocked in they could be sort of bobbed in. (508–09)

This almost Oulipian conceit continues across three pages and links, by end-note, to a long description of photographs of students hanging on the wall, which is perhaps even more stubbornly resistant to meaning and function.[31] Here, the listing artifice is intended to replicate the games played by a bored mind stuck in a waiting room, but it also illuminates important elements of Wallace's style. Perhaps the first thing to note is that the intentional structure of the passage, signaled by the desire to construct a list of blue items in the room, is shifted overwhelmingly toward Barthes' "catalyses" rather than the so-called "cardinal functions." More than this, the desire of the prose is to locate—dig up, uncover, reveal—potential catalyses, interruptions, and deferrals of the normal mode of narrative progression and explication, blurring what is supposedly important and what is disposable. The description of the room is willfully arbitrary; there is little of the natural forcefulness of a scene that needs to be described for effect, nothing that seems to impress itself upon the narratorial consciousness with any great purpose. It's as if Sherlock Holmes were looking with lament at a world where clues no longer mattered.

The cataloging of blue things is also used as a way to reveal whatever degraded cardinal points of the scene still exist, but almost as if the supposedly necessary narrative information (the names of the characters in the scene, where they are located) fleshed out the cataloging of detail, rather than the other way around. The plot information we need from the scene is that Michael Pemulis and Hal are in Charles Tavis' waiting room sometime after the debacle surrounding the Eschaton match, and the blue things are used as entry points to this information. We can see this most clearly on the level of sentence structure:

> And also the overenhanced blue of the wallpaper's sky, which the wallpaper scheme was fluffy cumuli arrayed patternlessly against an overenhancedly blue sky, incredibly disorientating wallpaper that was by an unpleasant coincidence also the wallpaper in the Enfield offices of a Dr. Zegarelli, D.D.S., which Hal's just come back from after a removal. (509)

The hierarchy Barthes describes is parodied. If the avowed point of the passage is to list the blue items, then the ordinary cardinal points are relegated to a secondary position, mere garnishes or afterthoughts. As readers, we of course know better than this and can immediately overturn the misdirection, siphoning out the crucial information and restoring the division between significant and disposable, plot, and decoration. We know enough to understand that a catalog of blue things does not constitute significant narrative information. But, one cannot help but ask, what if it did? Could we contend, perhaps, that here the list of blue things *is* the important information being communicated by the scene, that this noise does have a cardinal function, and that these details aren't important for what they provide, but for what they refuse?

To get at the heart of what Wallace is doing in this scene, as well as Hal's failed interview and other moments of flunking, it is important to explore the critical resonances of Barthes' terms and Wallace's play with them. In many ways, Barthes tacitly inherits a schema of literary value from Georg Lukács' reductive yet influential criticisms of the descriptive indulgences of the French "naturalists" Zola and Flaubert,[32] and modernists such as Joyce.[33] As I discussed in my introduction, for Lukács, description was fine if it also told a story (or, that is, if it *wasn't* pure description), as, for example, Tolstoy's depiction of a horse race in *Anna Karenina* did. But if a description only pictured, as Zola's description of a horse race in *Nana* did, then it was mere excess, and among other things signified the undesirable intrusion of the "style" of capitalism, with all its superfluities and excesses of production, into the form of the novel proper. Zola's preference for description over narration meant that his characters were "merely spectators" of the horse race, and "the events themselves become only a tableau for the reader, or, at best, a series of tableaux. We are merely observers."[34] Such thorough observation and description is pitted against the much more crucial functional impulse of the novel, which is to narrate, and also the role of the reader, which is to do more than merely observe, to be more than a passive spectator.

When Lukács complains about excess, another way to view the situation is that he is wanting to evacuate from the novel various qualities—stasis, meaninglessness, passivity, idleness, superfluity—that he considers to be pervading the world around him and that he thinks shouldn't be encouraged in the novel. That art is "the selection of the essential and subtraction of the inessential"[35] is obviously as much a critique of capitalist indulgences as it is an aesthetic judgment. It is not necessarily a certain mode of writing Lukács wishes to censure, then, but a certain set of qualities he finds unsuitable for the world as for the literary object. Boredom, stasis, and passivity are thrown out under the banner of description, whereas action and meaning are kept in under the name of narration. Description is the junk of the novel. But it is ultimately more of a code word for the ills of an increasingly commercial and materialistic society than a clearly defined mode of discourse.

Lukács' dissatisfaction with the supposedly spectatorial position encouraged of Zola's readers is actually not terribly dissimilar to the anxiety expressed in *Infinite Jest* about the passivity of television viewership. But what Lukács' dogmatism withholds from his contemplation is that Zola's excessive descriptions, and the act of representation itself, can do more than simply express or reinforce. As Jameson suggests—primarily reading

Conrad but his comments apply equally here—the overdescriptive writing of Zola and co. can "open up a space in which the opposite and the negation of [capitalist culture and epistemology] can be, at least imaginatively, experienced."[36] Jameson does concede Lukács' point that "faithful 'expression' of the underlying logic of the daily life of capitalism" may indeed risk making us feel "increasingly at home in what would otherwise ... be a distressingly alienating reality," retraining us "for life in the market system."[37] But he also believes that modern(ist) literature's increasing penchant for intractable passages of "trivial" description suggests a developing affinity and love for the resisting powers of what have, in a capitalist system that overdevelops the rational and functional parts of the mind, become "archaic" mental faculties, a kind of "psychic backwater" in the overrationalized modern world.[38] This backwater is a confluence of primarily qualitative processes of taste and aesthetics, as well as the irreducible experience of sense perception that can seem to offer no clear value in terms of exchange or use:

> The increasing abstraction of visual art [towards a pure sensory experience without semantic content] thus proves not only to express the abstraction of daily life and to presuppose fragmentation and reification; it also constitutes a Utopian compensation for everything lost in the process of the development of capitalism—the place of quality in an increasingly quantified world, the place of the archaic and of feeling amid the desacralization of the market system, the place of sheer color and intensity within the grayness of measurable extension and geometrical abstraction. The perceptual is in this sense a historically new experience, which has no equivalent in older kinds of social life.[39]

Thus, in Jameson's account, the importance of registering autonomous sensory experience via description increases in proportion to the expansion of market rationalization throughout the world and within the psyche. The logic of capitalism reifies the individual senses and makes each isolated sensory perception visible and tangible as a "semiautonomous" activity, but it doesn't necessarily find a way to quantify and rationalize sensory input. The "activity of sense perception," of which description is most often a vehicle, "comes to have little enough exchange value in a money economy dominated by considerations of calculation, measurement, profit, and the like."[40] The act of looking has been reified but not completely rationalized. And so the presence of ostensibly meaningless description in these works, and the kind of passive, idle subjectivities that accompany them, is, according to this account at least, not an embodiment of capitalist superfluity and excess as such, but evidence of a kind of cultural escapism, a fleeing into what areas are yet to be fully "colonized" by Tayloristic rationalization. For Jameson, the ultimate example of this is a style like Impressionism, which "discards even the operative fiction of some interest in the constituted objects of the natural world, and offers the exercise of perception and the perceptual recombination of sense data as an end in itself."[41]

Lukács, then, and to some extent Barthes, is operating on an understanding of the aesthetic object that is not only outdated, belonging to an earlier stage of cultural development, but one that neglects the "revolutionary" power of idleness and dysfunction in the novel. Following Jameson's reading, in contrast to Lukács, the way to stop novels becoming too capitalist would be to stop them becoming overly functional. Despite the risks of making its readership passive spectators, a heavily descriptive book harbors an irreducible excess—one that cannot be easily rationalized or made efficient via routinization. To be resistant, a book needs to load itself with Barthes' catalyses rather than cardinal functions.

Although this framework holds initial explanatory value when placed over Wallace's work, we need to be careful transplanting an analysis of what is essentially modernist writing onto a novel deeply ingrained in *post*modern social realities and postmodernist literary practices. In his later *Postmodernism* book, Jameson suggests that the fundamental difference between modernity and postmodernity is that modernism was characterized by an incomplete and hence uneven modernization of society and the human psyche, allowing for the presence of those "psychic backwaters" he discussed in *The Political Unconscious*. Postmodernism is to be considered as the completion of the modernizing process. The prefix "post" refers, then, to the end of the unevenness of capitalist development.[42] Following from this, Wallace's practice of description—at least the kind represented by the catalog of "blue things"—would not necessarily offer resistance to capitalist routinization. Instead, it would represent its progress. Jameson claims elsewhere that

> capital is in the process of colonizing that most remote part of the mind—the aesthetic—that traditionally seemed to resist its logic (being governed, as classical aesthetics taught us, by "purposefulness without a purpose"): on Mandel's account, then, consumer society would be a thoroughgoing push into this area of the mind—culture, the unconscious, whatever you want to call it—and a final rationalizing, modernizing, industrializing, commodifying, colonizing, of the non- or precapitalist enclave left surviving there.[43]

The type of description that Wallace employs, then, would manifest the same "rationalization" of the world from which it was trying to escape.

To return to Wallace's description of blue things quoted earlier, it is plausible to view the scene not as stubbornly resistant to function and narrative progression as we initially did, but as the expression of a sterile, bureaucratic gaze, one that quantifies the world like a machine and that has little time for the utopian sensory activity of, for instance, Conrad's impressionism. There is definitely a sort of sensory stubbornness to the passage, and a fascination with the abstraction of the color blue, but it can be instantly recoded as being symptomatic of a negative pathology like information addiction or some other bureaucratic malaise. Jameson's comments on Robbe-Grillet are here pertinent:

> Detail here no longer awakens the interpretative lust of Dali's "paranoiac-critical" method, where the very grain of gold sand, the individual beads of perspiration on the limp watches, promise an impending revelation. In Robbe-Grillet, for all the catastrophic temporality of the accumulated sentences, it is something closer to obsessional neurosis that declares itself, mindless compulsions not unrelated to workaholic efficiency, in which an absent subject desperately attempts to distract itself by way of sheer rote measurement and enumeration.[44]

We can discern this bureaucratic, "colonized" mode of looking in other stubbornly dysfunctional passages of *Infinite Jest*:

> Year of the Depend Adult Undergarment: InterLace TelEntertainment, 932/1864 R.I.S.C. power-TPs w/ or w/o console, Pink$_2$, post-Primestar D.S.S. dissemination, menus and icons, pixel-free InterNet Fax, tri- and quad-modems w/ adjustable baud, post-Web Dissemination-Grids, screens so high-def you might as well be there. (620)

This is not only a passage about a technology that facilitates obsessive observation, but a description filled with such emptily precise jargon that all its reader can do is, like the teleputer viewer herself, sit back, switch off their mind, and grow comfortably numbed by the onslaught of images flashed toward them by the screen of the page. It is more akin to the fine-print written on the back of a television box, complete with litigation-conscious warnings, than a description. This is what Alan Liu would probably call "information designed to resist information."[45]

Bartleby Returns

Yet, I think there is something different in other parts of *Infinite* Jest, moments that go beyond these possible encodings of its maximalism, and what makes Hal's narrative of institutional alienation so important. For regardless of how we might otherwise understand the many examples of refusal, breakdown, collapse, and seizure that punctuate the novel, they allow it an aesthetic experience unavailable to it elsewhere, justifying the novel's interest in detail and specificity. And we can see this most clearly when we combine Hal's narrative with the attention to the maximalist poetics of the novel we've been developing previously.

Late in the novel, Ortho Stice, a student at the Enfield Tennis Academy, has his forehead stuck to a hallway window grown icily cold in the predawn morning. He is literally glued to a screen, an avatar for all the teleputer nuts in this novel, as well as readers glued to its pages. By the time Hal (he is narrating in first person at this stage of the novel) comes upon him, the lower half of the window is fogged with Ortho's breath. Outside, seen through the unobscured portion of the window, the snow is a "white curtain endlessly descending" like the imminent end of the novel itself. But as Hal attempts to free Ortho from his painful bond with the glass, he spots an anomalous figure sitting out in the bleachers behind the show courts (867). The window is fogged by Stice's breath and the world outside is covered by the snow that's falling like a veil over our own curious vision, so we're told it's simply "impossible to tell the person's age or sex" (867). The figure effectively disappears from the novel's sight. Hal gives his attention to narrating the details of the Boston cityscape in the background of the scene that is framed by the window.

What it is that has Ortho stuck staring out a window in the early hours before sunrise is obviously an object of curiosity, both for Hal and the reader (although Hal, perhaps, is already in such a "fugue-state" that he couldn't care less). The figure seems the obvious goal of a broader narrative curiosity, especially when considered in relation to the other unexplained and ominous presences appearing at the fringes of ETA throughout the novel (the arrival of "Helen" Steeply, the imminent appearance of the *Assassins des Fauteuils Rollents* disguised as a rival tennis team, not to mention the "haunting" that has been troubling Ortho). Hal is narrating this scene and is faced with a decision: investigate who this figure is and play the "sport" of narrative, or look away. As we can see, Hal looks away, refusing to be curious, looking past the figure. Of course, his turning away risks only *increasing* our curiosity as readers, but he, and the novel that he is guiding, becomes more interested, intrigued, by what lies in the periphery of the window's frame, the play of peripheral visual data in his eyes. Narrative questions become subordinate to what is similar to an exercise of ekphrasis—a detailed description of a cityscape, framed by a window. But it's an ekphrasis with an inverted focus. Hal turns away from the questions in the foreground to provide us the background information instead—information we might struggle to find a use for, but which, the text tells us, we should perhaps learn to appreciate. Wallace is again reminding us of his interest in the catalyses of art rather than its cardinal points.

For a novel so interested in the negative aspects of addiction and entertainment, it's very tempting to see moments like these, filled with deflation and frustration, as a major part of its story, perhaps kernelling a somewhat quaint moral lesson about not getting all that we want. The form mimes the content. Indeed, many readers have used the text's play with such absences as a means of showing how the form of this novel emphasizes a particular thematic aspect of its content, the absence at its heart constituting the key to understanding the work as a textual performance.[46]

But to read the novel as permeated by meaningful holes and absences is to neglect the importance of what it actually provides us with, and is to look away from those details that occupy the place of the ones we stubbornly desire. For another way to view Hal and Ortho's scene, the description of blue objects in the waiting room, as well as the supposedly "missing" end of the novel, is that the text doesn't necessarily avoid telling us important information, so much as look elsewhere, toward other matters that interest it more. It is of course significant that the snowy figure Hal looks away from is sitting in the bleachers above the show courts, where coaches and others would sit to watch him play tennis. In turning away to record the rest of the vista—the "whole scene" (868)—he gives his attention to something other than being watched and made to perform for another's evaluation.

Not long after Hal looks out this hallway window, he starts to experience a vague sadness and panic similar to performance anxiety (896). These are the feelings that, we can assume, will lead to his failed interview at the novel's opening. But he also tells us that this "wasn't wholly unpleasant" (896). He starts to experience the world in a way that is disruptive to playing tennis, a panic that is disabling of the function for which he has been trained. But it is also enjoyable. Although Hal seems to feel guilty that he "didn't want to play this afternoon. ... Not even neutral, I realized. I would on the whole have preferred not to play" (954), it also awakens him "to a basic dimension" he had "neglected during years of upright movement, of standing and running and stopping and jumping." This new activity is, we'll recall, that of not doing anything, of lying down and being still.

But it is not just being still that excites Hal; it is also the freedom of a type of looking and registering of nonfunctional sensory facts that this immobility allows:

> Everything came at too many frames per second. Everything had too many aspects. But it wasn't disorienting. The intensity wasn't unmanageable. It was just intense and vivid. ... The world seemed suddenly almost edible, there for the ingesting. The thin skin of light over the baseboards' varnish. The cream of the ceiling's acoustic tile. The deerskin-brown longitudinal grain in the rooms' doors' darker wood. The dull brass gleam of the knobs. (896)

This is Hal cast as a reader of a maximalist novel. The narrative certainly gives us the option of understanding this experience as a negative development, the effect of Hal's marijuana withdrawal, for example. But to understand it as such would be to deny the enthusiasm with which Hal (and, by extension, Wallace) approaches these moments. It is the registering of banal data in the immediate present that liberates Hal here, or at least offers itself as an anti-purpose that fills in for the absence of his previous one—that of playing tennis. The novel's enthusiasm for dysfunctional description has climatically linked up with Hal's narrative arc: with the two combined, the text will soon reach its conclusion.

I think we are able to read this as a comment upon the novel's weariness with the "sport" expected of it, and confirmation of the relief that Wallace's frequent excursions into maximalist description allows him. Hal's narrative is ostensibly one of self-recovery, his learning to appreciate emotion and so forth, but it is also the story of someone becoming unsuitable for the professional world for which he is trained. It is his fall out of a mode of production, so to speak. At the beginning of the novel, Hal speaks in a way that is unable to be "sold." And the difficult, stubborn, almost terrifyingly indifferent passages of maximalist writing that fill the book are to be seen as expressions of a similar position, or at least moments in which Wallace allows himself to take a break from the pressures of being a novelist otherwise so keen to articulate the social, cultural, and interpersonal usefulness of literary objects.

This strand of the novel isn't confined to Hal's narrative, either, and we've done a disservice to *Infinite Jest* by only reading it through his character. Alongside Hal's move toward a catatonic flunking, Don Gately's narrative also dominates the final portion of the novel. Tellingly, he dominates it by doing nothing, by lying down in a hospital bed, unable to move, suffering from a gunshot wound. Despite what the novel warns us about being passive, it is only really interested in characters who are static or refuse action. As soon as Gately starts to positively act upon the world, working a job, entering a romance, and performing heroic actions (saving Randy Lenz from probable murder, for example), he is immediately immobilized for the remainder of the novel. His narrative progression is ultimately toward passivity.

The end of Gately's story is also the closing scene of the novel, and involves his memory of a particularly grisly drug binge that, like Hal's closing moments, marks a push toward stasis. If we are reading the novel for all the things that we are used to narratives giving us—conclusion, resolution, etc.—we will of course feel that this ending is an anticlimax, stealing the focus away from the central action. And indeed, in terms of the story of the novel it *is* anticlimactic. We've seen many similar vignettes of bad, junky behavior already and there is nothing terribly unique about this one. But never in Gately's narrative have we seen one that deals so explicitly with the connection between overwhelming, catatonic passivity, and maximalist description. Instead of the confluence of the narrative's "converging lines" of intent, a moment we're teasingly given snapshots of at opposite ends of the novel,[47] we are here witness to a refusal of narrative resolution that hinges on the description of a scene in "almost untakable focus" (980)—the apotheosis of maximalist writing.

Having, along with his companion Gene Fackelmann, binged on a veritable "mountain" of more-or-less stolen Dilaudid, Gately is set upon by a group of assailants sent to revenge his transgressions. As Fackelmann's eyes are sewn open a là *A Clockwork Orange*, Gately is injected with a drug nicknamed Sunshine and falls, with the help of one of his assailants, slowly to the floor. C, a junky thug organizing the elaborate payback, helps Gately down in such a way that he avoids sustaining injury to his head, and Gately gets "a rotary view of the whole room in almost untakable focus" (980). We are to understand that the detail of the "rotary view" overwhelms him.

The slow-motion, excruciatingly intense drug haze through which the scene is filtered is obviously intended to thematically emphasize the trouble substances have got Gately into, showing us his lowest ebb (after which he is "reborn" on the beach).[48] But from a formal perspective, it also forces upon the narrative a distinct mode of presentation, and, being the closing scene of the book, emphasizes it with finality. Gately becomes what is perhaps the prime subject (both thematically and formally) of the novel—an observer:

> The A.M. sun hung in the window, up and past the tree, yellowing. The bottles were the black-labelled boxy bottles that signified Jack Daniels. A churchbell off in the Square struck seven or eight. Gately had had a bad experience with Jack Daniels at age fourteen. The bland groomed corporate guy had inserted a different TP cartridge and now was getting a portable CD player out of the TaTung box while the pharmacist's assistant watched him. Fackelmann said whatever it was a total goddamn lie. Pointgravè or DesMonts took the bottle Chad taken from the tough girls and handed to Gately. The sunlight on the floor through the window was spidered with shadows of branches. Everybody in the room's shadows were moving around on the west wall. C also held a bottle. (976)

In his memory and his body, he becomes catatonically still. But the formal contrivance of a drug seizure, this moment of intense stillness and passivity, allows the narrative to close on the activity it seems to love most: registering detail, capturing a "whole scene" broken up into autonomous fragments of information that largely refuse to be drawn into a meaningful sequence. The bottles appear as a motif dispersed throughout the passage, almost as attempts to anchor it, but fail to make it meaningful in any ordinary sense. The sun appears in the first line of this passage but its influence doesn't appear in the room until near the end. A properly sequenced description might connect its presence in the window with the "spidered ... shadows of branches" falling across the floor, but this "narrative" flow is interrupted by other scattershot impressions, which themselves are interrupted by further details.

Jeffrey Karnicky has suggested that "moving toward stasis in Wallace's fiction is to undergo transformation. Stasis alters consciousness and provides a way out of a subjectivity that has become too much to bear."[49] Indeed, we certainly get the sense that reliving this moment involves some form of catharsis for Gately. But more than simply offering a way out of an oppressing subjectivity, it also gives the novel one final chance to emphasize the importance of its maximalist tendencies. Here, in the closing scene of the novel, we can see Wallace's two interests in direct conflict, as it were. On the one hand, this scene offers us a final example of the novel's thematic concern with addiction, a depiction of Gately's lowest ebb, his slump toward total, infantile helplessness from which he is to triumphantly rise in some future beyond the scope of the narrative. But on a formal level, this is also Wallace doing what he loves best: describing a room in "almost untakable focus." He enjoys when Gately is in decline, because it's also Wallace the maximalist who gets to be in full flight. We're meant to be shocked by Gately's stasis, but Wallace is excited by what it allows him as a writer.

Flunked

Wallace certainly knows a lot about what to do with words. But when viewed through its maximalism and the narrative threads that "naturalize" this mode of inquiry, *Infinite Jest* can be read as a novel about a writer who feels that the pressure to perform for an institution, a public, even just one's self, is often exhausting. There are moments throughout the novel when Wallace almost seems desperate just to be able to *write*, to pour words paratactically down on the page, to find relief in the basic activities involved in writing, and to temporarily refuse what else he is expected to do with words. And these are moments in which, almost invariably, his characters experience moments of intense breakdown, flunking, and failure. Having nothing else to do, nowhere to go, no ability to act otherwise, these characters become vehicles for the writer who simply wants to write, describe, and record detail, as if the other functions of his novel were put momentarily on pause. The importance of flunking is that, like in Hal's monstrous interview, it estranges and disrupts the processes of "assessment" so that for momentary instants a sort of freedom is allowed of the novel to be just what it is—a collection of signs, the record of the labor of writing—and for those characters and readers who find themselves within it to be just what they are. The writer asserts himself as one who simply writes, and wishes that this might be *enough*. Gone is the need to offer a complex and persuasive critique of a culture, to impress peers, to win grants, scholarships, and praise from institutions, and to reimagine a form that has been, in the last century, already reimagined to death.

The novel constantly searches for situations, figures, and themes that allow it the freest exercise of this maximalism. But it also ensures Wallace remains somewhat fractured as a writer, caught between purposes. On the one hand, *Infinite Jest* is uneasy with interviews and assessments, full of dysfunction; Wallace feels freedom in being allowed to remain detached, allowed to remain passive, to keep on writing free of the pressure to have the product meet the "grade." On the other hand, as we have seen in the opening section of this chapter, he is unusually articulate about his work and the social and personal value of literature. In the following chapter, we will see him attempting to resolve this potential impasse by developing a thematic concern that is more unified with his maximalist tendencies. *Infinite Jest*, however, remains a text defined by this tension.

Notes

1. Dave Eggers, "America in 2010: Everyone's Hooked on Something," *The San Francisco Chronicle*, February 11, 1996.
2. Ed Finn, "Becoming Yourself: The Afterlife of Reception," in *The Legacy of David Foster Wallace*, ed. Samuel Cohen and Lee Konstantinou (Iowa City: University of Iowa Press, 2012), 169.
3. Frank Bruni, "The Grunge American Novel," *The New York Times Magazine*, March 24, 1996, https://www.nytimes.com/books/97/03/16/reviews/wallace-v-profile.html.
4. Wallace, *Infinite Jest*, 832. In this chapter, subsequent citations for *Infinite Jest* are given in parentheses.
5. See, for example, Joelle's suicide attempt in Molly Notkin's bathroom (240).
6. Mark McGurl, "The Institution of Nothing: David Foster Wallace in the Program," *boundary 2* 41, no. 3 (2014): 32.
7. D.T. Max reveals that, when applying for colleges in his youth, "Wallace dreaded interviews. Life for him had the quality of a performance, and being called on to perform within that performance was too much. At the admissions interview [for Oberlin College] Wallace grew anxious. ... When the interview was over, Wallace went back to his hotel and threw up in the ice bucket." Max claims Wallace would later "transfer the scene into Hal's breakdown at the opening of *Infinite Jest*." D.T. Max, *Every Love Story is a Ghost Story: A Life of David Foster Wallace* (London: Granta, 2012), 13–14. Wallace's next book, *Brief Interviews With Hideous Men*, would be structured almost entirely around the interview format, a reflection, perhaps, of his increasing discomfort with his newfound celebrity.
8. Max, *Every Love Story*, 192.
9. Ibid., 193.
10. McGurl, *The Program Era*, x–xi.
11. Ibid., 48.
12. Larry McCaffery, "An Interview with David Foster Wallace," *Review of Contemporary Fiction* 13, no. 2 (1993): 131.
13. David Foster Wallace, "E Unibus Pluram: Television and U.S. Fiction," *Review of Contemporary Fiction* 13, no. 2 (1993): 171.
14. Adam Kelly suggests that "the essay-interview nexus became an inescapable point of departure" for readings of *Infinite Jest*. Adam Kelly, "David Foster Wallace: the Death of the Author and the Birth of a Discipline," *Irish Journal of American Studies Online* 2 (2010): para. 7, http://ijas.iaas.ie/index.php/article-david-foster-wallace-the-death-of-the-author-and-the-birth-of-a-discipline/.
15. David Foster Wallace and David Lipsky, *Although of Course You End Up Becoming Yourself: A Road Trip with David Foster Wallace* (New York: Broadway Books, 2010), 156.
16. For discussion of fears regarding the obsolescence of the novel as a form, see Fitzpatrick, *The Anxiety of Obsolescence*, and chapter 2 of Green, *Late Postmodernism*.
17. McCaffery, "An Interview with David Foster Wallace," 128.
18. Infinitedetox, quoted in Kathleen Fitzpatrick, "Infinite Summer: Reading, Empathy, and the Social Network," in *The Legacy of David Foster Wallace*, 194.
19. Fitzpatrick, "Infinite Summer," 195.

20. Mary K Holland, "'The Art's Heart's Purpose': Braving the Narcissistic Loop of David Foster Wallace's *Infinite Jest*," *Critique: Studies in Contemporary Fiction* 47, no. 3 (2006): 218.

21. Ibid.

22. To put it another way, the recent fascination with authors of "big" novels is perhaps to be seen as placing a demand of excessive labor on authors who want to be deified in this way. It is thus not unsurprising that long works are also commonly the most difficult, the most willing to "attack" the reader and resist his easy pleasures in what is perhaps the novelist's mutely expressed resentment for having to work so hard to achieve adoration. Mark Greif comments on this pressure to write big books and the form's relationship to literary achievement: "Thus an author who never produces such a mega-novel, like Philip Roth, remains oddly retrograde in the modernist and postmodernist trajectory of the art novel as a progressive form. Roth's midcareer moves in such a direction—toward the reckless and zany and nationally representative, albeit at shorter length, in novels like the significantly named *The Great American Novel* (1973) and *Our Gang (Starring Tricky and His Friends)* (1971)—are forgotten, not least because they seemed to be repudiated by Roth's later work. An author who produces a significant body of work in shorter books, like Don DeLillo, must push himself to produce one of the much longer, ceaseless-circulation-of-stories novels, in *Underworld* (1997), so that canon-makers can sort him in with the likes of Pynchon and Gaddis." Greif, "The Death of the Novel," 28.

23. David Foster Wallace, *The Broom of the System* (London: Abacus, 1987), 104.

24. David Foster Wallace, *Girl with Curious Hair* (London: Abacus, [1989] 1997).

25. David Foster Wallace, *Brief Interviews with Hideous Men* (London: Abacus, 1999), 123, 1.

26. David Foster Wallace, *Oblivion: Stories* (London: Abacus, 2005).

27. Although fiction writing is markedly absent from the novel, James Incandenza and his films are in some sense stand-ins for Wallace and his own art. James's story lacks the directness of the rest of Wallace's work's engagement with the practical realities of being "unfortunately, a fiction writer," but his career as an artist does seem to reveal Wallace's feelings about the relationship between art and institutional evaluation. James's films tend to either be absurd anti-films openly antagonistic to their audiences, or else sophisticated jokes aimed to poke fun at institutionalized film criticism. His genre of "found drama," in which a name is randomly picked out of a phonebook, and whatever happens to that person in the next hour and a half is considered to be the drama, eventually won him much institutional praise—until it was revealed as a joke (1028n145).

28. Such accusations of plagiarism or, more properly in Hal's case, a "helping hand," certainly speak to anxieties of the novelist who is keen to break free of his literary influences, but also those of the author who conducts research in order to get inside the head of his characters. As D.T. Max's biography of Wallace discusses, the inspiration for *Infinite Jest*'s Don Gately was a real recovering addict dubbed Big Craig. When Craig first met Wallace, he was skeptical because he felt Wallace was merely researching "material for a book." Wallace would not have been oblivious to this suspicion, and using other people's life stories in one's novel surely carries with it an uneasiness expressed in the allegations of plagiarism troubling the students.

29. Roland Barthes, "Introduction to the Structural Analysis of Narrative," *New Literary History* 6, no. 2 (1975): 247–48.

30. Ibid., 245.
31. See my introduction for a discussion of this passage.
32. Lukács, "Narrate or Describe?," in *Writer and Critic*.
33. Lukács, *Contemporary Realism*.
34. Lukács, *Writer and Critic*, 116.
35. Lukács, *Contemporary Realism*, 53.
36. Jameson, *Political Unconscious*, 225.
37. Ibid.
38. Ibid., 209.
39. Ibid., 225.
40. Ibid., 217.
41. Ibid., 218.
42. Fredric Jameson, *Postmodernism, or, The Cultural Logic of Late Capitalism* (Durham: Duke University Press, 1991), 366.
43. Fredric Jameson, *Jameson on Jameson: Conversations on Cultural Marxism*, ed. Ian Buchanan (Durham: Duke University Press, 2007), 19.
44. Fredric Jameson, *The Cultural Turn: Selected Writings on the Postmodern 1983–1998* (London: Verso, 1998), 108.
45. Liu, *Laws of Cool*, 356.
46. Samuel Cohen provides a neat synopsis of these various critical interpretations of the novel's ending. Samuel Cohen, "To Wish to Try to Sing to the Next Generation: *Infinite Jest's* History," in *The Legacy of David Foster Wallace*, 64.
47. See Wallace, *Infinite Jest*, 16–17 and 934.
48. Marshall Boswell contends that this final image of Gately lying on the shore suggests a strong notion of rebirth. Marshall Boswell, *Understanding David Foster Wallace* (Columbia, SC: University of South Carolina Press, 2003), 178–79.
49. Jeffrey Karnicky, *Contemporary Fiction and the Ethics of Modern Culture* (New York: Palgrave Macmillan, 2007), 121.

3   Data-Sickle

Maximalism and White-Collar Aesthetics in David Foster Wallace's *The Pale King*

The Terms and Conditions of Success

When the judges of the 2011 Pulitzer prize read David Foster Wallace's *The Pale King*, they felt its first paragraph alone was more powerful than the whole of any other shortlisted book they'd read.[1] This opening, originally published as a prose poem, offers a long and densely worded, second-person description of a mostly idealized rural landscape, listing the multitude of plants, insects, birds, and rocks that inhabit the scene, as well the imprint we make on the landscape as we watch it, the brand of our shoes "incised in the dew."[2] The section closes with an exhortation to "read these" things (4), which is, in effect, asking us to read the passage again. This command functions as a declaration of what any maximalist novel demonstrates as important—paying close attention to the world, listening carefully, getting everything and more down in prose that does justice to a sense of overflowing immediacy. It also tellingly maps changes in the scene of work in the age generally termed postindustrialism. The labor that we are to perform in this field is to *read*—to construct and manage the scene as information, rather than till its soil:

> Past the flannel plains and blacktop graphs and skylines of canted rust, and past the tobacco-brown river overhung with weeping trees and coins of sunlight through them on the water downriver, to the place beyond the windbreak, where untilled fields simmer shrilly in the A.M. heat: shattercane, lamb's quarter, cutgrass, sawbrier, nut-grass, jimsonweed, wild mint, dandelion, foxtail, muscadine, spine-cabbage, goldenrod, creeping Charlie. (3)

This is Wallace trying out a new voice, perhaps grown tired of his old one: the litany of product names, pharmaceutical brands, acronyms, trilled conjunctions and other literary pyrotechnics typical of *Infinite Jest* are replaced by an agricultural vocabulary, the invocation of a pastoral sublime that seems a respectful imitation of passages from Cormac McCarthy's *Suttree*.[3]

As any reader who has pursued the remainder of the novel knows, the reason this opening stands out so strongly is not just because it's the first that one encounters or that it contains especially beautiful prose. The passage appears so striking because, apart from one or two other brief sections like it in the early stages of the work, it is marooned amidst deliberately tedious descriptions of tax law, the internal monologs of exhausting characters, and a fascination with office places, accounting lectures, and bureaucratic bylaws. Indeed, whatever idyllic resonance lingers on after this opening passage is all but stamped out by a companion landscape described just a short time later—an airport so "uniformly featureless" that it looks as if it has been trodden on by a giant boot (29). It is this view of the airport that marks the arrival of the novel in its setting proper. For apart from its brief rural sojourn, most of *The Pale King* takes place in the claustrophobic offices and minds of employees at the Peoria branch of the Internal Revenue Service (IRS), narrating both real and fictional intricacies of tax law that influence society in ways overlooked or simply unknown by laymen, and that have generally fallen far below the threshold of novelistic interest. This is a novel about boring domains of life that at times sets out to be boring itself, as many reviewers of the work have duly noted.

As with the case of *Infinite Jest,* Wallace was once again relatively forthcoming about the intentions behind *The Pale King*, providing us with something of a formula—again, equal parts helpful and unhelpful—for unpacking the difficulties of the text and appreciating why it seems more interested in offices than the field. Indeed, many readers seem to enjoy Wallace's clear articulations of literary value just as much as they enjoy his writing. The almost schematic conception of literature's interaction with lives and society that Wallace promoted at various stages of his career is certainly attractive for dispelling doubts about the effectiveness of the form to enact real change in the world, quelling some of the anxieties of obsolescence studied by Kathleen Fitzpatrick and Jeremy Green, among others.[4] Here, in *The Pale King,* the "key to modern life" is not, as it was earlier in Wallace's career, having the courage to "endorse single-entendre values," or treat "old untrendy human troubles and emotions in U.S. life with reverence and conviction."[5] Instead, it is the ability to be "unborable" (438). In the "Notes and Asides" appendix included at the end of the novel, Wallace proposes that intense bliss lies in wait for those of us able to tolerate boredom (546). This is something of the abstinence counterpart to *Infinite Jest*'s warnings about excessive pleasure. Love boredom, learn to pay attention to the boring things around you, and you might fix your emotional problems.

Once familiar with these notes and similar sentiments expressed within the narrative proper, it doesn't take long to understand why so much of *The Pale King* takes place within the IRS rather than the idyllic field. We might also argue that the conceptual drive underpinning the novel is self-defensive in a manner that can make us cynical of its promotion in an "unfinished" novel. If boredom and paying attention are good, then to be a socially responsible and useful object, the novel has a duty to be dull, to be a challenge to concentration. Read in another way, any flaws we might judge of the work aren't actually flaws per se, but part of its project. So if the book fails to stir our interests or seems fragmented and unfinished, then *we* are failing it. And if the Pulitzer judges valued the novel for its unboring opening, they were valuing it incorrectly. Those parts of *The Pale King* that easily pique our interest would work against its outward thesis.

But apart from providing something of a rationale for a book that is not critiqueable, *The Pale King*'s focus on the benefits of boredom also allows Wallace to continue his promotion of the value of the maximalist literary object. *Infinite Jest* both opened and closed with scenes of flunking, revealing a tension between the novel's maximalism and cultures of evaluation. When placed alongside *The Pale King*, it appears that Wallace's enjoyment of stubborn maximalist prose has, if anything, increased: these pages are filled with more dense and jargon-filled descriptions, and Wallace has chosen a setting and subject matter that fits the mood of the novel's prose and thus intensifies the "dysfunctional" aspects of his writing, as well as the relief he seems to find in them. To create a textual experience of boredom and challenge the attention of his readers, Wallace foregrounds his maximalist tendencies as a writer.

But this increase of maximalist dysfunction comes with a marked decrease in the sort of tension we noted in *Infinite Jest* between wanting to have one's novel change the world and simply wanting to write. The detailedness of maximalist prose often means it flirts with some degree of tedium, but because boredom is theorized as desirable in *The Pale King*, never before has fiction's benefit—or, for that matter, "the key to modern life"—been so directly dependent on maximalist poetics, on long and information-filled sentences that describe beyond the needs of mimesis or desire. Finally, simply writing words, without having to worry much about their use, is felt to be enough to sustain the literary act. The connection between maximalist prose and the conceptual core of *The Pale King* means that it is explicitly a book about the importance of detail in literary writing, reading, and everyday life, even going so far as to propose what we might call an ethics of maximalism, offering ways that overspecific novels can be actively beneficial for readers.

The Pale King often lives up to its goal of providing boredom and a game of attention—indeed, Jonathan Raban suggests that parts are "so tedious to read that it would be a lot more interesting to be sifting through piles of other people's tax returns."[6] Based on the terms it sets itself, then, it's a very successful work. But whether it is able to illustrate exactly how this benefit is supposed to come from literary boredom is another matter entirely. To take Wallace at his word is probably to be too trusting. As Robert Potts puts it, "even Wallace didn't know which, if any, of the strands [of the narrative] would connect with each other, or how much of the existing material he would cut, and so we are left with a book which can only gesture suggestively at the suggestive gestures it might have made."[7] The boredom/attention thesis is, to an extent, one of these suggestive gestures, yet to find an entirely settled place in the narrative. Like Heidegger's conception of profound boredom,[8] to outline its benefit in too explicit terms might only undo its purpose, making boredom not boring enough, the challenges to attention filled with distracting anticipation instead. The premise remains vague by necessity. But it's also simply possible that, being unfinished, Wallace himself hadn't quite articulated exactly what it was about the dull pole of maximalist writing that captivated him, knowing the endpoint, but not the details. In fact, why *The Pale King* is especially interesting for our purposes is almost *because* of this unfinished status, in that we can see Wallace testing out new and different ways of understanding the work the maximalist novelist performs in contemporary culture, experimenting with the usefulness of detailed writing in the postindustrial environment. In one way or another, the novel can be taken as a scratchpad for thinking about what it is that literary writing might do in the twenty-first century, and one yet to conceal its notes and speculations behind the finish of a polished novel.

In what follows I will attempt to explicate, challenge, and deepen the "ethics" of maximalism proposed in *The Pale King* by showing that Wallace aligns the work of the novelist and his readers with that of the postindustrial professionals who are the focus of this text, figuring new and potentially vital ways that the detailed novel might function in contemporary culture. Its value, in the account I will propose in this chapter, is not entirely divorced from some notion of Heideggerian "profound" boredom and an ability to persist through walls of tedium, but it primarily depends on delineating ways the activities involved in knowledge work overlap and intersect with how we read in professional environments, and what reading and writing in a maximalist manner can change about our view of work in the so-called information age. Wallace uses maximalism to reflect on the complexity of class in the postindustrial workplace, where white-collar workers try to distance themselves from blue-collar labor at the same time that automation and outsourcing threaten to hurl them towards it.

Paperwork and the Novel

As discussed in the introduction to this book, in many ways the contemporary maximalist novel obsessed with detail begs to be seen as having strong ties with the putative information age, being judged as impressive and skillful in a time and place where information management is commensurately valuable. The ability to provide an exhaustive list of photographs hanging on a wall or blue things in a waiting room, as we find in *Infinite Jest*, is not primarily valuable for its mimetic function, but for the type of work on display: the stubborn and unflagging attention to the details of the world and the ability to record them with an enthusiasm that belies their dullness. As we saw in the previous chapter, there was no room for overdetailedness in Lukács' realism because excess could only be aligned with capitalist indulgence. Words, in that literary economy, were moneyed ornaments. But in contemporary maximalism, excess doesn't diagnose the wastefulness or commodity fetishism of capitalism. Lots of words are simply lots of information. And information in the postindustrial world is the tool of the worker. The fascination with big works and their authors seems to express an awareness of postindustrial economic power.

When we read novels, however, we generally expect something more than just information management. If we only wanted to be dazzled at how a text managed informational complexity, we could curl up on the couch with a tax return or a corporation's statement of earnings instead of a maximalist novel. We generally don't, because this sort of information management is too dull, too tedious for most of us outside the financial sectors. So we stand to be impressed by the maximalist novel's ability to rake in a plethora of information, *and* its ability to offer some amount of entertainment, pleasure, or meaning that denies or at least separates the work of the literary text from what we tend to consider to be the drudgery of real knowledge work. For all of their difficulties, *Gravity's Rainbow* and *Infinite Jest* are also very funny novels, of course, sometimes almost cartoonish in their sense of humor, populated by giant infants and adenoids, levitating tennis coaches and psychic military leaders. And much of what we read about such novels convinces us they are good for us in some manner that everyday knowledge work is not, worth more to society than bureaucratic documents of tedium, anyway. The maximalist novel thus stands to turn knowledge work into something worthwhile by mixing the management of data in with the presumed benefits of reading great literature, as well as the meantime stimulation of the emotions and imaginative faculties generally excluded from knowledge work.[9] Data management is ultimately able to be appreciated as something of an aesthetic activity. To engage these big works, one sometimes needs to read like an accountant, and so this activity becomes intermingled with ideas of artistic appreciation. This gradual confluence of data management and aesthetic work is confirmed by the growing popularity of other related artistic fields, such as "data jamming" and computer-assisted composition, that take the general premise of knowledge work—managing and monitoring information—to construct aesthetic experiences. We've seen similar developments in the critical sphere too, in works like Franco Moretti's *Graphs, Maps, Trees* and the broad field of the digital humanities.[10]

The Pale King's dominant setting (the offices of the IRS) should already tell us that it is acutely aware of this relationship to the current market and its dominant form of capital. In some way, it is self-consciously about the terms and conditions of maximalism's success as a mode of poetics. But the unique thing about this novel, as we have already intimated, is that its interest in boredom also largely denies the sort of pleasure and relief that usually accompanies artistic objects, separating them from a pure knowledge-work text. The imaginative and emotional faculties that usually accompany the processing habits of the mind engaging in maximalist works are, while certainly still present to some degree, significantly downplayed here.

Patricia Meyer Spacks has argued that boredom actually provides the impetus for novels and other works of art to exist, and so should probably be considered a "creative impetus"[11] rather than a stultifying force. As she puts it, "all endeavor of every kind takes place in the context of boredom impending or boredom repudiated and can be understood as impelled by the effort to withstand boredom's threat."[12] Still, it is most often a move *away* from boredom that is narrated in narrative art. Odysseus fixes to leave the island of Ogygia because he grows weary of a lack of "contending" (and of making love to the goddess Calypso—such are the burdens of familiarity). Similarly, when life on Jackson's Island gets too "slow and dull," Huck Finn heads back to the mainland "to get a stirring up."[13] A narrative text can only usually justify narrating boredom if it is temporary. As in D.A. Miller's understanding of the "unnarratable" nature of success, boredom is usually what happens at either end of a narrative (or before and after it), but not in its midst.[14]

In *The Pale King*, however, tedium is everywhere. Wallace seeks it out. While in *Infinite Jest*, characters were plagued by an excess of pleasure that needed to be resisted, here in *The Pale King* the world is mostly troubled by a plenitude of dull discomfort. The jobs of the low-level IRS employees we meet in the novel essentially involve sorting tax returns that are likely to earn government revenue from those that are not. But there is far less proverbial wheat than chaff, of course, which if nothing else tells us that the majority of the American population doesn't earn enough to really matter to the government. Lawrence Zelenak, a tax lawyer and former employee of the IRS writing for the *Michigan Law Review*, suggests that Wallace actually tends to paper over the potentially exciting aspects of the IRS worker's day-to-day in order to emphasize the tedious aspects of the job:

> There is a glaring omission from *The Pale King*'s examination of the tedium of work as a tax return examiner: the book never describes the thought processes of an examiner as he goes through a return and considers whether to order an audit of the return. ... Wallace might have omitted such a description out of fear of boring his readers, but that seems doubtful given Wallace's admirable willingness throughout the book to risk boring his readers in various ways. I suspect, rather, that he realized that a detailed description of the return examination process would have revealed that the job is not particularly boring—that it is, in fact, rather interesting in its own way—and that that would have undermined the novel's presentation of examinations as the epitome of boredom.[15]

This is not to say that such a job wouldn't still be dull and meaningless despite what Zelenak claims, as for many people the prospect of being stuck behind a desk analyzing financial records surely constitutes a vision of superlative drudgery (although it's not terribly different to the life of a writer or academic, a point we'll get to next). But it does appear that the more creative and potentially stimulating aspects of tax accounting are omitted in Wallace's portrayal of the IRS. There's potential detective work to be had here; the book just won't pick up the case. It prefers the chaff.

As such, unlike *Infinite Jest*'s characters, *The Pale King*'s subjects are not ruled and ruined by their hedonistic desires (even when, in Chris Fogle's case, which we will look at in detail later, they are taking drugs). Instead, they are obsessed with methods of managing the barrage of information in their lives both inside and outside of the IRS. Most of these characters also conveniently possess or have developed abilities that make them, if not especially suited to life in this world, reflections of it. They are, in one way or another, citizens of a maximalist world-text, and avatars for the maximalist novelist and reader who deal in information management. Claude Sylvanshine, whose excruciatingly detailed journey into employment at the Peoria IRS we follow in the opening sections of the novel, is supposedly a "fact psychic," a sufferer of a syndrome called "Random-Fact Intuition" (118). Fact psychics suffer intrusive thoughts consisting of "fractious, boiling minutiae that no one knows or could be bothered to know even if they had the chance to know" (120). So when Sylvanshine bites into a cupcake he knows "where it was made; knows who ran the machine that sprayed a light coating of chocolate frosting on top; knows that person's weight, shoe size, bowling average, American Legion career batting average; he knows the dimensions of the room that person is in right now. Overwhelming" (121). Marcel Proust's narrator's bite into a madeleine inspired an involuntary remembrance of many substantial things; Sylvanshine's cupcake-inspired journey is equally detailed, but overwhelming in its nullity. The novel is being deliberately cagey here too, for the psychological vocabulary it uses to describe Fogle's disorder clearly evokes the Freudian model of interpretation in which the most useless bits of information are always the most revealing. Fogle is almost a classical hysteric, refusing the advice of the analyst/novelist, which is to see in these "random" facts the unvoiced narrative of one's life. So to view Sylvanshine's ailment in another way, Wallace is signaling to us that the use of detail in this text has become largely disconnected from hermeneutic processes and values. Again, reading in *The Pale King* is not interpreting, but managing information.

Much of the early part of the novel is occupied by Sylvanshine's narration of his journey to the Peoria branch of the IRS, and in it Wallace recasts the archetypal modernist technique of stream-of-consciousness narration to further reframe the novel's relationship to information in this world of knowledge work. Throughout Sylvanshine's densely narrated airplane trip from Chicago to Peoria, we witness his anxious thoughts flitting about from one subject to the next, punctuated by failed attempts to focus on revision for an upcoming tax exam he's taking to gain a promotion (11). What we are presented with throughout this section is something like the postindustrial update of stream of consciousness, in which the real-time movement and unedited, natural disorder of thought does not express a radical modernist phenomenology or impressionism, as it did for Joyce, Virginia Woolf, and other writers, but is experienced by Sylvanshine as a source of anxiety. Sylvanshine wants to have a focused mind but cannot. He can't order his thoughts, can't remain undistracted, and so narratorial complexity is not liberation, as it was for modernists, but beckons imminent failure, a weak capability to be a successful knowledge worker. We can infer that Sylvanshine wishes he might be suddenly cast back into a novel by Dickens or Austen, where his thoughts and feelings could be structured and controlled by neater aesthetic forms. If only some other writer were around to narrate him.

Other employees *The Pale King* finds interestingly dull include Chris "Irrelevant" Fogle, Shane Drinion, and David Wallace, the supposedly "real" author of the text. Fogle has an eponymous passion for digression and providing extraneous information that bores anyone forced to listen to him but enriches his own life. The longest section of the novel is his very roundabout account of how he came to be interested in a career at the IRS, a monolog revealing that his digressive tendencies are an effect of his newfound passion for paying close attention to minutiae. We will return to Fogle's story at length later because it houses what I feel is the most crucial scene of the novel. Shane Drinion, a character with obvious autistic overtones whom we meet late in *The Pale King*, is such a close and perfect listener to a conversation partner that, absurdly, he levitates with the energy of concentration. His focus on the details of what is being said to him makes up for his inability to emotionally connect with others. He is himself empty of personality, but can "empathize" through unwavering attention.

David Wallace, whose supposedly autobiographical sections claim that *The Pale King* is a memoir of the real author's time spent as an IRS examiner, eventually becomes involved in a complicated and tedious administrative confusion in which he is mistaken for another David Wallace, this one a high-ranking IRS employee, and is thus treated with the deference a newbie would never ordinarily experience. Although David Wallace, unlike Fogle, Sylvanshine, and Drinion, doesn't have any announced personality quirks, his first-person sections of narration evidence an immensely fastidious, and often immensely tedious, attention to detail. These sections are also peppered with long and in-depth footnotes about literary contracts, tax law, and peculiarities of the 1980s IRS, recalling the style of (the really real) Wallace's other work (I'll try to head off any confusion in what follows by referring to the real author of *The Pale King* as Wallace, and referring to this character in the novel as David Wallace). The irony of the longest of David Wallace's sections—his narration of arriving at the Peoria IRS for his first day of work—is that, while he repeatedly tells us that he believes only "relevant" information is important to a novel,[16] and that his memory of the day is quite vague, he proceeds to give us almost nothing but tedious, irrelevant, and eidetically precise facts. He claims that he has no intention of inflicting on readers "a regurgitation of every last sensation and passing thought

I happen to recall." He is interested in "art, not simple reproduction" (259). But this is almost the exact opposite of what we read, as what follows is an anxiously detailed account of being collected from a bus stop in a car provided by the IRS (267–85). When taken individually, these passages of David Wallace's narration do not seem overly excessive or irrelevant, especially when compared to some of the densest passages of *Infinite Jest*. But when *every* paragraph in a fifty-two-page section is filled with such narration the overriding effect is deliberately excruciating. The tension of the section, and our experience of its tedium, is exacerbated by David Wallace's constant appeals to a disingenuous *minimalist* ethos, with his actual writing standing in stark distinction to the "art of relevance" he claims to be presenting. If in the past Wallace was admittedly anxious that readers were not going to understand important aspects of his work, and he thus felt pressured to guide them,[17] here he openly encourages us *not* to listen to what he (or his fictional avatar) has to say about reading his writing.

One of the implications of Wallace's decision to align the novel with tedium and work rather than "art," and one that *The Pale King* no doubt has great fun with, is that it forces us to consider why we would be impressed by a novel that is so often deliberately dull, but on the other hand be immensely frustrated and bored by the bureaucratic tedium of tax law and the sort of work that is performed within the IRS. Indeed, the novel asks us this difficult question over and over, refusing to let us sidestep it: why might some of us heap praise on the maximalist novelist's ability to manage vast amounts of data and complexity, but only see the rise of bureaucratic workers— who can presumably work with much more data than the novelist—as a lamentable development of contemporary society? Why, for example, might some of Pynchon's and Wallace's intensive, and information-rich descriptions stand to impress us, while the bureaucratic enumeration of the world only speaks to a hollowing out of life, the routinization of all spontaneity, fluidity, and chance that otherwise redeems the world as being beyond the control of the market? Why is the office worker such a target of ridicule, but the author who takes accounting classes to research a novel seen as some kind of savior of the contemporary scene? Is the difference only really the ideology bundled up with the aesthetic, these appeals to "art" that David Wallace hopes we will fall for? Because it seems that either we should love *both* the maximalist novel and the culture of bureaucracy, *or neither*. This is the quandary at the heart of this novel, which its engagement with the theme of boredom encapsulates so adroitly.

Reading Ailments

Many other novels set in the postindustrial workplace are also narratives of education and escape in which characters learn that there is more to life than efficiency and number-crunching. *Bartleby's* narrator discovers the deficiency of "humanity" in the world of offices and law documents; DeLillo's *Americana* quickly leaves offices behind to pursue the practice of art. But Wallace wants to remain in the hum of these spaces, not to flee. So if *The Pale King* is a novel of the office through and through, yet also seems to refuse the entertaining possibilities of aestheticized information management, what other work does it do in this space? How is it to insert itself into the postindustrial landscape as a useful object and resist becoming just another symptom of the culture it is examining? How does it justify its existence? Wallace offers at least two potential uses that I will investigate here. One has to do with attention and is relatively straightforward, whereas the other has to do with issues of class in the information age. We'll look at attention first.

There is an implied politics in many aspects of *The Pale King*'s proposed maximalist ethics, but one of its most explicit arguments is that our willingness to degrade knowledge work in favor of the novel marks an unwillingness to take the former's power and influence seriously. As Ben Kafka suggests, the "endless, repetitive stories about 'bureaucracy' [and] the pleasure we take in sharing them with one another, are often the closest we will ever get … to obtaining satisfaction from the state."[18] This is a situation that Wallace wants to change, and at the root of the problem, for him, is a failing of attention, an inability or unwillingness to perform the same close scrutiny of detail maximalism encourages. Wallace seems to follow Richard A. Lanham's suggestion that in an information economy the most valuable commodity isn't information itself, but the attention and brainpower needed to manage it:

> Economics … studies the allocation of scarce resources. Normally we would think that the phrase "information economy," which we hear everywhere nowadays, makes some sense. … But information is not in short supply in the new information economy. We're drowning in it. What we lack is the human attention needed to make sense of it all. It will be easier to find our place in the new regime if we think of it as an economics of attention. Attention is the commodity in short supply.[19]

Tracing this line of thought, in the metafictional "Author's Foreword" appearing partway through *The Pale King*, David Wallace tells us that if government laws and regulations can be written with sufficient complexity and dullness, then most citizens won't have the stamina to learn their ins and outs. Dullness and prolixity, then, are much more effective shields against protest and political action than secrecy (83). The implication here is that if the novel is to be a socially useful object, it can no longer have the luxury of being entertaining: by being dull and overly detailed, it forces us to contemplate the way our willingness not to think too hard about dull things, and to try and structure our life instead around entertainments, enables our exploitation.

Wallace also seems to engage here with Patricia Spacks' reading of boredom, in which the notion of the boring connotes a broad refusal of self-responsibility in modern culture. Boredom does not simply refer to an experience that lacks a sufficient degree of stimulation, but the predisposition to blame this lack of stimulation on outside forces, on one's society or immediate surroundings, rather than on oneself. For Spacks, expressing boredom is a way of situating the self in relation to the world in a manner that decreases self-responsibility for one's emotions and experiences.[20] It's plausible to view Wallace's interest in boredom as an attempt to engage with such notions, a lack of responsibility being one of the prime causes of addiction for characters in *Infinite Jest*, and, in *The Pale King*, a reason for the general public's lack of political agency.

It is telling that just a few pages after we are informed of the benefits of penetrating the barriers of "the dull and arcane" (83–84), we are offered a prolix passage typical of maximalist novels, filled with almost meaninglessly specific jargon:

> Conclusion of ACIRHRMSOEAPO Survey/Study 1–76—11–77: AMA/DSM (II)-authorized syndromes/symptoms associated with Examinations postings in excess of 36 months (average term of posting on report: 41.4 months), in reverse order of incidence (per medical/ EAP service claim per IRSM §743/12.2 (f-r)):
>
>> Chronic paraplegia
>> Temporary paraplegia
>> Temporary paralysis agitans
>> Paracatatonic fugues
>> Formication
>> Intracranial edema
>> Spasmodic dyskinesia
>> Paramnesia
>> Paresis. (87)

The list continues in a stubborn fashion. After being lectured to on the importance of paying attention to dull, opaque, and overdetailed tracts of information, we are immediately presented with a dull, opaque, and overdetailed tract of information as if asked to put this theory into practice, to see if we can pay attention, can penetrate the barrier of the "abstrusely dull" in the manner the book wants us to. This description is almost a challenge; here, the novel veritably dares us to not find it dull, and if we do, then to outlast it. If reading *Gravity's Rainbow* was good training in "negative capability,"[21] then reading *The Pale King* provides an obvious lesson in patience.

Tore Rye Anderson argues that the focus on attention foregrounded in such passages is a "red thread" that runs throughout all of Wallace's work, as well as that of his postmodernist forebears his fiction is seen to be in dialog with.[22] The political importance of dull and abstruse writing, and the agency that learning to deal with maximalist prose might instill in us, is just the latest in a line of critiques of, for example, the passive mode of viewership promoted by television and other media technology, and what appears more recently in diatribes about the negative influence the internet has on our minds and our relationships with others.

But, again, let's not take Wallace's word for this: we should try to put this lesson into practice, because if Wallace is testing us, then he's also testing the validity of his own premise. So, what can we glean from this list of opaque information if we persist through its opacity? What is there to learn that might be obscured by its potential dullness? The passage lists ailments encountered by IRS workers, presumably from the long periods of sitting and repetitive work in which they are engaged. These ailments and illnesses all seem to be markers of the loss of the physical control of the body or symptoms of its neglect. Paralysis, Parkinson's, tics—they represent the body acting beyond the control of volition, reasserting its right to be heard, to voice complaints about its neglect or misuse in an economy of the mental rather than physical (which might be a crude way of summing up postindustrialism). This list intended to teach us to pay attention is obviously reminding us to observe an overlooked consequence of knowledge work, which is the denigration of physical labor and the related health impacts this might bring, as addressed in the many recent studies warning us of the dangers of sedentary lifestyles.[23]

But this list of physical ailments also expresses an anxiety about the effects of living life as a *writer*, a worker who is also confined to a desk, forced to be still while managing an endless stream of paperwork. Moving and writing just don't work that well together, as anyone who's tried to do both at the same time can confirm. The protagonist of Paul Auster's *City of Glass*, for instance, grapples with this difficulty as he traces a suspect through the grid of Manhattan whilst at the same time trying to record his every movement in a notebook:

> walking and writing were not easily compatible activities. If for the past five years Quinne had spent his days doing the one and the other, now he was trying to do them both at the same time. In the beginning he made many mistakes. It was especially difficult to write without looking at the page, and he often discovered that he had written two or even three lines on top of each other, producing a jumbled, illegible palimpsest.[24]

That one must write while being still means that many of the health concerns affecting office workers in *The Pale King* map neatly over the workplace "dangers" faced by writers.

This brings us to one of the main effects of Wallace's writing in *The Pale King*: the drawing of symmetries between contemporary writers, readers, and knowledge workers, both in terms of their engagement with information and their working habits. Wallace doesn't just set his novel in the IRS because it's the most boring organization in contemporary America, but also because he sees its workers as figures that match writers and readers in contemporary culture, people who are also now likely to be knowledge workers of a sort, either laboring directly within educational or publishing institutions, or engaging in the collection, management, and parsing of information in a manner that can parallel the work of administrators. One of the most confronting sections of *The Pale King* is a columned description in which "Howard Cardwell turns a page, Ken Wax turns a page, Matt Redgate turns a page" (310) and not much else happens for several pages. This is not just a description of accounting work, but a mirror held up to all readers, reminding them of the repetitive nature of the physical activity in which they are engaged, which is normally overshadowed by the mental component of reading.

Setting this scene of page turning within the IRS offices has other purposes too, of course. As Stephen Schryer suggests, postwar America saw a rapid increase in a "new class" of academics, and a subsequent professionalization and systemization of literary reading, embodied, for example, in the New Criticism's attempt to make close reading more scientific, holding it aloft as the discipline's "specialized techne."[25] If we can propose that literary reading and writing have become somewhat similar to institutional knowledge work, performed within organizations that are increasingly indistinguishable from large corporations, then it's clear that whatever good Wallace believes is to come through persisting with knowledge work applies equally to reading literature. The postwar belief (or, as Schryer suggests, fantasy) that "technically qualified experts" can secure the public good,[26] instills in the reader of *The Pale King* a corresponding trust in the vitality of his or her "profession."

It's tempting to view Wallace's portrait of this situation—aligning IRS examiners and readers of his book in the same activity—as a critique of the routinization that such professionalism inevitably represents, but to do so is to ignore what Wallace thinks is the power that knowledge workers hold as professional concentrators. The important effect of *The Pale King* is that if lines of symmetry are drawn between readers and knowledge workers, then when interpreters of this novel are speaking of the text's ability to wrestle "directly with matters of real world politics,"[27] or demonstrate "the attention that American citizens must pay toward civic duty and maintaining their freedoms,"[28] they are also fantasizing about reading finally achieving this same "real" social and political usefulness. If paying attention is enough to instill political agency in a subject, as it is in Wallace's conception, then those citizens like literary professors and graduate students who are professional attention-payers, and whose superb scrutiny of detail is a requirement of their profession, can find a way of achieving political potency. They are at least able to situate the activity of reading at the forefront of political action. What is most exciting for readers of *The Pale King*, perhaps, is that it instills them with the feeling that the potential for activism has been right in front of them all along—merely a way of seeing. This again shows that maximalism is a type of writing that demonstrates *significant abilities* rather than objects of significance, and foregrounds something like the self-sufficiency of literary praxis. To develop agency, one doesn't have to engage particular fields of knowledge, but merely persist with turning page after page of maximalist prose while engaging in close reading and writing.

So if it is readers that Wallace is representing in his tax accountants, he's also asking for the development of a different kind of reading practice, one finally attuned to the ethics of a maximalist writing that, to reuse the ideas encountered in the previous chapter, celebrates Barthes' "catalyses" rather than "cardinal" functions, and is interested in the activity of reading as a way of training attention, rather than engaging with content. Indeed, much of the work the IRS examiners are engaged in throughout the novel can be taken as a metaphor for different approaches to literary reading. The fictional David Wallace's disingenuous claim that art should only focus on relevant information is, of course, contradicted buy the novel's opposing assertion that it is this preference for "vital" information that allows the most important facts and experiences to slip past our attention. The rhetoric of efficiency promoted by David Wallace—in idea if not word—is also repeated in several articles on *The Pale King*,[29] which find its point to be teaching us how to sort irrelevant information from important data. But to view the job of the reader as a sort of Maxwell's Demon, sorting meaningful from redundant information, is only to reinforce the view of literary experience that *The Pale King*, like other maximalist novels, is trying to subvert. Those at the Peoria IRS are informed that the point of their work is "not to catch every last little error and discrepancy," but just to "determine which returns give evidence of maximum auditability in terms of (a) profitability, and (b) expediency" (320–21). This seems the economy of reading apparent in an "ordinary" novel and model of criticism. But the maximalist novel promotes an engagement with detail that goes beyond the promotion of institutional efficiency and instead finds value in every last little detail.

Wall-Papering

The best way to deepen our understanding of what value maximalist prose brings to the culture of information management is through an investigation of Chris "Irrelevant" Fogle's story, which occupies the longest section of the novel. This relatively polished section of *The Pale King* follows Fogle's narration of how he came to work at the IRS, a story he relates to a camera as part of a survey of employee backgrounds. Fogle's experiences form a miniature bildungsroman of sorts,[30] and we see him progressing from an unfocused college graduate who suffers the tragic loss of his father, to a dedicated and responsible IRS employee in love with paying close attention to detail. Much of his story, and his eventual development of mental focus and self-responsibility, can also be read as a way of theorizing how this novel relates to the bureaucratic world of which it is indelibly a part. Fogle is ultimately used as a way for Wallace to tell a story about his proposed ethics of maximalism that also depends on readers practicing their own attention to detail in order to draw out its rewards.

Fogle begins his story as an unmotivated university student who drops out of an Intro to Accounting course because of the "combination of difficulty and sheer boredom," eventually withdrawing from college completely to try his hand at "so-called real jobs" (155). He works briefly as a security guard at a parking garage, a ticket attendant at Liberty Arena, and a cog in the production line of a Cheese Nabs factory, before finding these jobs too dull to continue. Boredom's obviously a big problem, the cause of his meanderings, but so is dissatisfaction with blue-collar forms of work, those jobs involving manual labor. The whole spectrum of employment seems alienated and ruined by dullness, so he eventually reenrolls in college.

In this manner, Fogle's story immediately appears to be one about anxieties of class in postindustrial culture, a world in which professionalism and knowledge work, as Stephen Schryer analyzes, are seen to offer an escape from the problems of older kinds of labor. Indeed, we can note that a fear of blue-collardom has preoccupied the knowledge workers at the IRS throughout the novel. Sylvanshine's vision of career failure in the early sections, for example, involved "pushing a wide industrial mop down a corridor lined with frosted-glass doors bearing other men's names" (16). It's not exactly clear what greater form of power or satisfaction being an IRS examiner will provide, beyond money of course, and so a fantasy of "new class" professionalism and its attendant benefits is surely operative in these characters' abhorrence of blue-collar labor. (The "frosted glass" in Sylvanshine's vision is partly a decorative feature, but also one that encourages the blue-collar worker to peer into the white-collar world at the same time as it refuses their gaze, cruelly policing class divisions). One of the clearest effects of the shift toward knowledge work in postindustrial culture is indeed the reciprocal feeling of dissatisfaction attached to traditional trades and occupations, as if to work them were to not reach one's full potential. Indeed, the novel's opening passage's exhortation to "read" the field rather than farm it expresses a similar ambivalence about manual labor.

Fogle's life progresses in this more-or-less haphazard fashion, but once he returns to college it begins to be broken by moments of drug-induced clarity that stand as counterpoints to his listlessness. Fogle is careful not to provide "an endorsement of drug abuse," but nevertheless acknowledges that substances were "part of the story of the factors that eventually drew [him] to the Service" (177). Here Wallace is conscious of *Infinite Jest*'s critique of addiction and is trying to carefully separate the two novels' treatment of substance use, or at least revise the earlier one to allow for more flexibility. *The Pale King*'s less anxious appraisal of drug use seems to affirm that there is something in the sort of noticing and stasis that the substances help Fogle achieve, and which also accompanied the experiences of Hal and Gately, that goes beyond the social critique of addiction contained in *Infinite Jest*. Rather than the collapse and fall from social grace that substances forced on the addicts in that earlier work, here drugs drive Fogle *toward* employment. The experience of intense focus they allow is likewise associated with a kind of valuable work in and of itself—the appreciation of fine detail.

Fogle's drug of choice is the stimulant Obetrol, his affinity for which has to do with the ability it gives him to concentrate intensely on his everyday surroundings. For Fogle, the drug eventually allows a breakthrough of sorts, enabling a focus that the "collage art" (155) of his patchwork early life lacked. Or, to put it another way, he is far less ambivalent about embracing stasis. That Fogle describes his academic transcript from these years as resembling a collage is of course significant when we consider a collage's relationship to the form of a fragmented novel like *Infinite Jest*, or the general canon of postmodernist writing and thought. If the "collage imagination" is, according to Lance Olsen's somewhat overblown definition, "committed to liberating juxtaposition, mosaic, conflation, fusion and confusion, Frankensteinian fictions, cyborg scripts, centaur texts, the narratologically amphibious writings that embrace a poetics of beautiful monstrosity,"[31] then its transgressive energy is here, in *The Pale King*, only a distraction, creating a "fuzziness and drift" (182) that disables the close attention to particulars one needs in order to resist being pulled along by the structuring powers of society. Rather than resisting anything, the politics and aesthetics of collage merely enable one to conform to the flow of the heterogeneous mixing of stimuli that is postmodern life, enabling one's attention to be constantly distracted, never focused on the banal and overly rigid fine print of life in which, this novel argues, the true structures of power operate in the meantime.

The drug Obetrol initially seems to solve Fogle's problem with boredom too, not through entertainment or distraction, but by bringing him much closer to an understanding of the way the experience masks a certain kind of relation to the world and work that is useful for the needs of a postindustrial, bureaucratic society. In one way or another, he learns to experience and appreciate the world as an overdetailed text. Although Fogle has previously been immensely frustrated with the "boring and meaningless" nature of most of everyday life, he now finds the prosaic filled with a veritable wonderland of neglected details. He breaks through the barrier of the dull, practicing the maximalist mode of inquiry as he stares at the "institutional color" of the paint on his dorm room walls:

> It was kind of striking. Their texture was mostly smooth, but if you really focused your attention there were also a lot of the little embedded strings and clots which painters tend to leave when they're paid by the job and not the hour and thus have motivation to hurry. If you really look at something, you can almost always tell what type of wage structure the person who made it was on. (182)

Although this description of a banal living room might ordinarily be tedious, the sense of profundity it provides Fogle suggests a transcendence of the ordinarily dull and commonplace world that made his early life so shift-less and meandering. But transcendence not figured as some sort of escape from, but dive *into*, a coming into awareness of the unrecognized details of the world. Boredom is not something to be relieved by the introduction of diverting colors (or by hanging an interesting artwork on the wall, for example). It's to be embraced.

I feel that the key aspect of the entire section, in this regard, hinges on Fogle's investigation of the wall paint. Despite it being beige, the color of this paint is not "neutral." It is an "institutional" color, the dullness of which is charged with a sort of motivation not to notice it, not to pay attention to the walls or the work that has produced them (and really, unless we acciden-tally put a hole in one, how often do walls truly factor into our awareness as objects of human construction?). The trace of the human that persists on the wall, however, tells us something different:

> It was kind of striking. Their texture was mostly smooth, but if you really focused your attention there were also a lot of the little embed-ded strings and clots which painters tend to leave when they're paid by the job and not the hour and thus have motivation to hurry. If you really look at something, you can almost always tell what type of wage structure the person who made it was on.

We have a vision of different types of textuality here. That Fogle scruti-nizes painting—what elsewhere is a high-art activity but is here present in its banal or unaesthetic mode (that is, as mere work)—is significant. The "embedded strings and clots" are seen as a signature of sorts, and one usu-ally overlooked by our preference for artistic rather than banal painting. But that it now *is* signed, suggests that wall painting is to be seen as a culturally meaningful practice in the world of this text.

Much of Wallace's writing in *The Pale King* should perhaps not be distin-guished, in terms of interest, from this kind of "painting." Such a point res-onates strongly with what has already been said of Wallace's reappraisal of boredom and dullness, but it also shows that the novel is interested in using maximalism to encourage the unearthing of something like the repressed class content of the information age. While we focus increasingly on the value that information provides to contemporary society, none of this value would be possible, of course, without the construction and maintenance of the office spaces and environments in which this type of work occurs. As with Gorz's argument that blue-collar, service-sector workers pick up the slack of those other citizens whose economic success allows them to neglect the physical labors of life,[32] there is a mass of people who are excluded from definitions of the information age and yet support its basic operations (imag-ine what chaos the absence of cleaners in an office would cause, for exam-ple, and yet they are hardly seen as an integral part of a knowledge-work organization). For that matter, the book industry is also supported by the creation, maintenance, and operation of offices and machinery, without which the dissemination and marketing of writing would not be possible. To value only the writers and editors of publishing houses for the creation of literary culture is to ignore half the equation, just as valuing high-art paintings over the walls upon which they are hung promotes something of a class imbalance in the view of art. An attention to information is not used by characters in *The Pale King* to only serve the development of commerce or the profits of an industry. Instead, like the list of ailments designed to de-neglect the physical component of knowledge work, Fogle's epiphany marks an attempt to widen the conception of the information age to include the work of those whose labor supports it.

White-Collar Heroes

Fogle's narrative offers us several ways of describing the novel's reevaluation of "the picayune, the meaningless, the repetitive, the pointlessly complex" (438), and of understanding the different uses of maximalist writing in the contemporary environment. But is this working-class epiphany hidden inside the institutional wall really only intended to get us to shift our attention away from all these knowledge workers and remember, instead, those working-class laborers whose voices are kept firmly offstage, cited only, as in Sylvanshine's anxious imagination, as a vision of failure? Possibly, but I don't think so—at least not entirely. If Fogle is seeing in order to realize the repressed content of the information age, he also fails this vision offered him, or at least he fails to do anything with it other than get himself a job at the IRS. Although Fogle learns to see the traces of this hurried and forgotten painter, it is only insofar as that painter becomes part of his preparation for employment. Fogle certainly sees what is "hidden" by the wall of dullness, but at the same time fails to see it as anything other than confirmation that he can now see in great detail and thus fulfill the demands of the world of knowledge work and succeed in the field of accounting. Any other noticing is left up to us as readers.

It's also possible to argue, however, that Fogle is being asked to recognize his ultimate fate in this world as being somewhat similar to that of the overlooked painter. In much the same way that the shift to postindustrialism left the manufacturing industry fragmented and struggling, so too does the historical moment the novel narrates put the skill of "deep" noticing promoted in Fogle's story at risk of redundancy. As David Wallace notes in his authorial confession, the year in which *The Pale King* is set saw "a climax of an involved intra-Service battle between advocates and opponents of an increasingly automated, computerized tax system" (82). In a long section describing the induction of new workers at the Peoria Regional Examination Center (REC), the employees are frequently reminded of the circumscribed nature of their role, not being examiners or investigators of tax returns in the relatively exciting manner Zelenak explained previously, but merely sorters of reports into two piles—one for returns likely to be profitable to pursue, and one for those that will not. They are certainly not "inspectors" tasked with noticing "every last little error or discrepancy" (320), such as the clots of paint on the wall Fogle prides himself on analyzing. Whatever Fogle learns in his epiphany will soon be redundant, performed with more efficiency by computers. Elsewhere in the novel David Wallace informs us that this already circumscribed job would be all but eradicated in 1987— two years after the action described in the novel—with the introduction of the computerized ANADA, an "Audit-No Audit Discriminant Algorithm" used to examine "nearly all individual US tax returns" (527). After 1987, David Wallace informs us, the Peoria REC all but closed down (527), and so the novel represents the end of an era for nonautomated examiners.

The ability to perform knowledge work is far from something that always holds power, and this is perhaps the true import of Fogle's scene. As Liu discusses in his account of the impact of mainframe computing on knowledge work, what might have initially been seen as a liberating machinery, enabling all workers in an organization to be engaged in a culture of "symbolic analysis and critical reflection … antithetical to the earlier industrial culture of deskilling and routinization,"[33] predictably resulted in another form of Taylorization in which the workers' knowledge was extracted and codified into computerized "management information systems," stripping people of power and agency once again and recreating the apparatuses of "generalized control" typical of the earlier industrial society.[34] The effect for lower echelon workers was another form of deskilling and the increased isolation and routinization of their workplace activities, turning them into not much more than factory laborers tasked with rote, repetitive tasks of data input, alienated from the output of their work. Rather than laborers with powerful skills of insight, they were only to do what the computer yet couldn't. So if the knowledge worker is king in the information age, he is also a pale one, worried for his future as much as the effaced working-class laborers onto whom so much fear is projected in *The Pale King*. Fogle's "discovery" of the hurried wall-painter also presents to him a vision of his own future.

To return once more to that idyllic field preoccupying the start of the novel, the enthusiasm with which its contents are enumerated through a poetry of information management is perhaps almost a paean, an elegy for the kind of seeing quickly being deskilled and routinized in the field of work in which the rest of the novel will be set. But the description of the precarious situation facing these IRS examiners also gives us a final, and perhaps the most utopian, sense of what is useful about encountering maximalist writing like Wallace's, at least as *The Pale King* figures it. As previously mentioned, the role of the knowledge worker in Wallace's novel is something of a figure for professional literary reading and writing. The workers sort tax returns based on whether they will provide significant revenue for the institution based on an economy of profit. But for someone of this world to then turn against this economy, and pay attention instead to information that is unprofitable, that is discarded, overlooked, and redundant, marks an attempt to step outside the office-world for a moment, and to search for a new frame of reference for looking at and appreciating work, life, and novels. The maximalist aesthetic, as practiced by Fogle and Wallace himself as a writer, offers the "unprofitable" detail as that which might take us out of the grand narrative of a society geared toward efficiency, and into a strange field of redundancy where we might discover, perhaps, a new kind of agency, a new way of managing and valuing things that have been delegated to a social and economic "backwater." Such is the moral of every maximalist story.

Notes

1. Michael Cunningham, "Letter from the Pulitzer Fiction Jury: What Really Happened This Year," *The New Yorker Online*, "Page Turner," July 9, 2012, http://www.newyorker.com/online/blogs/books/2012/07/letter-from-the-pulitzer-fiction-jury-what-really-happened-this-year.html#ixzz2HWuTrDVu. It wasn't powerful enough for them to confer the award, but impressive nonetheless.
2. David Foster Wallace, *The Pale King: An Unfinished Novel* (London: Hamish Hamilton, 2011), 4. In this chapter, all subsequent references to this work will be given in parentheses.
3. This is McCarthy: "Past these corrugated warehouse walls down little sandy streets where blownout autos sulk on pedestals of cinderblock. Through warrens of sumac and pokeweed and withered honeysuckle giving onto the scored clay banks of the railway. Gray vines coiled leftward in this northern hemisphere, what winds them shapes the dogwhelk's shell. Weeds sprouted from cinder and brick. A steamshovel reared in solitary abandonment against the night sky. Cross here." Cormac McCarthy, *Suttree* (London: Picador, [1979] 2010), 3–4.
4. Fitzpatrick, *Anxiety of Obsolescence*. Green, *Late Postmodernism*.
5. Wallace, "E Unibus Pluram," 193.
6. Jonathan Raban, "Divine Drudgery," *The New York Review of Books* 58, no. 8 (2011): 12.
7. Robert Potts, "In a Hall of Mirrors: David Foster Wallace's Less-Than-Final Text," *Times Literary Supplement*, April 15, 2011, 20.
8. Martin Heidegger, *The Fundamental Concepts of Metaphysics: World, Finitude, Solitude*, tr. William McNeill and Nicholas Walker (Bloomington: Indiana University Press, 1995), 136–42.
9. See Liu's *The Laws of Cool* for a discussion of how modern industrial culture ushered in a "complete system of emotional labor management that disallowed workers any 'productive' emotion at all." At the heart of this was the development of the restraint and "cool" of postindustrial office workers, an emotional identity tied to a sense of class distinction, aimed to differentiate them from the unruly, lazy, and hotheaded blue-collar laborers. Liu, *The Laws of Cool*, 94–99.
10. Franco Moretti, *Graphs, Maps, Trees: Abstract Models for a Literary History* (London: Verso, 2005). See the recent article by Daniel Allington, Sarah Brouillette, and David Golumbia for an argument that positions digital

humanities as a "neoliberal tool." For the authors, in the digital humanities "technical expertise trumps all other forms of knowledge," transforming the study of literature into an activity that better suits the needs of industry. Daniel Allington, Sarah Brouillette, and David Golumbia, "Neoliberal Tools (and Archives): A Political History of Digital Humanities," *Los Angeles Review of Books*, May 1, 2016, https://lareviewofbooks.org/article/neoliberal-tools-archives-political-history-digital-humanities/.

11. Patricia Meyer Spacks, *Boredom: The Literary History of a State of Mind* (Chicago: The University of Chicago Press, 1995), 3.

12. Ibid., 2.

13. Mark Twain, *The Adventures of Huckleberry Finn* (London: Vintage Books, 2007), 60.

14. D.A. Miller, *Narrative and Its Discontents: Problems of Closure in the Traditional Novel* (Princeton: Princeton University Press, 1981).

15. Lawrence Zelenak, "The Great American Tax Novel," *Michigan Law Review* 110, no. 6 (2012): 979.

16. See, for instance, 257n3.

17. See Lipsky, *Although of Course*, 156.

18. Kafka, *The Demon of Writing*, 79.

19. Lanham, *Economics of Attention*, xi.

20. Spacks, *Boredom*, 11.

21. McHale, *Constructing Postmodernism*, 82.

22. Tore Rye Anderson, "Pay Attention! David Foster Wallace and his Real Enemies," *English Studies 95*, no. 1 (2014): 17.

23. See, for example, James Vlahos, "Is Sitting a Lethal Activity?" *The New York Times,* April 14, 2011, http://www.nytimes.com/2011/04/17/magazine/mag-17sitting-t.html?_r=0.

24. Paul Auster, *The New York Trilogy* (London: Faber and Faber, 1987), 62.

25. Stephen Schryer, *Fantasies of the New Class: Ideologies of Professionalism in Post-World War II American Fiction* (New York: Columbia University Press, 2011), 31.

26. Schryer, *Fantasies of the New Class*, 31.

27. Marshall Boswell, "Trickle-Down Citizenship: Taxes and Civic Responsibility in David Foster Wallace's *The Pale King*," *Studies in the Novel* 44, no. 4 (2012): 464–65.

28. Ralph Clare, "The Politics of Boredom and the Boredom of Politics in David Foster Wallace's *The Pale King*," *Studies in the Novel* 44, no. 4 (2012): 444.

29. See, for example, David Letzler's "Encyclopedic Novels and the Cruft of Fiction: *Infinite Jest*'s Endnotes," *Studies in the Novel* 44, no. 3 (2012).

30. D.T. Max reveals that at one stage Wallace considered releasing Fogle's story as a stand-alone novel. Madras Press did this in 2013, publishing *The Awakening of My Interest in Advanced Tax: An Excerpt from The Pale King*, which was a novelized version of Fogle's story. Max, *Every Love Story*, 294.

31. Lance Olsen, "Notes Toward the Musicality of Creative Disjunction, or: Fiction by Collage," *Symplokē* 12, no. 1/2 (2004): 130.

32. Gorz, *Critique of Economic Reason*, 5–6.

33. Liu, *The Laws of Cool*, 110.

34. Ibid., 112.

4 Just Maximalist Things

Nicholson Baker's *The Mezzanine* and Objects of Curiosity

Wear and Tear

A broken shoelace is only a minor inconvenience. It might cause a shoe to become annoyingly loose, slip off your heel as you make your way to the supermarket to buy a replacement. If you happen to be a runner in the Olympic Games, it might make you lose a race, disappoint some fans. But that's about the worst of it. Nicholson Baker's *The Mezzanine* is a novel that takes a broken shoelace very seriously, however, as it does the malfunctioning of other relatively benign and inconsequential objects—drinking straws with too much buoyancy, ineffective hand driers, unpopular shampoo brands. Logic would have it that *The Mezzanine* is then also an inconsequential novel, a text of domestic trivialities and pedantry. And as if mirroring this narrative content, it is also a very small book, the outward antithesis of other maximalist works studied here. Barely 100 pages long and confined in time and space to an uneventful lunch break and a trip up an escalator, it looks like a novel of the miniature or minimalist, the Blakean grain of sand, rather than the gigantic, excessive, door-stopping maximalism of Wallace and Pynchon.

Even the briefest engagement with what lies between the covers of *The Mezzanine* should convince anyone that a label of superficiality is an uneasy fit. Small spaces, objects, and details certainly fascinate Baker, but for him hasty hierarchies of size and value generally only speak a laziness of attention. When looked at more closely, a broken shoelace offers the chance to undertake an expansive examination of cause and effect, a plastic drinking straw the impetus to meditate on the whims and economics of commercial design, and an office stapler the pleasures of serious aesthetic appreciation. If anything, the almost claustrophobic dimensions of this novel—its restraint of both length and subject matter—enable it to become something akin to an echo chamber of complexity, increasing in density as it shrinks in scope. Don't judge a book by the width of its spine, would be the moral.

To properly understand why a broken shoelace isn't just a triviality, and why we are also able to consider that Nicholson Baker is one of the most interesting and vital maximalist writers of the contemporary scene, we first need to turn to another thinker for whom an untieable shoe might also have held a great deal of significance. Martin Heidegger once considered that when an object is found to be broken, its attributes and the web of relations in which it is woven can become suddenly visible:

> When we concern ourselves with something the entities which are most closely ready-to-hand may be met as something unusable, not properly adapted for the use we have decided upon. The tool turns out to be damaged, or the material unsuitable. In each of these cases *equipment* is here, ready to hand. We discover its unusability, however, not by looking at it and establishing its properties, but rather by the circumspection of the dealings in which we use it. When its unusability is thus discovered, equipment becomes conspicuous.[1]

When an object or a tool breaks, we want to find out why, and we do so by contemplation of the varied uses to which the piece of "equipment" is put. In the process, behaviors previously ignored become salient, equipment taken for granted become conspicuous. In Heidegger's conception, it is not just the unusable object that becomes a focus of attention, but the over-looked world (of behavior, of intention, of production and design) of which it is part. The small movements and relations surrounding the object that were for all purposes invisible, now rush suddenly into focus. A spanner is thrown in the works, but a great deal becomes apparent as it grinds to a halt.[2] Brokenness repairs an oversight of unthought activity.

This passage of Heidegger's lies at the heart of Bill Brown's "thing theory," where things "name less an object than a particular subject-object rela-tion" that becomes graspable when objects "stop working for us" and the nature of our relationships with them become clear.[3] But it also offers a neat description of the plot of *The Mezzanine*—or at least what semblance of plot can be said to exist in the novel. The narrator Howie's shoelaces have broken within two days of each other and he wonders what vast system of variables could have led to such an occurrence. The broken laces open out to a series of similarly overlooked relations and developments that have been underfoot his whole life, yet often very distant from consideration. The interesting thing is that, in agreement with Heidegger's theory, the bro-kenness enables Howie to undertake this project, which would almost be impossible were the problem not literally "at hand." The broken laces make "the variables of private life seem suddenly graspable and law-abiding."[4] Breakage allows the object to be scrutinized, and this excites Howie because it allows other objects to appear similarly graspable, rule-governed, and lawful. The shoelace becomes a lens through which the complex interactions of daily life are able to be viewed. Many of Howie's other meditations and investigations are made available by similar breakages: either direct damage to an object's physicality, or else errors of design, mutations of use, breaking of norms, and so forth. And although such malfunction can be inconvenient, for a writer bent on comprehensiveness, which, as we will suggest through-out this chapter, is certainly an apt description of Baker, it enables a sort of epistemological "reaching" that stands to have an overwhelmingly positive effect. Importantly for *The Mezzanine*, brokenness illuminates.

The Mezzanine is set mostly in a shopping mall and an office, and, so, as with Wallace's *The Pale King*, draws the spheres of the corporate, the artistic, and the personal very close together, situating the novel as a mediator between different cultural fields. But, like *The Pale King* again, it also claims for itself the task of reinvigorating overfamiliar domains of everyday life that might ordinarily be considered mundane and trivial. In both *The Pale King* and *The Mezzanine*, a maximalist attention to detail possesses the power to both break *and repair* whatever objects, places, and relationships fall under its gaze, rendering visible their hitherto inconspicuous details in a manner that encourages a fuller, richer appreciation of the world of which they are a part.

If the smallness and scope of *The Mezzanine* doesn't fit into our ordinary idea of maximalist writing, however, it's because it challenges assumptions, such as Stefano Ercolino's, that it is "difficult, if not impossible, to imagine a maximalist novel that is not long."[5] Although maximalist writers commonly produce outwardly large novels such as *Gravity's Rainbow* and *Infinite Jest*, my argument throughout this book has been that there need be no connection between maximalism and novels of particular dimensions. Maximalism exists, first and foremost, as a mode of inquiry, an enthusiasm for the inclusion of detail and its benefits that overrides other "sport" of the novel. And far from just being another example of maximalism, Baker's writing also tends to succeed in areas where our other novelists reach impasses. Although, like Wallace's *The Pale King*, *The Mezzanine* is set partly in an office, it is far less troubled by the attempt to turn this antithesis of the aesthetic world into a subject of novelistic interest. This is never a place of boredom or tedium for Baker. His attention to detail and deftness of description enable him to turn the most outwardly dull objects or events into ones of intense interest, and the difference between Wallace and Baker is that there is no presumption in Baker's novel that these objects of inquiry are dull to begin with.

My somewhat polemic appreciation of *The Mezzanine* as maximalist is important here not just because it gives us the opportunity to revise our understanding of a style of writing and its textual features, which is a relatively unimportant exercise on its own. As we will see, *The Mezzanine*'s humble setting, subject matter, and form—the modern office and shopping mall, the staplers, shoelaces, and hotdogs of life, the small takeaway-sized novel—allow us to figure a relationship between the maximalist mode of inquiry and its popularity in the contemporary landscape that lends *The Mezzanine* not just a mimetic function, but a practical usefulness for those who inhabit the ubiquitous spaces in which the novel's narrator finds himself confined. For starters, the novel's unintimidating smallness and interest in everyday objects like shoelaces and hand driers can make the ordinary habitat of office workers and mall shoppers seem reassuringly rich with material for literary adventure, putting the stuff of serious intellectual pursuit firmly within the grasp of the humdrum everyman. The epitome of such a transformation—the rendering exciting and worthy of what is otherwise commonplace and trivial—is Howie's historicizing of the shift from paper to plastic drinking straws, a passage worth quoting at length:

> I stared in disbelief the first time a straw rose up from my can of soda and hung out over the table, barely arrested by burrs in the underside of the metal opening. ... The whole point of straws, I had thought, was that you did not have to set down the slice of pizza to suck a dose of Coke while reading a paperback. ... How could the straw engineers have made so elementary a mistake, designing a straw that weighed less than the sugar-water in which it was intended to stand? Madness! (4n1)

Anyone who has ever sat at a McDonalds sipping a Coca-Cola can find within their own experience the material for serious cultural analysis. Howie is eventually able to tie this investigation in with the development of slosh caps on soft drinks served at fast-food chains, which have the benefit of cutting down on spillage of liquid while also allowing the frustratingly buoyant plastic straws to remain gripped in place by the "little cross in the middle, which had been the source of some unhappiness in the age of paper straws" (5n1). The period of transitional discomfort is thus resolved when various commercial pressures (the possibility of manufacturing cheaper plastic straws and cutting down on cleanup costs) align to accidentally forge a solution to the original floating drinking straw problem. Just as in *Gravity's Rainbow*, there are "thousands of details" to get hold of here, but there is very little of the accompanying anxiety that troubled Pynchon's characters.

The attention *The Mezzanine* pays to trivial consumer objects like drinking straws means the maximalist novel here becomes something akin to a user's guide to the enrichment of life in the postindustrial day-to-day. The novel attempts to repair our relationship to commodities not by encouraging us to revise our reliance on them, as in a standard critique of consumer culture, but by encouraging us to forge a healthier relationship with them, one centering on the personal autonomy that can be enacted through a maximalist appraisal of detail. The lasting effect of Baker's work is, in this regard, not Wallace's stoic acceptance of the dull, but a sort of epistemological optimism—a confidence in one's ability to grapple with the complexity of the late-capitalist landscape. The unanguished, cheery confidence of *The Mezzanine* is even perhaps where it is most unique among other works of contemporary literature. Don DeLillo's Jack Gladney noted a "dull and unlocatable roar ... just outside the range of human apprehension" during his adventures at Blacksmith's shopping centers.[6] Although it might be a valid impression, it certainly doesn't offer us much of a way to navigate contemporary America without ironic detachment or critical contempt. Baker's maximalism offers us a different approach, one that translates the "roar" of culture into a clear and parsable language.

Trashy Books and Corporate Aesthetics

But all this is to come. To begin, we don't need to interpret the intricacies of *The Mezzanine* in order to understand the unique view of maximalism and its relationship to the world of commodities, consumers, and shopping malls that Baker promotes. In several articles and a nonfiction book alongside which the enthusiasms of *The Mezzanine* should be read, Baker has developed what we can again call an ethics of maximalism, a campaign for the preservation of any and all information and objects produced by a culture. In an illustrative essay titled "The Charms of Wikipedia,"[7] Baker sets about trying to rescue obscure Wikipedia articles flagged for deletion because of what is deemed their uselessness. Although what use an entry on, say, the Jitterbug telephone might have is somewhat unclear, what stands to be lost with its deletion is, for Baker, greater than the esoteric facts recorded in it. If nothing else, these obscurities record that somewhere, someone in the world was interested enough in a matter to contribute to the giant joint-publishing text that is Wikipedia. And this fact of personal interest, this enthusiasm for life and knowledge, is what needs to be defended, because it is what is lost in a world dominated by standardizing processes and industry-bred norms of efficiency and usefulness. The fact of an article's "irrelevance" is, for Baker, a *charm*, a strangeness that burns bright amidst the standardized. It is to be defended because it speaks to an aura that will only exist in the world so long as there are "loose, baggy monsters" like Wikipedia (and the maximalist novel) to house it.

In a similar series of articles and a book critical of the ethics of modern library administrations (or, at one remove, the corporatization, in the form of technologization, of libraries), Baker has spoken out against the purging of millions of library books considered to be no longer of cultural value.[8] Defenders of this sort of deletionism cite economic factors—that space is quickly becoming a scarce resource, and as we move into the digital age it becomes less necessary to have physical books anyway. Baker rebukes the attitude behind this management of cultural value, claiming that many texts have a use precisely because of their obscurity: "We till around in great collections looking for things that have lain unnoticed—the urge to search through obscurity is basic to scholarship. And if the research libraries don't keep it—don't keep copies of the stuff that we as a people publish—nobody else is going to do it. It just won't happen. We can't depend on businesses to save our past."[9] Although the digital age can act as a successful repository for much of this overlooked knowledge (as the "charm" of Wikipedia demonstrates), Baker's main concern is that, in the case of the San Francisco Public Library at least, hundreds and thousands of books that had not found a digital home were simply being tossed into a landfill, their existence, and the possibility of new understandings they housed, effectively erased. A maximalist approach to archiving is, for Baker, not indulgence and wastefulness, but a protection of the future of human knowledge, a proclamation that the lessons of the past are never exhausted.

Baker was criticized in a letter written by this library's fund-raising "affinity group" for speaking out against the decision to restructure their collection. The letter accused Baker of

> anti-Semitism, because I had used what were, the letter charged, Holocaust references by mentioning the so-called Deselection Chamber and by calling the book purge a "hate crime directed at the past." And the audience that "cheered [me] on" were, according to the letter, "intellectually dishonest, disrespectful to the library staff, and insulting to all Jewish, gay and lesbian, and other individuals who suffered the actual Holocaust." Over the next several weeks, this letter began to appear on the desks of newspaper and radio editors.[10]

Although these accusations are hyperbolic and enact a somewhat disingenuous claim to offense, again there is a small amount of truth in that Baker does seem to equate the destruction of cultural artifacts with the destruction of life, or at least the traces of those who once lived. In Baker's thought, everyone has the right to persist in traces, but corporations (or the corporatized society), with their cost-cutting obligations,[11] feel they have the right to unwrite and efface them for reasons beyond what can be considered practical necessities.

A fear of the loss of information certainly motivates Baker's thought here (explaining why he founded the American Newspaper Repository in 1999, a place to house discarded archives), and is what makes his frequent association with the minimalist canon again so misguided. But it almost seems that the more fundamental fear that lies behind this anxiety about the loss of information is for the loss of human passion and charisma. What scares Baker is the erasure of the work of a mind, filled with all of its strange and heterogeneous enthusiasms and quirks, because of economies that put premiums on space and duration, even in relation to cyberspace where no such restrictions should reasonably apply. A maximalist ethics becomes a defense of the inefficiencies of human understanding and passion, recognizing the necessity of the junk as much as the giant and defending the full spectrum of cultural participants.

Baker's argument in these essays suggests that the business world penetrates literary culture not only in terms of commercial influence—those budget and profit-geared decisions affecting the publication, circulation, and marketing of certain works—but in regard to what information is kept alive and preserved in libraries. Ironically, Baker suggests that it is actually the new breed of library leader's fascination with a kind of "management lit"— the writings of business gurus promoting different brands of corporate strategy—that is driving this deletion of the charms of the obscure and the unmaximalization of cultural archives. It's a battle of books against books. In "Truckin' for the Future," Baker discusses that Ken Dowlin, the head of the San Francisco Public Library, is a devout fan of business theorists like Everett M. Rogers, whom Dowlin calls his "guru for change."

Baker notes that one of Everett's books suggests four ways to transform an organization—"by destroying it, by restructuring it, by changing the individuals within it, and by introducing new technology."[12] In the age of knowledge work, efficiency here is figured as the reduction of information as a means of managing it more successfully. But claims that the restructuring of library collections occurs to promote efficiency is perhaps more of a submission to the rhetoric of management gurus than a reasoned response to changing circumstances and cultural needs. As Baker points out, libraries are overly willing to spend millions of dollars on new computers and other information-technology equipment, only to have them become obsolete in a few short years. And yet books, which can store information for hundreds of years with minimal maintenance, are somehow seen as inefficient. The rhetoric of business authors influences the erasure of other writers deemed to be less relevant to corporate aesthetics.

The Miniature Maximalist

As this interest in rescuing the cultural discards suggests, Baker's fiction is pervaded by a concern with politically charged, maximalist thoroughness, set on a quest to avoid overlooking—and hence deleting—any possible object of study. As Ross Chambers puts it, after reading *The Mezzanine*, it becomes apparent that "the writing mimes … something like a potentially limitless, descriptive comprehensiveness."[13] There are, admittedly, at least two moments in *The Mezzanine* when Baker's narrator does feel it proper to advise *against* comprehensiveness—one is in relation to editorial footnotes in the *Norton Anthology of Poetry* that destroy the deliberate strangeness of words like "polypi" (122); the other is in response to a scientific pronouncement that seems to put the brakes on Howie's dream of understanding the intricacies of shoelace wear. But this last, at least, which Howie finds "exhilarating," seems to be taken as a heightening of the challenge rather than a true concession to "skepticism" (132).

If such aspirations of comprehensiveness pose difficulties for archives and libraries, they will obviously affect the form and style of a hundred-page novel. Indeed, a desire for comprehensiveness certainly shapes the content of *The Mezzanine*, but also impacts its form. For starters, it explains the peculiar narrative shape of this work, which tends to circle around a relatively motionless center in an endless stream of digressions and detailed descriptions. As Chambers suggests, Baker's desire for thoroughness "produces the whole text as a 'veritable infarct of narrative cloggers.'"[14] It is almost as if forward momentum brings with it a hastiness that is unpalatable for Baker's maximalist tastes. As his narrator Howie states, "under microscopy, even insignificant perceptions … are almost always revealed to be more incremental than you later are tempted to present them as being:"

> It would have been less cumbersome, in the account I am giving here of a specific lunch hour several years ago, to have pretended that the

bag thought had come to me complete and "all at once" at the foot of the up escalator, but the truth was that it was only the latest in a fairly long sequence of partially forgotten, inarticulable experience, finally now reaching a point that I paid attention to it for the first time. (9)

The circling back and forth of this narrative attests to a desire not only to present some true and comprehensive account of objects, feelings, and relationships, but a thorough representation of *how* such accounts are arrived at. The process and experience of discovery is something worthy of accurate inclusion, not just its results. Again, the specifics matter. This will become especially important in our discussion of *Room Temperature* in the following chapter.

This ethos of comprehensiveness guiding Baker's writing discloses an impasse *The Mezzanine* inevitably encounters, however, and for which its miniaturism is to be seen as crucial. Howie wants to tell us *everything* about the contents of his CVS Pharmacy bag and a broken pair of shoelaces, but it means he can't tell us anything beyond these small moments unless the book is to grow to unmanageably immense proportions.[15] The "miniature" size, setting, and timespan of this novel is thus a space of containment that usefully limits its infinite expansion, but also allows for an increase in density and specificity. Baker's aim is to move closer rather than expand his scope, as being able to see things in "high definition" matters more than being able to see a large amount. We might also consider that the compression of focus is a form of risk-management, allowing Baker to affect maximalist mastery in a small and relatively contained space, without having to move out into the wider world where objects aren't necessarily available for close and comfortable scrutiny. The space that exists in *The Mezzanine* is a heavily anthropocentric one that responds to the needs of an agent seeking to view the world as ultimately "graspable" in human terms, as if its components were building blocks able to be arranged and rearranged like in the play of children. What I'll argue in this chapter is that the "mastery" affected by Baker is intended to have a meme-like function, inspiring others to (re)discover an enthusiasm for the close scrutiny of their relationship with objects. The humanizing function of Baker's maximalist gaze is thus deliberate and purposeful, rather than lazily anthropocentric. But what I'll consider in the next chapter is that such mastery might equally be viewed as a compensatory retreat from the uncomfortable contemplation of one's broader inability to effect change in a world defined by systems of power that dwarf the individual. Playing with staplers and drinking straws allows for a fantasy of control that the individual viewed in the context of the globalized world of late-capitalism emphatically lacks. If, as McGurl suggests, miniature-maximalism provides a "special effect of individual autonomy in a world dominated by massively trans-individual systems,"[16] it achieves this, in Baker's case at least, by sequestering a small portion of the world and filling it with calming fantasies of intellectual ability.[17]

If Baker has a weapon in his quest for a tightly compressed comprehensiveness, it is description. *The Mezzanine* progresses largely by the description of objects, experiences and small, semiautonomous events that are linked to other descriptions of objects and experiences in a process that generates a movement miming narrative progression, but which is really a sort of descriptive linkage. Although the epistemological fastidiousness of *The Mezzanine* allows it few opportunities to achieve the "excitations" typical of traditional narrative art—suspense, peripeteia, catharsis, some sort of drama that would redeem the banality of the everyday spaces in which the novels take place—the obsessive and impossibly precise descriptions are nevertheless able to infuse its deliberately static stories with such rich, emotional density, that were Baker to attempt to offer a more conventional plot, we would surely feel he was cheapening himself.

The problem a writer beloved of description usually faces is that descriptive art tends to be viewed as ornamental. As Svetlana Alpers claims, art that focuses on description has historically been viewed as the poorer cousin of narrative art, giving "attention to the surface of the world described … at the expense of the representation of narrative action," and unable to observe the dynamic quality of "human emotion."[18] Alpers endeavors to vindicate descriptive art from such charges, and this is, broadly, the path Baker must tread, too. In *The Mezzanine*, his risk is further compounded by the novel's subject matter—the everyday matters of middle-class, corporate America, often seen as some sort of existential wasteland of humanity. But if there is emotion to be found in these novels—and there is a plenitude of it—it is overwhelmingly because of maximalist description, the careful, intense observation of the world, rather than narration.

These issues aside, any charges of triviality or ornamentalism Baker's work might elicit are ultimately overcome by its grounding epistemological effect. As Ross Chambers suggests, his investigations into the "trivial" matters of life frequently "cause in the reader a certain shock of pleasurable recognition ('Yes, that's true') combined with awareness that one had never attended to things that, in one's own child-like fashion, one had nevertheless noticed."[19] This novel doesn't necessarily depend upon the introduction of unique and fascinating objects of study to generate interest, then, but on our tendency to overlook the natural complexity of even the most banal objects that surround us—the shoelaces and drinking straws of life. Baker's meditations perform a sort of epistemological realignment on readers that encourages them, for small moments, to fall off of the perpetual motion machine (the escalator, to use the guiding metaphor of *The Mezzanine*) that is life in a world filled with constant sensory bombardment. Ultimately, the slow, careful attention that he encourages through maximalist description is figured as a form of resistance to a world that would lure us toward consumption of always newer things (the narrative payoffs of consumer life), and that would have us "spend" our attention on only the shiniest objects. Similar to Wallace's argument in *The Pale King*, our willingness to view objects and experiences as mundane can simply be a consequence of our failing attention, our inability—or refusal—to give proper focus to the complexities of the microscopic textures of daily life. Rather than a celebration of a maximalist way of seeing for its own sake, then, Baker's work offers maximalist vision as a necessary practice of resistance, in the vein of Michel de Certeau's "practice of everyday life" or "making do."[20] As we will see, close and unswerving observation is an act that reveals an amount of autonomy we possess in the modern world, and that we might otherwise be inclined to overlook and "delete." The maximalist mass of information assembled in *Gravity's Rainbow* overwhelmed readers; in *The Pale King*, it put them to sleep; in *The Mezzanine*, it repairs and refreshes. Maximalism is here a tonic, stimulating a fresh appetite for reality in which broken shoelaces, drinking straws, and shampoo bottles figure as main courses.

The Invisibility of Objects

The usefulness of Baker's maximalism is the attention to detail he promotes, but it gains its full effect because of the nature of the objects and experiences that form the subject matter of *The Mezzanine*. Shoelaces, staplers, and shampoo bottles are such ideal objects for Baker to investigate because as well as being so thoroughly everyday and overlookable, the nature of their commodity form tends to doubly preclude their contemplation. Even though much of life in contemporary America is intimately involved with these things, there is, strangely, very little appreciation of them as specific objects, both inside and outside of literary works, which is partly why the critical movement of "thing theory" has enjoyed recent popularity. In novels, they occupy the background of descriptions, signifying verisimilitude only in the passive manner of Flaubert's barometer. In everyday life, they are just as liable to be overlooked and discarded, replaced, overwritten, like those obscure Wikipedia articles or esoteric library books flagged for deletion.

Familiar objects like drinking straws and shoelaces are, as Marx once put it, "at the same time perceptible and imperceptible by the senses"[21] and thus naturally engage a maximalist curiosity like Baker's, one intent on overcoming the cultural tendency to overlook and dismiss cultural artefacts as trivial. Indeed, in Marxist terms, commodities seem to encourage us not to think about their specifics too much (at least in ways other than anticipation and desire); they are cast in a sort of epistemological fog that clouds the details we aren't really supposed to need to know.[22] As Lukács puts it, "the individual object which man confronts directly, either as producer or consumer, is distorted in its objectivity by its commodity character."[23] Despite this masculine, aggressive "confrontation" with the object that Lukács figures, the siren-like commodity steers our eyes away from its true nature toward the mystifying allure of its auratic song. The point is that, although consumer objects ostensibly advertise their individuality (and indeed offer an ideal of personal difference as part of their purchase) and claim that their qualities are available for scrutiny (with their lists of ingredients, warnings, and so forth),[24] to many of us they appear mostly abstracted and reified. In essence, this abstract quality that predominates, at least in a society in which the commodity form has become universal, is one of formal equivalence or homogeneity. As Lukács claims, "in so far as the commodity form facilitates the equal exchange of qualitatively different objects, it can only exist if that formal quality is in fact recognized."[25] *Recognized* is the important word here, highlighting the epistemological oversight commodities not only encourage but depend upon: we recognize the formal homogeneity of consumer products over and above their specificity. And the important point for our study is that this formal equivalence of the commodity form is what we generally come to "see," rather than the much more immediate physical qualities of objects and their uses.

As with the broken shoelaces and obsolescent drinking straws, *The Mezzanine* engages with the delicate physical qualities of consumer objects to return to them some of their lost specificity. But that Howie's investigation of shoelaces and drinking straws can seem so stunningly observant implies that it is not simply the nature of objects themselves that are obscured by the commodity form, but also the behaviors associated with them. That we all use toothbrushes, for example, seems to cover over the fact that twice a day we scrub food scraps from our teeth and gums. That we use branded toilet paper seems to hide the fact that we clean away fecal matter from our bodies after defecating (and indeed, the sterility and homogeneity of the toilet seems designed to mentally bracket the fact that we must, like those animals so beneath us, defecate at all). That we hurtle down a freeway at a hundred miles an hour in a metal shell is similarly obscured by the idea that we are travelling in a car. And cars, of course, are becoming increasingly like the home, insistent on a denial of the fact that we are travelling at all, as if to be "on the road" were now some sort of trauma rather than the liberation it was for older generations such as the Beats. The commodity form affects these activities in such a way that their physicality and immediate purpose is masked. So, when participating with commodities, we almost become one ourselves, or at least are encouraged to forget the specifics of the activities in which we are engaged. Indeed, the nervous excitement Howie feels while walking through a CVS pharmacy (113), witness to people buying embarrassingly personal items, stems from the store's position as meeting place of the intimately personal and the outwardly sterile and abstract. It is a place where the personal realm bracketed by the homogeneity of commodities is unavoidably present—a space where the abstraction threatens to collapse, and people likewise risk devolving back into messy and physically complex bodies, full of awkward ailments, fluids, and functions.

Although there is certainly a lot of truth in Lukács' claim that the commodity form conceals "all the immediate—qualitative and material—character of things as things,"[26] it is perhaps not surprising that we are so frequently given to overlooking their complexities, as well as the intimate, personal activities in which they are involved, when we consider the now deeply sedimented ambivalence toward consumer objects in contemporary thought. As John Fiske has argued, the "complexity and subtlety of the roles played by commodities in our culture are all too easily dismissed by the concept of a 'consumer society.'"[27] In this respect, the concept of commodity itself becomes a homogenizing force. By labeling something a commodity, it can indeed *only become* homogenous. The concept limits the complexity of the object it defines, and only increases whatever abstractions it might have already been subject to, overlooking any concrete significance that might persist despite its form. The general critical antipathy toward commodities certainly has an important political function, yet it does inevitably work against many of the intentions of a resistant politics. It is something of a Catch-22: one needs to describe the system, but in doing so unavoidably constructs it at the same time. As Timothy Bewes suggests in a similar context, reification is a reified and reifying concept itself, becoming a "mystical, autonomous and inevitable process … impermeable to political intervention."[28] Instead of enabling a person to see their implication in the mode of production, reification exacerbates and "imbues with a tragical character" the "alienation of subject and object."[29] We could suggest similar things of the notion of the commodity. If commodity culture is seen as something to be resisted and deconstructed, our antipathy toward it encourages us to downplay the extent to which our lives are deeply interwoven with these things, if only to defend against the anxiety that they are somehow bad for us, and to maintain a utopian wish that we—the thinkers able to see through the commodity form—might remain impervious to them. Those critiques that at once ask us to study the commodity form yet distance ourselves from its influence can have the more immediate effect of encouraging us not to take our dealings with these objects seriously enough. And by enacting a somewhat moral judgment of commodity culture, we risk restricting a fuller contemplation of their role in our lives. The effect for novels, likewise, is that any such attempt to put a commodity center-stage in a character's life is usually accompanied by the sense that they are suffering from some sort of obsessive neurosis reeking of a complete abandonment to capitalism.

To get an example of the way Baker's maximalist mode of inquiry is employed to break and unsettle the foggy aura of the commodity form, we can turn to Howie's investigation of a date-stamp:

> It was a self-inking model: at rest, the internal dating element, looped with six belts of rubber, held its current numerology pressed upside down against the moist black roof of the armature. To use it, you set the square base of the machine down on the piece of paper you wished to date and pressed on the wooden knob (a true knob!)—then the internal element, guided by S curves cut out of the gantry-like super-structure, began its graceful rotational descent, uprighting itself just in

time for landing like the lunar excursion module, touching the paper for an instant, depositing today's date, and then springing back up to its bat-repose. (32)

The attention to detail certainly breaks the otherwise inconspicuous object up into a complex system of forces, movements, and parts, allowing it to be appreciated as an intricate object that belies its outward simplicity. Howie never really treats this as a simple and singular object, preferring instead the experience of its individual aspects: "Now I touched the date-stamper's belts of rubber numbers, which were updated by little metal thumb-wheels; the belts that correspond to days were entirely black, but the belt that corresponded to the decade was still red-rubber-colored and new, except for the 8, which was sticky with ink" (33). He reveals the stamp's complexity as a physical system by beginning a tactile engagement with its details.

Although we have probably all used a stamp before and have observed much the same mechanism that Howie is describing here, it's doubtful that we've ever seen one in a novel in any way other than a passing mention. This absence has hardly seemed like something in need of addressing, however. Indeed, the fascination Howie displays with the banal object is almost intended to be initially anomalous, but perhaps also to entice us through this perplexity, to make us curious about what motivates the almost sensual engagement he has with the stamp. It's unclear exactly *why* he needs to describe it; but that it *is* notated in such excited detail creates the feeling that there is perhaps something we, as readers, are missing out on here, some quality of insight or enthusiasm that Howie possesses which we also might gain access to if we pay as close attention to this object as he does. The key aspect of this description is, in this regard, its implied enthusiasm. The maximalist excitement for detail offers Howie a quiet comfort, and we should probably be curious about testing it out for ourselves. So we read along and follow the movements of the prose, the intricate outlining of the stamp's mechanics. By the end of the description its significance is probably still unclear to us, but we've hopefully become interested ourselves nonetheless, almost mesmerized by the mechanisms of the tool and the prose that dissects it. It's very difficult to be bored by this description, anyway. And, in this manner, Baker's detailedness again works in something of the opposite manner to Wallace's in *The Pale King*. *The Mezzanine* is largely a sustained attempt to get us enthused about objects with which we have previously had little or no interest. And while it therefore seems to assert a similar thesis to the one outlined in *The Pale King*—that the dull walls of life can be places of immense interest, for example—it doesn't admit that these things are dull to begin with. The novel challenges us, instead, to keep up with the enthusiasm it models, to never feel that there's a barrier of boredom that we are forced to tolerate and penetrate. Howie is oblivious to dullness; for him, it simply doesn't exist.

At a later stage in the novel, Howie ventures into the shampoo aisle of a CVS pharmacy with similar results:

> emotional analogies were not hard to find between the history of civilization on the one hand and the history within the CVS pharmacy on the other, when you caught sight of a once great shampoo like Alberto V05 or Prell now in sorry vassalage on the bottom shelf of aisle 1 B ... Prell's green is too simple a green for us now; the false French of its name seems kitschy, not chic, and where once it was enveloped in my TV-soaked mind by the immediacy and throatiness of womanly voice-overs, it is now late in its decline, lightly advertised, having descended year by year through the thick but hygroscopic emulsions of our esteem. (114)

There's definitely some degree of absurdity here; finding analogies between shampoo bottles and the history of civilization almost seems parody of what this novel is otherwise trying to achieve. But Howie is at the same time earnest, and we cannot help but feel that his seriousness has a point beyond a satire of consumerist obsession or a valuation of quirkiness. Like those books discarded from American libraries, Prell maintains a value despite its commercial irrelevance. That particular brands of shampoo are on the wane, falling out of favor, illuminates the "hygroscopic emulsions of our esteem" (114), the complex mixture of personal preference and external influence that dictates enthusiasm and taste. In the first instance, Howie's shampoo historicism becomes available to him because he sees brokenness in the brand of Prell: it is no longer valued, so its existence as a commodity has begun to flicker, illuminating the contingency of commercial appeal and consumer desire. It enables Howie to see what he does desire by making apparent what he doesn't. The process also enables him to see the form— and the fickleness, if he chooses—of that desire, giving the shampoo not just a mute, static existence, but an emotional character.

Although this brokenness allows the shampoo to become epistemologically conspicuous, at the same moment it threatens this newfound salience because of the market's refusal to keep broken objects in stock. As Howie meditates, "once everyone had died who had used a certain discontinued brand of shampoo, so that it passed from living memory, it no longer would be understood properly, correctly situated in the felt periphery of life" (115). So Howie's meditations are then to function as a record of all these broken things, transcribing their embedded knowledge before they are wiped from history. Baker is once again seeking to rescue the cultural discards from deletion, and the maximalist novel here becomes a cultural archive.

When a person develops an idiosyncratic use for these products, one which goes beyond the intentions of design, the materiality of the objects becomes similarly conspicuous, its commodity form broken, and its specificity repaired. *The Mezzanine* gives us many examples of the development of product uses that transcend the intentions of their original purpose in such a manner. But more than simply revealing the overlooked particulars of objects, such descriptions develop a portrait of a forgotten autonomy, the agency we have to use these products *against* their design. Howie calls such developments "a mute folklore of behavioral inventions, unregistered, unpatented, adopted and fine-tuned without comment or thought" (95):

> Nobody could have predicted that maintenance men would polish escalator handrails standing still, or that students would discover that you can flip pats of pre-portioned butter so they stick to the wall, or that tradesmen would discover that they could conveniently store pencils behind their ears, or later they would gradually *stop* storing pencils behind their ears, or that windshield wipers could serve as handy places to leave advertisement flyers. (95)

We can add to this list Howie's youthful and bizarre habit of poking holes in sanitary napkins and urinating through them (113). These acts of inventiveness suggest something similar to what Raymond Malewitz has called "rugged consumerism," in which, despite being "alienated from sites of industrial productivity," consumers find "alternative ways of practicing their skills by creatively misusing, repairing, and repurposing the objects in their environments."[30] The importance of broken commodities, and of breaking them through either misuse or maximalist attention, is that they are the sign of someone having the autonomy to do so—as well as the possibility to act against the "rules" of use that ask us to modify our behavior to suit the needs of things. Ernst Mandel suggests that, despite its global spread, late capitalism is still "a hybrid and bastardized *combination* of organization and anarchy," rather than a perfect system of homogenized and immutable production and control.[31] Commodities still possess this potential "anarchy" of misuse. And it's a potential of which Baker's maximalism constantly strives to remind us.

So the broken object offers us at least two things: the sudden salience of the details that constitute it and an opportunity to recognize and employ a neglected agency that the maximalist engagement with it reveals. The object is freed from the tyranny of the concept; and the subject is freed from the determining relationship the concept likewise traps him in. By giving voice to a "mute folklore," Baker delineates the way our everyday, prosaic actions evidence a level of autonomy that resists simple subjection to capitalist reification and its stubborn means/ends culture. As John Fiske suggests, commodities are "not just objects of economic exchange; they are goods to think with, goods to speak with."[32] And Baker's point seems to be to get us to do just this. As Fiske suggests elsewhere:

> The fact that the system [of capitalism] provides only commodities, whether cultural or material, does not mean that the process of

consuming those commodities can be adequately described as one that commodifies the people into a homogenized mass at the mercy of the barons of the industry. People can, and do, tear their jeans.[33]

The effect of brokenness, in the end, brings us to recognize the autonomy we already possess in a system so supposedly pervaded by commercial interests that the individual "is not able to modify the process by his own activity."[34] Maximalism rescues the modern subject, in Baker's novel, by breaking everything around him, forcing him to rebuild his life through an examination of how it is he actually lives.

A Little Attention

The ultimate point of Howie's detailed meditations, then, is not to study the variables of wear on shoelaces or the history of shampoo placement, as much as he does earnestly value doing so. He does want us to appraise our lives with these things, but to do so to draw out an overlooked autonomy in a world supposedly governed by the rules and demands of capitalism. It is clear that Baker wants these meditations to operate as something like case studies for the important uses of the maximalist mode of inquiry available to us in the contemporary world—indeed, wants to exhibit to us the many *reparative* functions of a mind elsewhere humbled by intimations of its epistemological limitations. As with the example of the stamp, it's not even that Howie needs to reveal an overlooked sense of autonomy, so much as an enthusiasm for observation that can perplex us with its excitement, and entice us into paying attention to the specifics for ourselves.

As stated previously, Baker's books wouldn't succeed were it not for our general insensitivity toward (or at least inability to articulate) these small details belonging to what is demarcated as the realm of the trivial. That a description of a stamp or the shift from paper to plastic straws seems so preternaturally observant obviously depends upon an inverse correspondence in our ability—or, perhaps more importantly, willingness—to undertake such observations ourselves. For it is not that we are necessarily unfamiliar with the topics Baker investigates—again, Chambers asserts that *The Mezzanine* often elicits "a certain shock of pleasurable recognition"[35]—but that we have *learned* to overlook their significance. As such, it becomes clear that for it to have its intended effect, *The Mezzanine* almost depends upon its readers being alienated in some degree from the particulars of their everyday environments. Although, of course, Baker's work would read much differently for a reader from a less developed nation than North America, probably appearing as something like a field guide to the peculiarities and indulgences of middle-class Westerners, for both readerships the effectiveness of *The Mezzanine* depends upon the strangeness of those things and feelings hidden behind the notion of the "familiar." Our interest in the book's maximalism is a sign that many of us fail to be cognizant of relations of production that are extremely close to us, that are literally underfoot. Its maximalism retrains us to notice the specifics.

Although Lukács has occasionally been positioned as the strawman of my study of maximalism, the project of *The Mezzanine* seems not altogether dissimilar from his understanding of the defetishizing and dereifying effects of realism. Like the totalizing realist work, Baker's maximalism aims to reconfigure man's life under capitalism, freeing him from a relationship to the commodity form that has encouraged a skewed view of reality. In Lukács' terms, Baker's art could be said to depict "the subtlety of life," offering a "richness beyond ordinary experience" by breaking "the old abstractions."[36] In a capitalist society, "a special intellectual effort is required for a man to see through this fetishizing,"[37] and the practice of maximalism would be such an effort. But while for Lukács the role of art is to remind us of the importance and autonomy of our social relations and to overcome our fascination with things (i.e. commodities), Baker's maximalism encourages us to use a fascination with consumer objects to realize autonomy, or at least just a sense of enthusiasm that isn't governed by the market. If, as Eagleton suggests, commodities seem to "exist for nothing and nobody in particular"[38] and efface the traces of human production embodied in their materiality, Baker encourages us to forcefully own them in a way beyond purchase, to break their false autonomy and write our own onto them. In the world seen through Baker's novels, paying attention to particulars is a dereifying, defetishizing activity; if one commits to it, he or she will eventually break the laziness of attention that is a symptom of the ascendance of commodity form and a consequence of the ambivalence to commercial culture in the manner Fiske describes. So it's not just that broken objects allow for a maximalist investigation; the maximalist mode of inquiry effectively breaks them, makes them visible again.

The setting and subjects of *The Mezzanine* are obviously very American, but thanks to the global spread of capitalism, American literature is able to extend its relevance across the planet in a form of imperialism that is here, if nowhere else, able to liberate more than colonize. If readers are fans of Prell shampoo, drinking straws, and American shopping malls, then they can certainly feel buoyed by the attention Baker pays to these objects and locations, but the rest of us still stand to gain something beyond the particulars. By focusing on objects more than the relations between people—the opposite of what Lukács advises—*The Mezzanine* enables its mode of inquiry to be transplanted to any perceivable environment where commodities are found. They are everywhere now, of course, and so with the maximalist mode of inquiry we are able to turn these objects into something like portable dereifying devices, things always at our side that we can "break" with a maximalist attention to detail whenever we need to remind ourselves that we make these things, they don't make us.

What becomes clear here is the use value of the maximalist text as something other than a mimetic device. *The Mezzanine* portrays the positive values of a mode of inquiry attuned to specifics above and beyond any particular object it represents. Baker's quest for specificity and comprehensiveness can be valued not only in relation to the particular content of its investigations, but for the example of epistemological optimism it models. We can appreciate this text as a kind of performance, then, a demonstration of certain activities that, the novel suggests, can be valuable for negotiating contemporary life. The comprehensiveness of this work never leaves us feeling insufficient or not up to the task. If anything, the opposite is true. While *The Mezzanine* is so often about brokenness, from a reader's perspective it has a much stronger reparative function.

Notes

1. Martin Heidegger, *Being and Time*, tr. John Macquarrie & Edward Robinson (Malden, MA: Blackwell Publishing, 1962), 102.
2. The cover of Baker's latest collection of essays, *The Way the World Works*, depicts just this—a spanner wedged in between cogs. Nicholson Baker, *The Way the World Works: Essays* (New York: Simon & Schuster, 2012).
3. Bill Brown, "Thing Theory," *Critical Inquiry* 28, no. 1 (2001): 4. This moment in Heidegger's work has also recently formed the backbone of Graham Harman's "speculative realism," in which Harman describes something he calls tool-being and object-oriented ontology. Graham Harman, *Tool-Being: Heidegger and the Metaphysics of Objects* (Peru, IL: Open Court Publishing, 2002).
4. Nicholson Baker, *The Mezzanine* (London: Granta, 1988), 15. In this chapter, all subsequent references to this text will be given in parentheses.
5. Ercolino, "The Maximalist Novel," 244.
6. Don DeLillo, *White Noise* (London: Picador, 1985), 36.
7. Baker, *The Way the World Works*, 188–205.
8. See the essays in the "Libraries and Newspapers" section of *The Way the World Works*, and Nicholson Baker, *Double Fold: Libraries and the Assault on Paper* (New York: Random House, 2001).
9. Baker, *The Way the World Works*, 134.
10. Baker, *The Way the World Works*, 124.
11. Which, Baker suggests, are misguided anyway. In a speech given at the opening of a new library at Duke University, Baker pointed out that it costs only around three dollars to store a book in a library, whereas it costs around one hundred dollars to have a book digitally scanned. The premiums on space are also disingenuous: "And it's compact, too—2.5 million books go in here, and across the street, an even bigger building is devoted to doing the laundry." Baker, *The Way the World Works*, 130.
12. Baker, *The Way the World Works*, 116.
13. Ross Chambers, "Meditation and the Escalator Principle: On Nicholson Baker's *The Mezzanine*," *Modern Fiction Studies* 40, no. 4 (1994): 798.
14. Ibid., 799. "Veritable infarct of narrative cloggers" is a quote from Baker's book on John Updike, *U and I: A True Story* (New York: Random House, 1991), 72.
15. Chambers argues Baker leaves some observations "less developed" to "provide raw material for future social historians"; this might also be one of Baker's solutions to this potential problem of infinite expansion, inviting others to become involved in his work. Chambers, "The Escalator Principle," 795.

16. McGurl, *The Program Era*, 380.
17. On the idea of calmness, the smallness of the book also suggests, importantly, a desire on Baker's part to avoid exhausting his reader, which again distinguishes his maximalism from writers such as Pynchon and Baker. If *The Mezzanine* were a thorough account of an entire day or week that filled a thousand pages, the novel would soon tire out in its reader, making them unwilling to be inspired by its maximalism in the way Baker intends (which, as we'll get to later, has a lot to do with encouraging them to use a maximalist mode of inquiry to enrich their own lunch breaks and office hours).
18. Svetlana Alpers, *The Art of Describing: Dutch Art in the Seventeenth Century* (London: John Murray, 1983), xxi.
19. Chambers, "The Escalator Principle," 795.
20. Michel de Certeau, *The Practice of Everyday Life*, tr. Steven Rendall (Berkeley: University of California Press, 1984).
21. Quoted in Georg Lukács, *History and Class Consciousness: Studies in Marxist Dialectics*, tr. Rodney Livingstone (London: Merlin Press, 1971), 86.
22. When we are confronted by their details, such as in the technical information section of a television's user manual, they are often presented in such an opaque fashion and small font as to be practically unreadable.
23. Lukács, *History and Class Consciousness*, 93.
24. Susan Willis suggests that product packaging is a window onto the purchased object, offering up "a naked view of the commodity to the consumer's gaze." Susan Willis, *A Primer for Daily Life* (London: Routledge, 1991), 4. Packaging also enables us both to see and not see the enclosed object. The packaging often supplies the "aura" that surrounds the object, the necessary ground against which the commodity need always be seen. The image of packaging (part of which we might consider the brand logo) is somehow imaginatively carried around with the object even when its wrapper is discarded, an aura that frames the object for the entirety of its life (who can think of a McDonald's hamburger, for example, without picturing the packaging?). Packaging also turns trash into free advertising.
25. Lukács, *History and Class Consciousness*, 87.
26. Ibid., 92.
27. John Fiske, *Reading the Popular*, 2nd ed. (Hoboken: Taylor & Francis, 2010), 23.
28. Timothy Bewes, *Reification, or The Anxiety of Late Capitalism* (London: Verso, 2002), 9.
29. Ibid., 9.
30. Raymond Malewitz, "Regeneration through Misuse: Rugged Consumerism in Contemporary American Culture," *PMLA* 127, no. 3 (2012): 527.
31. Ernst Mandel, *Late Capitalism*, tr. Joris De Bres (London: NLB, 1975), 502.
32. Fiske, *Reading the Popular*, 25.
33. John Fiske, *Understanding Popular Culture* (Boston: Unwin Hyman, 1989), 25–26.
34. Lukács, *History and Class Consciousness*, 87.
35. Chambers, "The Escalator Principle," 795.
36. Lukács, *Writer and Critic*, 39.
37. Ibid., 69.
38. Eagleton, *Ideology of the Aesthetic*, 9.

5   Housebound

Domestic Excess in Nicholson Baker's *Room Temperature*

Homeliness

The ABC television series *Castle* is implausible for many reasons, not the least of which is its premise of a successful mystery writer becoming a de facto member of the New York Police Department, solving crimes alongside a homicide detective. Despite its deliberate absurdity, the show does express something useful about the writing life nonetheless—that there exists at its core a tension between the practice of a "slow" craft demanding long periods of stillness, quiet, and isolation, and what it is otherwise seen as "real" adventure (and work). Although Richard Castle gets to join in the hunt for dangerous New York criminals, putting the skills he has developed as a writer to use beyond the page, the reality is that a lot of authors spend rather boring lives, chained to desks, and most often at home. The eclectic fiction of J.G. Ballard contrasts to the humdrum Surrey house in which most of it was written. For much of his career, David Foster Wallace wrote in a room painted black in his unassuming house on the outskirts of Bloomington. In terms of literary history, the humble domestic environment is the engine of creative production even if writers tend to tell stories about the outside world and the adventures it beckons.

Historically, the domestic has been subject to an ambivalent cultural coding, often seen as a place of retreat or decline, and mostly inseparable from the category of the feminine. As Paula E. Geyh discusses, however, houses are gendered in an overdetermined way, given maternal qualities, but also entrusted with the protection and reproduction of the patriarchal family and all of its laws and strictures. The home is sometimes figured as a prison for women (Perrault's "Bluebeard" being the most obvious example, *Jane Eyre* a close second), and is thus a space that serves the needs of masculine aggression.[1] But it can be a complex space for men too, who often seem ambivalent about remaining within the home, perhaps for fear of being "feminized" or denied the masculine adventures of the outside. Raymond Carver's narrator in "Cathedral," for instance, seems to use the home as a retreat from the pressures of competition with other men, which is partly why he is so anxious about his wife's blind friend Robert entering his safe space.[2]

Nicholson Baker's *Room Temperature* is a novel about Mike, a man sitting inside his home while nursing his baby daughter, and it embraces the ostensible dullness of its setting with maximalist expansiveness. Like *The Mezzanine*, *Room Temperature* is a small novel that approaches the tiny details of life with enthusiasm and a keen eye for the overlooked. It thus stands to be read in a very similar fashion to Baker's earlier book, with Arthur Saltzman even describing it as "something of a sequel to *The Mezzanine*."[3] Shifting his focus from the shopping mall to the family home, Baker now provides us with a narrator who spends his time in a novel—all of twenty minutes in his world—sitting in a rocking chair, nursing his newborn daughter. Once again, Baker works hard to show us that humble domains of everyday life are not detached from theatres of worldly significance, but register them in subtle ways we can learn to pay attention to. Mike gives us an almost knowingly absurd example of this brand of maximalist investigation when he attempts to trace the "history" of a puff of air through a room:

> if I kept looking, could I detect and read the vestigial pulsations inflicted on this yard of air by the movements of Patty's pen the night before as she described yesterday's Bug-delights in her notebook, or those of Gibbon's agitating feather as he scribbled the closing words of his history of the world two hundred years before?[4]

An attentive maximalism can enlarge even the most trivial event into one of global standing, if its author chooses. As in *The Mezzanine*, the ostensible dullness of this situation is counteracted by the ambitious investigations Baker offers.

We cannot help but get the sense that Mike's attempted extrapolation of the living room's air sees Baker poking a little fun at his earlier narrator Howie, so confident in his ability to discover the cause of his broken shoelaces. And indeed, *Room Temperature* is a subtly different novel than *The Mezzanine*, questioning both the method and the content of its investigations by offering a different example of what maximalist poetics can provide readers of the contemporary novel. *Room Temperature* tends to tackle questions that aren't necessarily solvable with the same sort of close attention to mechanics and usage that *The Mezzanine*'s Howie paid to shoelaces, shampoo bottles, and drinking straws. As with Mike's historicizing of the puff of air, which eventually runs into a "stifling limit to understanding" and a realization of the impossibility of such detailed scholarship (54), or his hopeless attempt to "read" what his wife Patty is writing by listening to the noises her pen makes, many of *Room Temperature*'s investigations end only in frustration, or at least a sense that there is more to be captured than an impossibly close scrutiny of detail alone can account for. As Saltzman suggests, *The Mezzanine* was interested in the technicalities of products and design, governed by an "emphasis upon mechanical engineering and office-related technology."[5] *Room Temperature* seems far more preoccupied with details that evade observation. This is as much a study of the limitations of the maximalist mind as it is a celebration of it. As we will see, many of the objects of study that fascinate *Room Temperature* are intangible, or at least not graspable through sight or empirical sensation. They are only observable as a complex set of interrelations, effects, and feelings that need to be experienced rather than described, unable to be notated or expressed regardless of how much detail one uses. Here, Baker's maximalism goes beyond presenting a view of overlooked particulars and seeks to penetrate into what is perhaps *unlookable*, that which evades description, even at its most maximalist.

The domestic confinement of *Room Temperature* initially makes its comparison to more obviously maximalist works such as Pynchon's and Wallace's seem strained. A common understanding of maximalism is that it engages with the imagined totality of a culture, attempting to include the range of styles, forms, and experiences that constitute it, and this can hardly be done through the investigation of one man's domestic microcosm. But we can note in Baker's second novel a trend in contemporary maximalism—if not fiction in general—that will become increasingly dominant in the decades after its publication, making *Room Temperature* more important as a literary landmark than its humble appearance implies. As registered in Pynchon's recent novels *Inherent Vice* and *Bleeding Edge* (narratives concerned with family life and domestic environments much more than usual in Pynchon's oeuvre), fiction since the millennium has tended to mark a retreat away from the grandiosity of international politics and apocalypses—the typical subject matter of "ambitious" postwar American writers—toward the more intimate, contained, and inward-looking domains of the domestic and everyday. Some of the most successful literary works of recent years are Karl Ove Knausgaard's *My Struggle* series (which we'll discuss in the Conclusion as an example of Scandinavian maximalism), Elena Ferrante's Neapolitan novels, and the literary "soap-operas" that are Jonathan Franzen's recent works. All of these novels, and particularly Knausgaard's, have a focus on domestic affairs that occur within a relatively small radius from the home, registering global political events and developments only through the filter of a local lens.

It would certainly be possible to read this supposed "domestic turn" as a reaction to the events of September 11 and the fifteen years of continuous wars that have followed. Knausgaard is particularly interested in the intensive description of banal minutiae in a way that is often confoundingly engaging, and his work could be seen to use the comforting certainty of the "at hand" as a way to retreat from a more difficult global perspective in the new millennium. Although Baker's novel was published more than a decade before the fall of the World Trade Center towers, its domestic focus does still seem to express a loss of certainty regarding how global affairs occur or are to be understood, preferring the safety and certainty of the family home. It's significant that, in the passage quoted previously, Mike connects his attempt to trace the history of a puff of air to Edward Gibbon's account of the fall of the Roman Empire, domestic analysis here displacing the work of grander political and social commentary and becoming invested with much the same hopes. The loss of ability to master the postwar landscape in the confident manner of Gibbon perhaps results in Mike's domestic turn.

But whatever domestic shift we're witnessing in contemporary fiction is perhaps also a reflection of how male writers are envisioning their position in the social field. As Geyh states, part of the interest in Marilynne Robinson's 1980 novel *Housekeeping*, a very different novel to Baker's but nonetheless related through its interest in domesticity, was found in Robinson's portrayal of "unhousing," the attempt, by women, to "pass out of the household and forsake the patriarchal family" and its boundaries and fantasies of stability.[6] This female subject of liberatory transience and wandering is complemented a decade later by Baker's confining of a man to the domestic sphere and its conterminous duties, a mirroring that links these two novels despite their differences in style and tone. In one sense, Baker's casting of a male in the role of primary carer is progressive, reflecting the rise of the "stay at home dad" and the move of more women into the workforce. This is a very contemporary vision of domestic labor, and Baker obviously celebrates the fluidity of gender roles that *Room Temperature* captures. But if this novel marks a happy degendering of the domestic environment, it occurs without much recognition of the space's troubled past, with Mike allowed to be someone along the lines of a naïve interloper, a tourist that has not had to live through the hardships experienced by the setting's "original" inhabitants. Baker's narrator is allowed to find excitement in this space because it is only one of novelty—Mike remains detached from the history of oppression, violence, and discontent housed in the domestic's gendered past, and he can embrace this world with the enthusiasm of the innocently curious. That this space has had to wait for a male writer to be "maximalized" further suggests a caution in regards to how we should approach the novel, or at least a reminder that we need to temper the fascination we might have for its maximalism with an awareness of its social context.

Pond or Petri Dish

We can introduce Baker's unique approach to maximalism in *Room Temperature* by looking at one of the key meditations of the novel—Mike remembering a picture he once saw of a frog cloned from the intestinal cell of another. When pictured side by side, these frogs appeared almost identical but for a small yet crucial difference: "a disturbing and somehow gastrointestinal pallor in [the clone's] mottling, and an unhealthy, pear-shaped, I-was-raised-in-a-petri-dish-and-know-little-of-mud-and-reeds type of body that betrayed its origins" (41). It is from such small, barely perceptible differences that very grand things stem, however. This artificial frog, Mike tells us, permanently influenced his "theory of knowledge:"

> I certainly believed ... that with a little concentration one's whole life could be reconstructed from any single twenty-minute period randomly or almost randomly selected; ... but you had to expect that a version of your past arrived at this way would exhibit, like the unhealthily pale frog, certain telltale differences of emphasis from the past you would recount if you proceeded serially, beginning with "I was born on January 5, 1957," and letting each moment give birth naturally to the next. The particular cell you started from colored your entire recreation. (41)

Described here are two kinds of novels. One seems a muted reference to a work such as *David Copperfield*, where the narrator begins the tale of his life at the very beginning and proceeds in a more or less linear fashion. The other, which we find in *Room Temperature* and *The Mezzanine* before it, discovers in a seemingly random "twenty-minute period" enough substance to illuminate the contours of an entire life, to reconstruct it from a single cell. In *Room Temperature*, Mike spends the afternoon in a rocking chair feeding his infant child and trying to imagine the passage of his breath through the room, unearthing enough substance in the moment to motivate a wide-ranging and intricately connected remembrance of things past. The echoes of Proust are audible, but in a much different timbre.

This anecdote of the frogs is curious, however, because far from legitimizing Baker's own style of writing and its subject matter as it compares to those more traditional, linear ones, it is actually quite anxious about this method of knowing the world and one's life. So what on the one hand is a celebration of the epistemological powers these nonlinear and digressive novels demonstrate, is also a worry, a concern that their method might be enfeebled and unnecessarily artificial when compared to the Dickensian tactic of "letting each moment give birth naturally to the next" (41). Like the frog cloned from an intestinal cell and thus forever marked by an intestinal pallor, a life described from the perspective of a single moment is bound not only to be colored by this origin, but carry with it inerasable signs of artificiality (which in the end is a marker of inaccuracy, a failure to be truly comprehensive in the art of recreation). Rather than the more "natural" linear narrative, the extrapolative narrative is, like the clone, an artificial, technological construct, a mere man-made object of literary experimentation and not the impartial mirroring of nature one was after. It is an enfeebled mimesis.

It soon becomes clear that the image of the cloned frog raised in the Petri dish risks standing for Mike too, who spends his afternoon and the whole book seated in a rocking chair, hidden from the outside world and all of the "proper" experiential texture it offers. So when Mike looks at the frog and notices its impoverishment, Baker is also seeing the potential risk of setting his novel within such a tightly demarcated domestic sphere, one which is generally figured in fiction as a place where one hides from the "real" world and attempts to escape from its complexity through housework or some form of destructive stasis (watching television and smoking pot, in the example of Raymond Carver's "Cathedral"). It is telling that the family home in *Infinite Jest*, far from being a space of safety, is most often a place of sexual and physical abuse, and in order for her adventures to begin, Pynchon's Oedipa Maas had to give up her domestic duties, leaving behind Tupperware parties and fondue.

We should be wary of conflating Mike's view that linear narrative is the most accurate form of recreation with Baker's own beliefs, however, because his writing frequently shows us all we miss out on if we only approach the world in a straightforward fashion. And indeed, like *The Mezzanine*, *Room Temperature* is a celebration of complexities of relation and knowledge that a more linear narrative would struggle to account for. Perhaps Mike's claimed preference for the Dickensian narrative is simply colored here by his fascination with watching his newborn child (referred to only by the nickname Bug) grow, the baby asleep in his arms throughout *Room Temperature* periodically reminding him of the linear progression that the growing body signifies so neatly. The linearity of the body here pressures the circularity of the mind into conformity with it.

There is more complexity to this photograph of frogs than a weighing up of narrative form, however, or of deciding in which manner one wishes to write their novel. When we look closer at Mike's memory of the frogs, we can see that the aspect of the cloned amphibian that worries him most is that it visibly lacks experience. What is missing in the scientific reconstruction is the color that having a "real" life lends to an organism; the clone carries with it the signs of its nonexperience, of having been raised in the safety and sterility of a Petri dish. Although the objective physicality of the frog can be replicated by an almost perfect, scientific form of mimesis (figured as the technique of cloning, in what is to be taken as a metaphor for something like the Holy Grail of maximalist specificity), to provide a truly complete copy one must offer something that a purely objective eye will inevitably miss: the impossible-to-cheat color of experience, the hue of life itself. Although the outward qualities of the frog have been cloned, the cloning ultimately remains incomplete, and the copied frog speaks only of the method's flaws.

If *Room Temperature* can be viewed as similar to the cloned frog in its narrative structure and claustrophobic encasement, being an extrapolation from a single cell of life rather than a complete linear history, it should also be understood as an attempt to transcend the cloned frog's limitations, supplementing its experiential paucity with a unique maximalist intensity that operates by capturing those aspects of life that are usually felt to lie *beyond* literary description. As we'll see throughout this chapter, spurred by Mike's dissatisfaction with the cloned frog, the novel attempts to capture those experiences that the process of cloning leaves behind. And, as such, it provides a revision of the maximalism practiced in Baker's earlier work. The key investigations in *Room Temperature* narrate what occurs when maximalist description exhausts itself, yet still knows that there is more to be "seen." Here Baker seems to realize that sometimes in order to see the world in high definition, to capture all of its overlooked details and recreate it perfectly on the page, we can't rely on specificity alone. At some point, no matter how detailed we are, description will always fail to capture something. We must provide that which exceeds description, which is something along the lines of what Brian Massumi calls the "missing-in-discourse of also-sensed quality," those aspects of life that exceed "a restricted empirical field."[7] In one sense, this is then a novel about the limitations of maximalism when figured as a desire to empirically record as much of the world as possible, to put it all directly within the grasp of the novelist and his reader. But, in another sense, it is also to be seen as maximalism's continuation, its intensification into realms beyond the merely descriptive or cataloguing. It is precisely because of Baker's eye for comprehensiveness that he notices the limitations of his descriptive, empirical maximalism, just as Mike's keen eye for detail enables him to discern the paucity of the cloned frog. His need for being precise enables him to see the imprecision of an otherwise perfect method.

Initially, Baker's concern with what remains ineffable to empirical description might seem to jar with his maximalist belief in comprehensiveness. Indeed, in *The Mezzanine*, Howie argues that vague impressions have been "mistakenly exalted by some writers as something realer and purer and sacredly significant than intellective memory."[8] That Baker is so determined to "roar something defiant" against the ordinary limits of understanding (54) means his novels frequently show a distaste for the tropes ineffability and "imaginative failure"[9] that a great deal of other contemporary fiction relies upon for rhetorical effect (especially those of the minimalist canon, but also, as in Wallace's and Pynchon's work, those maximalist novels orbiting a key epistemological aporia). To make "particular entities and meanings ... powerful because vague, intense because unrealized,"[10] as James Guetti once put it, would be sheer laziness for Baker, a rhetorical cop-out working against what his novels value.

It makes for an interesting comparison here to place Baker's relationship to vagueness and ineffability alongside that of another master of the meditation, W.G. Sebald. Although in terms of subject matter and tone these writers differ immensely, stylistically they do share many similarities of form. Both employ digressions that oppose linear narrative movement and organization, both are fascinated by overlooked particulars, and their texts are primarily staged as meditations rather than plots, replicating the circular movements of memory and thought. Whereas Sebald is a poet of the decline of the postwar West, Baker is something akin to the bard of the shopping mall and suburban microcosm. But, as said, there are major differences in their projects, one of the key ones being their relationship to ineffability.

Sebald's meditations frequently hinge on moments in which his narrators and characters become overwhelmed by "deep impressions" that outstrip any kind of linguistic or epistemological function:

> It was an utterly incomprehensible spectacle which moved me deeply.[11]

> Those square and circular smokestacks, and the countless chimneys from which a yellowy-grey smoke rose, made a deeper impression on me when I arrived than anything else I had previously seen, said Ferber. I can no longer say exactly what thoughts the sight of Manchester prompted in me then[12]

> Why exactly this lagoon of oblivion had spread in him, and how far it extended, had remained a mystery to him however hard he thought about it.[13]

This brooding romanticization of ineffability would be unacceptable to Baker and his desire for comprehensiveness. There is, on the whole, very little of this mood in Baker's work, and I think this is partly able to explain why his novels tend to be neglected in consideration of literary innovation, even though many of his techniques have been employed by subsequent writers such as Wallace. *The Mezzanine* is peppered with footnotes, and Wallace's story in *Brief Interviews with Hideous Men* about a boy freezing time to indulge in masturbation fantasies ("B.I. #59") builds upon Baker's 1994 novel *The Fermata*. Indeed, *The Pale King*'s encouragement to find the boring and trivial aspects of life infused with an "immense bliss" is precisely what *The Mezzanine* had achieved more than a decade earlier, but with none of the existential fanfare or angst that seems to be necessary if one wants to be taken seriously as an artist. Vagueness simply aggravates Baker, and has more to do with laziness than a serious engagement with Sebald's "deep impressions." Indeed, after reading Baker's work, we are given to feel that the romanticization of ineffability might just be a cover for a much more real failure of patient insight, returning us to Richard A. Lanham's notion of the "scarcity of attention" in the information age.[14]

So, if *Room Temperature* attempts to either supplement or overcome empirical limitations, as with Mike's attempt to study the invisible currents of air flowing through a room or to read his wife's handwriting by listening to the sound of her pen scratching against paper, then it needs to be careful not to stray into the posturing that vagueness often leads to in literary culture. In general, it seeks to avoid doing this by supplementing any descriptive shortcomings it encounters with what we might call the "experiential" quality of the narrative, its intention to perform—through its movements, cross-references, and complexities—those aspects of an object that remain resistant to an empirical field. This novel, which strives to represent the unrepresentable, is careful to proceed in a manner that assures us these questions *are*, in the end, answerable, but just in ways that a more "scientific" form of literary cloning would miss.

A Door-Stop Novel

Although the cloned frog (and the novel confined to a suburban home) might seem pale because of its lack of engagement with the world outside the Petri dish, it nevertheless exists as a pure, uncoded body of feeling. From its perspective, all that we consider to be meaningful experience still exists as a gloop of strange, exciting, and diffuse sensations yet to be codified. The familiarity of concepts is yet to mediate its empirical engagement with the world. All details are fresh, unprecedented, and striking. So although, in Mike's account, the clone is "impoverished," it is also extremely sensitive to every stimulus, no matter how trivial. It's a veritable *tabula rasa*, and able to find pleasure in the most banal of experiences.

It is of course not insignificant that throughout *Room Temperature* Mike's baby daughter stays nestled in his lap, mostly asleep. The baby is present as a similarly "uncoded" apparatus of feeling, an explorer of the world yet to be numbed by habituation, yet to experience life in any way other than an anarchic chaos of exciting tensions and intensities.[15] At one stage Mike describes Bug's birth as an "amphibious" emergence (42), emphasizing her connection with the frog. Bug also tends to display a relatively inexplicable fascination with simple sensation that reflects the novel's guiding enthusiasm for the "missing-in-discourse," as well as its fascination with otherwise uninteresting aspects of life. Mike is surprised, for instance, that her favorite toy is a rubber aspirator that she squeezes to send air whooshing into her face (42). Her enjoyment of the air is a sheer love of affect that confounds her parents.

The domestic, as it exists in this novel, is a space that allows for many experiences and enthusiasms similar to Bug's seemingly arbitrary enjoyment of intensities of air. The domestic microcosm—the home, the spousal relationship, the miniaturist novel—is analogous to the womb, and so Mike and his wife Patty are perhaps to be seen as possessing a similar sort of subjectivity to Bug, harboring all sorts of peculiar enthusiasms as they emerge into the outside world and retreat back inside their home, bringing new objects and experiences with them. Because of its insularity, the domestic space also becomes a sort of echo chamber of shared experience in which meanings and memories intertwine and overlap in a collective stew, discrete definitions becoming impossible. The enclosed space of the domestic leads to intensification—the production of ever more information—rather than entropic stasis or emptiness. Here, the home becomes a sort of maximalist machine, proliferating textuality outward that soon hits a wall and bounces back in on itself, reconfiguring its code as it ricochets around its cage.

Typical of Baker's novels, this messy complexity brings with it a sense of challenge—a desire to name, control, and separate domestic experience into precise categories. To take just one of many examples, while reflecting on the early stages of his and Patty's life together, Mike notes that the domestic experience that pleased Patty most was reserving a drawer to hold colored candles, whereas what pleased him most was "owning five wedges of dark-red rubber to shove under the doors" (25). Mike's seemingly arbitrary enthusiasm for the red of these door-stoppers sets off a chain of associations through which he attempts to explain why this particular color brings with it so much pleasure. Initially, Mike tries to find a relational context and content for the feeling, comparing the color to the red of air hoses at gas stations, lids of peanut butter jars, and toilet plungers, among other things (25). This attempt to explain the significance of the color extends into a complex and tender recounting of domestic intimacy. In the early years of their relationship, Mike grew determined to display an interest in the "sophisticated colors" cherished by Patty, expressing his love for her by way of adopting her interests. This anecdote eventually ends up explaining one of Mike's other inexplicable enthusiasms for color, mentioned earlier in the book and which previously remained unexplained. In this earlier instance, Mike grew fascinated by the color quality-inspection slips he had found in the pockets of a tweed jacket. Mike arranged the slips "like a bouquet of dried flowers" and presented them to Patty in a mock-romantic gesture (14). It is only later, in this attempt to account for the pleasure of the "brick red" door-wedges, that we understand whence his enthusiasm for the inspection slips came—an attempt to "prove to Patty that I was making progress in my ability to find things in the world that she would like, and bring them to her as gifts" (25).

This explanation seems to provide a sound-enough account of the related door-wedge pleasure, but is soon undercut by another, even more revealing anecdote about his mother's love for mixing paints (especially a combination of red and yellow—resulting in a "brick red," presumably), which is itself a testament to the unexplained power of color to provide excitement:

> she used old peanut butter jars as receptacles, and sat cross-legged in the side yard pouring imperceptibly different yellow-greens from one jar to another, refining the color that she wanted for the porcelain-knobbed dresser in my sister's room, though the young technician in the paint department at Sears had with apparently scientific precision injected what seemed to me a perfectly acceptable series of squirts of yellow, cyan, and magenta from the paint organ into a white base, according to the recipe in a notebook for the sample chip my mother had matched to the border of a cloth calendar. (31)

The mind's idea of color exceeds its real-world correlate, and his mother's attempt to recreate this idealized hue cannot be realized through the "scientific" method of the technician and his recipe.[16] So, once again, Mike's enthusiasm for the red door-wedges is thrown back on an "also-quality" of the color that exceeds explanation. As in Mike's statistical breakdown of the (he suspects) slightly forced enthusiasm Patty shows in response to the inspection strips he presents to her, there is a rational explanation for the majority of the excitement, but there still remains an irreducible "15% genuine pleasure in the colors" (31), a pleasure that exceeds all words, memories and histories that would try to contain it.

Although attempts are made to explain the reasoning for these enthusiasms, they are always ungrounded by the narrative's constant shifts in time and space as Mike connects memory to memory in an attempt to explain his experience of the world with precision, so that every sensation gives rise to another possible explanation, which gives rise to yet another, and so forth until eventually we are left with something like Lacan's eternally moving "chain of signifiers" rather than a stable explanation. It is deliberately ironic that Mike purchases the door wedges to enjoy the "simplicity" of the door stop as a tool, its job of "enforcing stability" (24), yet the wedges' color suggests a complexity of feeling that is far from simple or stable and is ungrounding in its ability to flow across time and space. Rather than try to explain the specifics of the pleasure as Mike does, Baker attempts to provide readers observing Mike's attempts with an experience of the pleasure. What ultimately seems pleasurable about the color is the sense of interconnection it evokes, its ability to connect a range of spatially and temporally disparate events and experiences. The feeling of interrelation, and the proliferating associations and connections that the color triggers, is what Mike's account provides at the same time as it appears to fail to describe his enjoyment of the color effectively. Developing in place of an ordinary answer is a sense that the reason these colors emote so strongly for Mike is because of their ability to recall a field of interrelations that is experienced as a kind of closeness, or comfort, a home. What seems like an arrival at ineffability is actually an answer in a different sense, and one a more definite explanation would perhaps overlook.

Negative Space

The complexity of this shape of definition, and of the feelings that are described by it, is given unity by the book's engagement with a larger quagmire of representation associated with the notion of "negative space." As Mike encounters it, negative space immediately offers itself as a metaphor for the sort of gaps and unfilled content of life that Baker's novels compulsively want to fill, but it is also an anchoring point for the novel's interest in experiences of excess, what we might call, following Massumi again, the "missing-in-discourse of also-sensed quality," as well as the shifting interrelations they evoke.

Mike tells us that one of his earliest encounters with the idea of negative space was in the art lessons his mother, a teacher at an art gallery, used to trial on him and his sister in their youth. One of the more "impossible assignments" she set them was to draw the inside of a pillow (20). It is partly an absurd task, almost similar to a kōan in the difficulty it presents to conceptualization. Nevertheless, throughout the novel, we read of Mike's various struggles with the challenge, which he eventually solves in a fit of competitive desperation (albeit somewhat disingenuously, he admits): "Finally, defeated, knowing I was cheating, I sketched a primitive pair of lungs, resembling the ones in the ad for Primatene Mist, and an arrow pointing to them that said 'From a pillow'; for, as I explained to my mother, the only way to know the real nature of the inside of a pillow was to breathe in its air" (56). Although on one hand Mike is obviously aware he is doing little more than admitting defeat, in the wider context of the book he is proposing a solution that is not so facile.

To understand Mike's solution and why it is important for this novel, it probably first needs to be placed in comparison with his sister's effort. To address the challenge, Mike's sister draws pictures of a pillow on a bed with "a wedge cut out of it to show the cross section of messy feathers" (55). His sister's solution to the problem is a traditionally realist one, relying on a static visual relationship to an object, one that takes the perspective and instruments of human sight as its guiding measures. But his sister's pillow cross-section is also bound up with an impossible *hyper*realism, an intensification of the realist urge that undoes its claims to objectivity. Cross-section drawings seem at once to speak of the objective powers of observation and at the same time cancel this power, or at least admit the limits of it by employing an impossible fantasy of observation. A cross-section allows us to see through what we ordinarily couldn't and, importantly, to see an inside unaffected by the removal of its outside, offering an imaginary vista not otherwise achievable. It is a picture of an object with a hole in it, but a hole that does not really exist as part of the object. A cross-sectioned drawing of a spaceship, for example, is not a picture of a spaceship missing a wall, and nor is Mike's sister drawing a pillow with a hole in it. If the pillow did have a hole, its insides would probably be spilling out, and thus would not be the inside any longer. The cross-section is thus an image of objectivity breaking down in order to satisfy the desire to see an inside and outside simultaneously. On one hand, the drawer of a cross-section seeks to faithfully represent the entirety of the object, but on the other wishes to intrude upon the desired realism with a device that expresses a fantasy of something like x-ray vision.

Mike's first attempts at solving the problem try to avoid this quagmire by representing the inside of the pillow from *inside* the pillow, rather than outside. This drawing cannot serve sight in any ordinary sense, but nor does it have to engage in the hyperreal fantasy of cross-section. He imagines this drawing as a "mass of loops" or "the record of the pencil's tactile encounter with every feather and inner boundary" (55). It is clear here that Mike's idea of representation is guided more by how being inside a pillow might feel, rather than what it would look like from some impossible "view from above" that could also somehow see through the exterior of solid objects— the gaze of a superman perhaps. A record of the movements of the pencil as Mike's hand felt around inside the pillow, a bizarre form of cartography that involves a confluence of senses (tactility, sight, proprioperception, and breath all working together in an experiential jumble), would for him be much more realistic than a quasi-scientific cross-section. He theorizes the rationale behind his method in the following manner:

> I needed to catch in the sketch some of the sensation of reaching inside a new chicken and pulling out the giblets ... or of plunging a knife into a new jar of peanut butter and creating complex comma-shaped hollows as you brought a gob of deeper butter upon the end of the blade. (55)

As with cloning a truly identical frog, to accurately draw an object, one needs to factor in the full component of its experiential texture, not just those aspects that best suit the chosen representational medium. As Mike notes, while drawing his pillow he "broke the over-sharpened pencil almost immediately, trying to enter the paper and scoop into a third dimension; and yet three would have fallen almost as short" (54). The missing dimension seems to be something like the experiential, that which exceeds a sort of one-to-one visual copying or mimesis. The command to *draw* implies an agreed-upon mode of viewership, an assumed praxis of observation insepa-rable from a broadly realist ideology, but one that is difficult to persist with here, at least for Mike (and Baker), who fears the loss of information that occurs through inaccuracy. Representation must describe the intersection of the empirical and experiential if it is to be truly complete—this seems to be Mike's point.[17]

This quagmire of representation is, of course, intended to reflect back upon how novels attempt to capture the world through written descrip-tion. Maximalism confidently expresses an ability to empirically cata-log the world as information, seen, for instance, in Wallace's persistence with describing dull collections of photographs or blue items in a waiting room, or in Pynchon's obsession with historical minutiae. Through Mike's attempts to account for the pleasure of colors and represent the inside of a pillow, Baker proposes a model of literary description that introduces the added "dimension" of experience to supplement representations that usually depend on sense data. And the solution Mike comes up with—the drawing of lungs and the accompanying suggestion that the only way to "know the real nature of the inside of a pillow was to breathe in its air"—is much more complicated than a simple description of the experiential texture of the pil-low: it is a description that turns the entire novel into a performance of a sort, an attempt to describe, in expanded form, the experience of negative space Mike is attempting to capture. *Room Temperature* wants to recreate, for the reader, the feeling of what the inside of a pillow "looks" like, not just represent it analogously.

The first mention of Mike's drawing task is itself a digression nested in a more primary anecdote about Mike's attempt to grasp, through just the sound of pen on paper, what his wife Patty is writing each night in her notebook by focusing on the "negative space" (or silence) between her words. As with his later dream of reconstructing the objects in a room by studying the miniscule movements of air, it involves the fantasy of an almost superhuman power of mind (20). After the drawing challenge is "solved" some forty pages later, it once again becomes nested in the meditations on Patty's writing (indeed, Mike's attempts to read Patty's writing bookend his attempts to draw the inside of the pillow). But now this negative space between words is no longer marked by the sound of her moving hand, but by the noise of commas: "one evening, as with my eyes closed I listened to her write about the Bug ... I thought I could detect the particular sound of a comma just before a pause in her penmanship" (58). This is a small victory for Mike in terms of his attempt to "read" with his ears (and again, as in the pillow challenge, it is a limit of sight that he is attempting to overcome, freeing himself from optical dependence), but it also involves Patty's writing in a web of associations that flow through the book and appear in various guises in almost all of Mike's fascinations, forming a "series of loops" that formally mimes the experience of being "inside" the pillow.

The comma, of course, is a visible rendering of negative space, paradoxically signifying an absence of presence. It is also a grammatical simulation of the space required to take a breath whilst reading aloud, or, in Mike's experience of playing a horn (58), a musical notation indicating a brief pause or separation within or between phrases. For the horn player the comma is an "oasis of respiration" (66). Although the book doesn't offer this interpretation, in relation to musical tuning a comma also refers to the small adjustments made to certain intervals in order to achieve "just" or perfect intervals (generally in relation to major thirds, as in quarter-comma meantone tuning). This practice is compared to the compromises of the now-standard equal temperament (by which, for example, modern pianos are tuned) in which all intervals are equivalent but none are truly "just" or perfectly tuned.[18] Taken through this rather discursive route of associations, a comma then relates back to the barely perceptible difference between the cloned and natural frogs, the slight imperfection that worried Mike so much in his youth. Such is the logic of the book that here on page sixty-six a comma is also compared to the shape of Bug's head, nostril openings (at one point Mike worries excessively that being caught picking his nose might be beyond the bounds of domestic tolerance [89]), a tube of antifungal ointment (which Mike notes is in the room with him on the very first page of the book), and airplane wings in cross-section (elsewhere Mike tells of his love for making "chop shop" versions of model airplanes [6]). Earlier in the book, before the significance of commas becomes clear to us, the imprints left by a knife scooping peanut butter from a jar are also described as "complex comma-shaped hollows" (55), and this reference reoccurs, tellingly, in the description of Mike's desired experiential solution to the pillow problem.

The result of this web of associations is that every time a comma is mentioned it also references air, breathing, model planes, nostrils, Bug, peanut butter, and the inside of a pillow, recalling the entire chain of associations. And the same goes for any of the other things associated in this web. For example, in answering the pillow problem by saying that the "only way to know the real nature of the inside of a pillow was to breathe in its air," this breathing in of air connects to the grammatical comma, the pause in which the horn player takes breath, the air flowing through the room, the drops of peanut butter that look like commas, as well as the shape of airplane wings seen in cross-section. The web expands and expands, and is recallable by any one of its elements. By answering the task of drawing the inside of a pillow by suggesting it depends upon breathing in its air, then, Mike implies that the only way to describe the inside of a pillow is to experience a vast web of connectedness, which is what the pillow "looks" like in a more experiential sense of representation, rather than its visual image.

The book, then, *is* the inside of the pillow figured as "some sort of mass of loops." The experience that is "missing-in-discourse" is captured by the novel, but exists only as the performance (the reading) of its narrative. And this book-pillow is then the description of that which exceeds description as the ordinary novel knows it. It succeeds in this task not by gesturing toward an ineffable quality of reality that escapes encoding in the novel (the romanticization of excess as practiced by Sebald, for example), but by performing it through the structure of the book. The analogical complexity of the narrative traces the experiences that escape mimesis figured as cloning (to return to the frog anecdote), and enables them to be experienced without the fantasy and inaccuracy of cross-section. At the very least, we arrive at a type of mimesis that a focus only on the observable information of the world would miss. Baker's lust for comprehensiveness is sated once again, and the maximalist mode of inquiry is now able to record even those details which lie beyond direct observation.

Notes

1. Paula E. Geyh, "Burning down the House? Domestic Space and Feminine Subjectivity in Marilynne Robinson's *Housekeeping*," *Contemporary Literature* 34, no. 1 (1993): 106–7.
2. Raymond Carver, *Cathedral: Stories* (New York: Vintage Books, 1984).
3. Arthur Saltzman, *Understanding Nicholson Baker* (Columbia, SC: University of South Carolina Press, 1999), 33.
4. Nicholson Baker, *Room Temperature* (London: Granta, 1990), 53–54. In this chapter, all subsequent references to this text will be given in parentheses.
5. Saltzman, *Understanding Nicholson Baker*, 33.
6. Geyh, "Burning down the House," 112. Marilynne Robinson, *Housekeeping* (London: Faber, 1981).
7. Brian Massumi, *Parables for the Virtual: Movement, Affect, Sensation* (Durham: Duke University Press, 2002), 234.
8. Baker, *The Mezzanine*, 109.
9. James Guetti, *The Limits of Metaphor: A Study of Melville, Conrad, and Faulkner* (Ithaca: Cornell University Press, 1967), 157.

10. Ibid., 156–57.
11. W.G. Sebald, *The Emigrants*, tr. Michael Hulse (London: Vintage Books, 2002), 166.
12. Ibid., 169.
13. Ibid., 174.
14. See Chapter 3.
15. Lacan, however, argues that even before we are born we enter into the Symbolic order of society, laden with expectations and meanings by our parents and others: "Symbols in fact envelop the life of man in a network ... so total they they bring to his birth ... the shape of his destiny; so total they they give the words that will make him faithful or renegade, the law of the acts that will follow him right to the very place where he is not yet and even beyond his death." Jacques Lacan, "The Function and Field of Speech and Language in Psychoanalysis," *Écrits: A Selection*, tr. Alan Sheridan (London: Routledge, 2001), 74. In this way we already exist—as a sign, an expectation, a desire, a fear—before we are born. But this interpellation into the Symbolic, while definitely affecting the infant in more-or-less tangible ways, is far from a complete socialization. One can be more than what one is expected to be. Indeed, the process of growing up is precisely that of managing (both assimilating and resisting) the "language" of expectation into which one is born.
16. This is similar to Massumi's discussion of David Katz's color-patch experiment, in which the mind's apprehension of color exceeded any attempted approximation of it, resulting in test subjects being unable to match a blue color-strip with what they felt was the blue of an absent friend's eyes. Massumi, *Parables for the Virtual*, 208–30. We also can't help but think here of Wallace's description of blue things in a waiting room, which was discussed in Chapter 2. Color in that scene, however, beckoned no kind of experience; it was offered merely as an abstract organizational criteria.
17. A pillow—an object with a distinct exterior and interior—seems also to be analogous to a human being, and the challenge of Mike's task is the one faced by life writing in general: how to record the inner experience of life as it intersects with an exterior world in the form of writing.
18. See, for example, Ross W. Duffin, *How Equal Temperament Ruined Harmony (And Why You Should Care)* (New York: W.W. Norton & Co., 2007).

6 Mindless Pleasures
Playlists, Unemployment, and Thomas Pynchon's *Inherent Vice*

Hyperlinking

When *Inherent Vice* was published in 2009, it came accompanied by two curious things, at least for a Thomas Pynchon novel. The first was a book trailer voiced by the author in a lovely beatnik drawl, marking just the third time his voice had been broadcast in the media (the other two occasions occurring on *The Simpsons*). You can still watch the trailer on YouTube.[1] The second accompaniment was a playlist of songs, "designed exclusively for Amazon.com, courtesy of Thomas Pynchon," with the tracks available for purchase on the store's website:

> Larry "Doc" Sportello is a private eye who sees the world through a sticky dope haze, animated by the music of an era whose hallmarks were peace, love, and revolution. As Doc's strange case grows stranger, his 60s soundtrack—ranging from surf pop and psychedelic rock to eerie instrumentals—picks up pace. Have a listen to some of the songs you'll hear in *Inherent Vice*—the playlist that follows is designed exclusively for Amazon.com, courtesy of Thomas Pynchon. (Links will take you to individual MP3 downloads, full albums, or artist pages).[2]

This "Amazon Exclusive" might interest us for several reasons. Superficially, it gives the impression that Pynchon has finally given in to "the man," cutting deals with the leader of cyber-trade monopolization and the supposed enemy of bookstores and publishers the world over (if the doom and gloom of 2014's Hachette controversy is to be believed[3]). The appearance of Pynchon's voice and mix-tape also affirms that in today's literary economy the author can no longer remain entirely aloof. This famously private writer has finally been drawn into the publicity game, moving closer and closer to revealing himself to the market as it grows hungrier and hungrier for whatever surrounds the literary object. The book itself seems to be no longer enough to satisfy literary interest; the weaknesses of its peculiar commodity form—its resistance to advertising and product placement, the difficulty in leveraging it to sell other commodities—weighs ever heavier and draws more supplementary material into the market. The situation leaves us wondering if we might even see a dust-jacket portrait on some future Pynchon novel.

But the playlist of songs has another interesting implication when we consider it in relation to the way Pynchon's novels have tended to be read in critical communities. I argue that this playlist ultimately allows us to use *Inherent Vice* to reevaluate not only Pynchon's writing, but what the general "employment" of academic readers of his works should be in the new millennium. As I hope to show, the playlist is not as important for what it provides, as for what it doesn't—what it refuses.

But to do all of this, it is necessary to first think about how the experience of reading *Inherent Vice* compares to that of Pynchon's other novels. To look back to 2006, it's probably safe to say that some casual readers let out a sigh of exasperation when his previous novel *Against the Day* was published, being his longest and most sprawling book yet. But many scholars let out cries of glee, it seems, knowing well by 2006 how to tackle Pynchon's excesses. As an ambitiously maximalist-historical novel in the vein of *Gravity's Rainbow* and *Mason and Dixon* before it, *Against the Day* has proved an overly fertile source of work for readers in the professional Pynchon community: here's a book for which the academy indeed seems *needed*.[4] Such hypothetical labor-potential housed in the immensity of *Against the Day* and other Pynchon epics also translates into real-world profits, of course. If one is able to do the work, writing explications can enable one to land a better job or strengthen one's résumé, which, if we want to be skeptical, is the shadowy "other" purpose of almost all literary criticism today.[5] Back in 1976, Edward Mendelson pointed out that "critical industries built upon the exile, obscurity or illegality of Dante, Rabelais, Cervantes, Melville and Joyce now provide food and shelter for many hundreds of scholars and critics, and will doubtless continue to do so, no matter how stormy the economic climate becomes" (1274).[6] He offered Pynchon's work as providing much the same academic meal-ticket, with a caveat due to the novelist's treatment of Weberian routinization:

> A comparable industry is already beginning to develop around Thomas Pynchon. Uniquely, however, among encyclopedic authors, Pynchon calls attention to just this kind of critical industry in the course of his own work. Unlike Joyce who—outside *Ulysses*, in letters and over cafe-tables—welcomed and encouraged the creation of a Joycean cartel, Pynchon warns of the rise of bureaucracies and of their social and economic roles. His warning is timely. Recent criticism almost entirely ignores its own economic and political motives. Although most critics surely write out of love for their subject, most critics also hope to gain some sort of profit, some sort of place for themselves, as by-products of their works of love. But how many critics can bring themselves, in their criticism, to acknowledge this?[7]

To collapse the critical enterprise into an economic motive is reductive. But even when summarizing the plot of a novel such as *Against the Day* calls for a professional (Pynchon himself is said to have blurbed the book, as he was rumored to have done for *Inherent Vice*), the maximalist novel's function as a wellspring of specialized employment opportunities is obvious. We thus need to think of novels like *Gravity's Rainbow* and *Against the Day* as not only stylistically excessive, but containing an excess of critical value that readers can sell on the market for some figuration of profit—be it literal income, or the respect of their peers (which is perhaps just income waiting to happen).

There are, of course, many aspects of a big novel such as *Against the Day* that appeal to professional study, and often the pleasure of the book comes from just this possibility of it having many aspects. But one of its key sources of excitement, as with *Gravity's Rainbow* and *Mason and Dixon*, is Pynchon's engagement with historical knowledge—the novel's details and references, the often obscure and erudite data of the world that compose the background of Pynchon's literary landscapes and invite further exploration. As Amy J. Elias puts it, these novels are "stuffed to the brim with historical facts,"[8] and this certainly engages the attention of many Pynchon readers.

Pynchon's enthusiasm for historical detail can be exciting when it teaches us things we might not have otherwise known,[9] but as readers it also allows readers to feel a sort of vicarious intellectual accomplishment. Detailism—as both a style of writing and reading—can offer itself as a way of asserting one's power as a writer or audience. As Alan Liu suggests of cultural criticism's "reverence for detail," it is "in part a sustained allegory for individualism," revealing "a hidden agenda of Western individualism not clearly distinguished from … an original-pragmatist nostalgia for the colonial or nineteenth-century frontiersman of can-do sufficiency."[10] For Liu, in such accounts people are "personified details."[11] The power we bestow upon the detail to influence and shape the meaning of the text makes up for the loss of power that the reader, and the "person" in general in postmodernity, stands to feel in relation to the whole of which he is part.

Take, for example, Justin St. Clair's article on *Against the Day*, "Binocular Disparity and Pynchon's Panoramic Paradigm." St. Clair begins by affirming with some excitement that "there is no denying that … this novel is another adventure in encyclopedic erudition."[12] He then continues to reveal the significance of Pynchon's reference to a series of panorama paintings, disclosing the history of what, following Richard Oettermann's account, St. Clair claims is the first visual mass medium. Whether or not St. Clair reveals anything interesting about the novel through this reading is not at stake here (he does); what the detail allows him to feel is:

> First, most people simply do not know that the panorama was arguably the dominant visual mass medium of the nineteenth century. In fact, many contemporary media buffs would be hard pressed even to describe the form. And while it may be argued that contemporary visual media aspire toward the panoramic, I would offer that they do so in ignorance of the medium that engendered the terminology.[13]

First, claiming that most people failed to know that something was "arguably" the most dominant visual mass medium is such a weak assertion that one wonders if it really means anything. St. Clair cannot even commit to knowing it beyond argument himself. But to get to the point, are we to take from this footnote that St. Clair *was* one of the erudite few who knew lots of things about the panorama before reading Pynchon's novel, that he was historically enlightened? It doesn't really matter either way: it is clear that what Pynchon's encyclopedic erudition can offer readers, above all else, is the demonstration of a felt intellectual triumph, a display of Liu's "can-do sufficiency" on the frontier of intellectualism.

Redundancy Package

Unlike *Against the Day* and *Gravity's Rainbow*, *Inherent Vice* reads like a relatively unacademic, stoner comedy. By being full of details anyone can know without great effort, this book largely refuses appeals to intellectual triumph like St. Clair's. It is set in a 1960s California similar to the one through which Oedipa Maas frantically dashed in *The Crying of Lot 49*, and where *Vineland*'s Frenesi became involved with the radical film collective 24fps. *Inherent Vice*'s protagonist, Leo "Doc" Sportello, a young but seemingly washed-up P.I., is reminiscent of *Vineland*'s Zoyd Wheeler, the hippie-burnout he may very well grow up to resemble. Rather than Werner von Braun, B.F. Skinner, and panoramic paintings, however, this novel's historical referents are Country Joe and the Fish, Godzilla, and the LA Lakers. Indeed, as the Pynchon Wiki community has adroitly demonstrated, it's possible to reconstruct the novel's historical timeline by tracing its references to real-world basketball matches, which seems something of an antischolarly exercise.[14] But perhaps the most bountiful of *Inherent Vice*'s historical references are the songs of the era that blast out of every radio and car stereo in the novel—*those* songs that Pynchon's Amazon playlist so helpfully sourced for readers.

What is Pynchon up to here? Joyce wanted to keep scholars riddling forever, but is Pynchon, by sourcing his own references, sending his scholarly devotees a redundancy notice? The mainstream nature of the novel's historical data (basketball matches, pop music, Hollywood films) is nothing terribly new in Pynchon's oeuvre, which has always toyed with both low and high culture. But that Pynchon (or Amazon with his permission) has organized a lot of the novel's real-world referents for easy access seems to suggest that the author is keen to derail or at least meddle with the sort of reading his novels have offered some professionals in the past.[15] And indeed, compared to the ever-growing list of articles and books devoted to *Against the Day*, *Inherent Vice* has but a few; the academy remains largely silent.[16] This novel doesn't immediately open itself to scholars and their ways of seeing.

So if casual readers let out a sigh of relief when this relatively accessible, brief, and straightforward Pynchon novel was published, then academics, we are to infer, were disappointed or at least dismissive. Empirically, this novel has offered them far less opportunity for work; it has *un*employed them. Even the *Cambridge Companion to Thomas Pynchon*, published in 2012, three years after *Inherent Vice*, contains only a few cursory remarks on the novel, whereas the rest of the works have dedicated chapters. We are free to assume that the editors couldn't get anyone to write about it at length. Although reception of the novel in trade publications has generally been very positive, the lack of critical considerations reveals to what extent *Inherent Vice* either fails to stir the interests of the academy, or frustrates the work they might do.

If Pynchon enacts this severance of employment, it's not because he views all of his detail-hunting readers with antipathy, of course. His past novels have openly encouraged critical annotators like Steven Weisenburger and St. Clair, among many others. If anything, Pynchon seems to adore detail as much as his readers. But there does seem to be a slight uncertainty creeping into the game, a staleness appearing in the gambit between the maximalist writer and the reader of difficult detail.

One possible explanation for this uncertainty is the Internet. Although *Inherent Vice* is set in the late 1960s, the book demonstrates a consciousness of the epistemological implications of today's cyberculture, particularly our ability to easily organize, store, and retrieve vast amounts of complex information. At the center of the narrative lies the slightly ominous presence of a primitive computer network located in the office of Doc's friend Fritz Drybeam, a debt collector. This sprawling mess of equipment is hooked up to "ARPAnet," the forerunner of today's World Wide Web. To Doc, it looks like a "science-fictional Christmas tree."[17] But this network is growing, as "all over the country, in fact the world, there's new computers getting plugged in every day" (54). By the novel's end, it's clear just what power this network has—the power to put investigators like Doc out of business, for instance. As he admits with what he hopes is merely sarcasm, "guess I better learn something about this or I'll be obsolete" (365).[18]

As with most Pynchon novels, there is more uneasiness than joy accompanying the hardening of technological power. Fritz's young apprentice Sparky ruminates that the surveillance and search powers of the computer network are to be feared rather than celebrated: "someday everybody's gonna wake up to find they're under surveillance they can't escape. Skips won't be able to skip no more, maybe by then there'll be no place to skip to" (365). That "skips" can't skip means there'll be no need for skip tracers like Doc, nor presumably his story that we are reading. The freedom to move unwatched is also the freedom to load one's text with tiny bits of data that elude easy definition, that slip between the fingers of literary sleuths, eliciting adventures of the kind Doc—and annotators of obscure detail—embarks upon. But in the Internet age, this all changes. Detective work is infinitely easier, yet also dehumanized once human foibles and uncertainties are no longer part of the process.

In one sense, what Doc is seeking throughout the novel is to affirm the continued relevance his special skill set—the uncomputerizable functions of a loose and sketchy mind. Readers likewise are searching for a way of experiencing a Pynchon novel when any Skip—an obscure historical tidbit, or a forgettable character who pops up sporadically within a 1,000-page epic—can be traced with a search engine in a fraction of a second. The Internet and eBooks might make critical work a lot easier in this regard, but also offer far less experience along the way. This type of reading becomes a labor largely free of laboriousness, a work that only produces results, not the slow learning that comes through toil and practice. As Doc's Aunt Reet prophesizes, "someday ... there will be computers for this, all you'll have to do's type in what you're looking for ... and it'll be right back at you with more information than you'd ever want to know" (6–7). And, of course, she is correct. When I can now search my Kindle version of *Gravity's Rainbow* for all mentions of the word "light," then part of what makes reading a big book such a unique and challenging experience is lost—big books aren't so big after all. That none of Pynchon's novels—at least up until 2013's *Bleeding Edge*, set in New York City in 2001—have taken place in a world where the Internet is truly dominant, suggests to what extent his poetics and storytelling have depended upon difficulties with information management that are far easier to avoid on a Googled earth. What is appealingly historical in all of Pynchon's earlier novels, then, is the looseness of mind and knowledge that a hardened cyberculture seems to no longer allow. The ability to know too much too easily ruins the journey, and intrudes upon the kind of chaotic excess that has bewildered and excited Pynchon's characters since Oedipa Maas found herself struggling with all of the "crowding in" details of Pierce Inverarity's will.[19]

Inherent Vice's contiguity with the electronic "mind" also cancels, or at least troubles, whatever fantasies of triumphant individualism might have accompanied reading Pynchon's earlier novels. So although there's nothing wrong with continuing to construct readings around Pynchon's use of historical detail, to fill such readings with claims of intellectual triumph is now slightly misguided. As Jonathan Franzen suggested in a 2010 article in *The Guardian* proposing "rules" for aspiring fiction writers, "when information becomes free and universally accessible, voluminous research for a novel is devalued along with it."[20] The demonstration of polymath brilliance loses some of its shine when all readers have easy access to Wikipedia.

The maximalist novel itself also faces a crisis in this climate. To excite and challenge its reader, it can no longer simply be a massive compendium of data that attests to the author's powers of research or the general citizen's impotence in the face of an overloaded world. And as Pynchon seems to suggest with his beating-us-to-the-chase Amazon playlist, this crisis should encourage us to change the way we seek employment as readers of these novels. Although Pynchon partly mourns the loss of scholarly difficulty signaled by the disappearance of the charisma that Doc and the recalcitrant details of a text embody, he nevertheless shifts the focus of reading and writing maximalist novels away from noting the thousands of details that swirl disorientatingly through them. Readers cannot triumph over the computer in quantitative research. So, we should ask, what other jobs might the maximalist novel offer them?

Wise Guys

Reviewing *Inherent Vice* for the *London Review of Books*, Thomas Jones describes what he considers "the weirdest thing of all" about this novel:

> the thought that somewhere out there in one of the beach towns of LA County, never very far away from wherever Doc is carrying out his desultory investigations, somewhere among the dopers and the surfers and the hippie chicks, among the dentists and lawyers and loan sharks, among the voters who put Nixon in the White House and Reagan in the Governor's Mansion in Sacramento, Thomas Pynchon is secluded at his typewriter, at work on *Gravity's Rainbow*.[21]

It is thus difficult not to feel that *Inherent Vice* reapproaches the concerns, interests, and passions motivating Pynchon when writing that masterwork of postwar literature. The later novel is a reflection on a career, perhaps even a life. Many of the themes and ideas that appear in *Inherent Vice* are certainly classic Pynchon subject matter. Early on, we get references to a place called Vineland, obviously the setting of the eponymous novel, as well as "chums" and Old West paraphernalia, which are allusions to *Against the Day*.

But *Inherent Vice* also revises these old stomping grounds. The main revision occurs in its questioning of the authenticity of the countercultural or hippie movement of the 1960s. Pynchon's interest here is not in the exciting chaos and complexity of a culture, but its settling into a kind of unenergetic homogeneity. As Doc Sportello's frequent worries reveal, even for someone living in the sixties there's a divide between what things used to be like, and what they are now in their degraded, mass-marketed, and media-disseminated forms. People strike the poses of resistance, singing along to anthems of change, yet "Doc wondered how many would have recognized revolution if it had come up and said howdy" (356). Affirming this cynicism, early in the novel Richard Nixon appears on television to claim that "if it's Fascism for Freedom? *I ... can ... dig it!*" (120), and we can feel all the hippies wince in unison.

But the problem isn't just the appropriation of edgy styles by the media and authority figures; the growing lure of the gentrifying middle class also has an influence. On the novel's first page, Doc's ex-hippie, ex-girlfriend Shasta Fay Hepworth pays him a visit, "looking like she swore she'd never look" (1). The narrative begins because of Shasta's relationship with a real-estate mogul and her mutation into a "flatlander," a term meant to suggest her betrayal of the beach and its undulating, unpredictable surf. Doc's attempt to help her with her problems, and later find her after her disappearance, is thus also a quest to reclaim the culture he fears is being turned into units for sale (which literally happens to the old haunts of the Artesia Crips [16–17]), or else is changing so much that it now does the selling itself.

Doc finds his own enthusiasms tainted by this collapse of idealism and authenticity, experiencing a sort of hippie disillusionment. Before the novel's hectic action begins, he stands looking at a painting hung on his wall of a "Southern California beach that never was—palms, bikini babes, surfboards, the works. He thought of it as a window to look out of when he couldn't deal with looking out of the traditional glass-type one" (6). Sometimes when watching the painting, or the view of it outside the window, things "would light up … and promise that the night was about to turn epic somehow" (6). But in this particular moment no such epic foreshadowing occurs: "Except for tonight, which only looked more like work" (6). The beach is just business, the real cleaved irreparably from its aesthetic idealization.

For a novel that pines nostalgically for authentic, free-wheeling excess, it is strange that in many respects *Inherent Vice* is the least unruly and difficult of Pynchon's novels, especially, as already suggested, in regards to its treatment of historical detail. This is not to say that the novel is necessarily *un*excessive—if Raymond Carver had written it, we would assume he had gone mad. But compared to such gigantic and effusive works as *Against the Day* and *Gravity's Rainbow*, it is far more restrained, even conventional.

Such restraint can be most clearly felt in several formal aspects that make *Inherent Vice* seem determinedly different from those works of Pynchon's past. First, the narrative is focalized almost exclusively through one character, Doc Sportello, and takes place almost entirely in one temporal and geographical locale, Los Angeles, California (with a brief trip to Vegas), at the very end of the 1960s. Pynchon hasn't had such unification of perspective and location in a novel since *The Crying of Lot 49*. Despite the drug haze that pervades it, *Inherent Vice* is also quite ontologically stable: unlike other Pynchon works, the line between fantasy and reality is always quite clearly drawn. As Thomas Hill Schaub suggests, *Inherent Vice* contains "abundant fantasy—but it is *just* fantasy, lacking the subversive implications it has for Oedipa and the reader in *Lot 49*."[22] For critics that join Pynchon and postmodernism at the hip, this clear line rather uncomfortably implies that his novels are no longer as archetypically postmodernist as they once were, at least if we consider that postmodernist fiction, in Brian McHale's formulation, is driven by ontological uncertainty. In *Gravity's Rainbow*, for example, we were given access "only to provisional 'realities' … always liable to be contradicted and canceled out."[23] Although many of the transgressions of reality were signaled directly by the text, as when Slothrop took a trip down the toilet under the influence of sodium amytal, or when Pirate Prentice encountered a giant adenoid while dreaming another character's dream, some were much sneakier. For McHale, the best example was the Mrs. Quoad incident. What early in the book was reported to us as a real and entirely plausible encounter was later shown to be most likely a fantasy, with serious implications for the ontological integrity of the novel's plot.[24] Unlike *Gravity's Rainbow*, however, *Inherent Vice* is very ontologically stable, and is relatively uninterested in satirizing the hermeneutic management of novels.

One of the reasons for this stability is, ironically, the constant drug use that pervades *Inherent Vice*. On almost every page, Doc Sportello smokes marijuana, and yet the constant acknowledgment of the pot haze filling the novel disarms what would ordinarily be the confusing and jarring intrusion of Pynchonian unreality and absurdity. The drugs introduce a degree of ontological stability by clearly demarcating fantasy from reality, and the explicit drug use keeps the novel grounded by allowing any strange intrusion to be explained away as a temporary hallucination. As such, to repeat Schaub, although plenty of fantasy haunts the novel, it is *merely* fantasy. The line between real and unreal is always clearly drawn. The drugs, then, have a sort of anchoring, framing function, providing information that contextualizes any estranging elements of the novel, enabling them to be justified and explained away as having not occurred. It puts contextualizing borders around fantasy, providing ontological scare quotes of a sort. As a result, there's almost no bleed between ontological domains; we always know when something is a trip, and when it is just real life.

This emphasis on frames and contextualization forces us to question and weigh up the validity of different interpretations of Pynchon's relationship to the politics and aesthetics of postmodernist fiction. Perhaps, we are left to infer, *Inherent Vice* refuses a more experimental or challenging exterior because what were once "dangerous" and nonconformist modes of postmodernist writing are now nothing more than hollowed-out images and tired tropes, just like the poses of resistance struck by the late-60s counterculture. From such an idea, many questions follow: does *Inherent Vice* seek to represent the theme of cultural routinization by employing relatively restrained prose, providing a list of historical sources, and offering a fastidiously stable sense of reality? Or does the novel knowingly draw attention to its restraint to tint the "steadiness" of its world with a sense of irony, and thereby grow unsteady? If so, is the novel then to be read as a lament, a nostalgic pining for a less routinized and bureaucratic world? Or is this simply Pynchon moving on? As Doc's policeman friend Bigfoot Bjornsen informs him early on, this time he might have stumbled into something "too real and deep" to hallucinate his way out of (22).

If taken seriously, Bjornsen's words suggest that in *Inherent Vice* Pynchon builds upon what Shawn Smith sees as the critique of postmodernist textuality contained in *Vineland*. For Smith, in *Vineland* Pynchon expressed a "belief in the incompatibility of postmodern culture and progressive politics," a critique mainly centered on televisual mediation and the consequently "fluid textual boundary between reality and fantasy" that characterizes everyday life in postmodernity.[25] In *Vineland*, as in every other Pynchon novel besides *Inherent Vice*, the line between fantasy and reality is hopelessly blurred. But for Smith, this is not a liberating textual tactic that would free us from the tyranny of an oppressive realism. Instead, the intrusion of textual fantasy into the domain of reality only *"represses* our perception of what is real" (110). The "difficulty of seeing what is politically and historically real and what is not" is no longer a critique of a dull and conservative view of what constitutes reality or the truth, but a critique of postmodern life and its mediation by the hyperreality of television, cinema, and advertising (112). The only thing fantasy helps us escape from today is the uncomfortable fact that escapism makes us better consumers.

Smith's argument focusses on *Vineland*'s portrayal of a student riot at Berkeley and the subsequent police murder of Weed Atman. The event is captured on film by Frenesi and the 24fps film collective—or, at least partially captured, as the camera seems to malfunction at the crucial moment of Weed's death.[26] For Frenesi and others in the collective, the medium of film offers revolutionary potential in its ability to document reality and capture something essential about a moment, but Smith argues that Pynchon views this belief as, at best, an expression of a more fundamental social impotence, and, at worst, a reluctance to undertake "real" acts of resistance. Smith argues that the group's proposal of "guerrilla cinema as a tool of revolutionary praxis" only reveals its "misguided belief that the camera will bring it closer to its dreams of liberation."[27] In reality, "24fps deals only in simulacra of revolutionary action. The group's belief in the political utility of images is part of the text's metahistorical explanation for why sixties political activism 'died' while the repressive power structures it opposed flourished."[28] In Smith's view, political art is a poor substitute for "real" political action.

But Smith fails to capitalize on the full potential of his own argument here, neglecting to understand the extent to which the depiction of Frenesi's filmmaking involves a reflection on Pynchon's own art's relationship to radicalism and resistance. If Smith's argument is true, then *Vineland* critiques its own status as an object of resistance and likewise points toward its political impotence. But I don't think this is accurate. Smith's tacit assertion that physical action is the only form of "real" resistance ("Brock [Vond], Pynchon implies, is the *real* revolutionary because he is willing to use actual guns instead of the figurative 'guns' used by the ostensibly revolutionary 24fps"[29]) seems to jar with Pynchon's distaste for aggression and violence. One of the points of writing political novels, surely, is to affirm that there are ways to "fight" other than coming to blows. The revolution needs to be "televised" in radical ways as much as it requires radical participants.

If there is a problem of complacency here it is to do with the spectatorial role the viewers of this film adopt. Prairie and the others who watch the film in the novel's present moment do so in a "prehypnotic" state,[30] lulled into passivity by the images. The problem is not with the representation of this moment of revolutionary praxis, but with the passive way viewers who, in the televisually mediated present of the novel's 1984, observe these spectacles as mere images. If we are immune to their effect, then there's not a problem with the medium, but its reception.

When we witness *Inherent Vice*'s restriction of fantasy, it is certainly plausible to understand the novel as intensifying the critique of postmodernism that Smith sees in *Vineland*. Reality and fantasy were fluid in *Vineland*, whereas in *Inherent Vice* they are clearly demarcated; Pynchon's distaste for televisual hijinks is hardening. As with his downplaying of historical referents, Pynchon refuses readers the pleasures of "classic" Pynchonian textuality by not allowing them to speculate about the ontological integrity of the text.

But although this argument seems plausible enough, there are aspects of *Inherent Vice* that should make us feel that it still genuinely pines for a time when textual "reality" was allowed to be looser, when fantasy and excess weren't just the signs of the mediation of contemporary society. And if it is a critique of postmodernist play, then *Inherent Vice*'s stability is also, in this line of thought, a potential lament. Indeed, the more we look at the novel, the more we notice that there is actually a particular anxiety of framing that flows through it and subtly disrupts any tendencies toward restriction and steadiness. Pynchon is certainly keen to show that there is a clear boundary between fantasy and reality, but at times the separation appears strained. Consider the following example. Roughly halfway through *Inherent Vice*, Doc runs into Japonica Fenway, the wayward and probably insane daughter of a wealthy family, and a girl whom Doc was once hired to locate. When they meet again in the present of the novel, Doc is visiting a strange dental surgery that seems involved in a typically Pynchonian conspiracy, at which Japonica also arrives for an appointment. They exchange a brief greeting, then the text shifts to an omniscient point of view that seemingly steps out of Doc's focalization in order to present Japonica's recent experiences at a rehab center called Chryskylodon, as well as on dates with the dentist Rudy Blatnoyd, a benefactor of the institution. To get the sense of the specific formal tensions in the passage, it is helpful to consider a lengthy sample:

> So, Dr. Rudy Blatnoyd, out on a first blind date with Japonica at the Sound Mind Café. [...] The Japonica sitting with the older man in the funny velour suit was actually a Cybernetic Organism, or cyborg, programmed to eat and drink, converse and socialize, while Real Japonica tended to important business elsewhere. [...] Dr. Blatnoyd, escorting her out through a roomful of disapproving faces, only grew more bedazzled. So this was a free-spirited hippie chick! He saw these girls on the streets of Hollywood, on the TV screen, but this was his first up-close encounter. No wonder Japonica's parents didn't know what to do with her—his assumption here, which he didn't examine too closely, being that he did.
>
> "And actually, I wasn't too sure about who he was till I came in for my first Smile Evaluation ..." At which point in Japonica's reminiscing, in popped the lecherous toothyanker himself, zipping up his fly. (173)

Pynchon plays up the implausibility of this digression fitting within the frame of Japonica's reminiscence to Doc: the passage doesn't fit the suggestion that this is all just reported speech, focalized through his point of view.

In an older Pynchon novel, the story of Cyborg Japonica would be simply allowed to run loose, disrupting the ontological integrity of the text, affirming the novel's postmodernist sense of play and leaving Doc behind without a second thought. But *Inherent Vice* attempts to force this excess back into the too-small container of "Japonica's reminiscing," and, in turn, Doc's focalization. There is more information and perspective here than can be contained in whatever Japonica has narrated to Doc, and so the suggestion that this is just him listening to Japonica reminisce seems quite jarring and forced. The subtle falsity of this attempted containment should alert us to the fact that the conventions here are strained. The novel anxiously provides this anchoring frame, but also hints at its oppressiveness.

Such ontological frames are self-consciously flawed, I believe, to give us glimpses of what textual reality used to look like in Pynchon's past, and to create the feeling that the novel's stability is slightly oppressive. But they are also used by Pynchon to create a precedent for the introduction of a more troubling sense of unreality than would otherwise occur in his novels. In one such moment, Doc thinks he sees the mythical lost continent of Lemuria rising from the ocean:

> Being on the way to visit Adrian Prussia, he'd decided not to smoke much, so he was at a loss to account for the sudden appearance, rising ahead, of a dark metallic gray promontory about the size of the Rock of Gibraltar. Traffic crept along, nobody else seemed to see it. ... People in this town saw only what they'd all agreed to see, they believed what was on the tube or in the morning papers half of them read while they were driving to work on the freeway, and it was all their dream about being wised up, about the truth setting them free. What good would Lemuria do them? (315)

This eruption cannot be contained within the otherwise strict reality or hallucination binary because Pynchon is careful to point out here that Doc had decided "not to smoke much." It's one of only a few moments in *Inherent Vice* in which the intrusion of fantasy cannot be explained away as a drug hallucination. The significance of this moment resonates in its pointed questions: "What good would Lemuria do" for these "wised up" citizens? Would they even see it? In this moment of Lemuria rising, the previous ontological restraint of the novel disappears. So what is Doc witnessing? What "unexplained" possibilities of the text still persist? In a novel that has elsewhere been so careful to offer only contingent fantasy, Lemuria threatens to erupt into the narrative with the same force it would erupt into our own world.

Here, Pynchon's engagement with postmodern mediation pushes past the terms Smith ascribes to it, becoming more akin to David Foster Wallace's critique of the epistemological pleasures of postmodern(ist) irony. As much as Wallace's dissatisfaction with irony was related to the mood's barring of sincerity in favor of "cool detachment," it was also a critique of knowingness, of being "wised up." Even though many postmodernist advertisements and texts contain absurd and fantastic elements, for example, they are also *obviously* absurd and fantastic, designed to draw attention to their ridiculousness and make viewers feel as though they know something that the people in the texts do not. Readers are encouraged to feel as though they can see through the mechanics of fiction, and gain pleasure through this act. But this access to the "truth" is, of course, itself just another fiction aimed to mislead them into commercial pliancy:

> [TV can] ease that painful tension between Joe's need to transcend the crowd and his status as Audience member. For to the extent that TV can flatter Joe about "seeing through" the pretentiousness and hypocrisy of outdated values, it can induce in him precisely the feeling of canny superiority it's taught him to crave, and can keep him dependent on the cynical TV-watching that alone affords this feeling.[31]

Something of this is pointed out as Lemuria erupts into *Inherent Vice*, and offers another explanation for why the text is so laden with contextualizing frames. On the whole, it seems as if *Inherent Vice* gives us so much contextualizing information to explicate itself *before* we are able to declare which parts of it are true or false, so as to thwart the desire for what Wallace calls "canny superiority." The contextualizers are disillusioning in their containing of fantasy within the frame of drug-induced hallucinations, but they also destroy the "dream" of having a text that needs significant figuring out in the way readers of Pynchon are used to. The novel beats the "wised-up" reader at their own game.

Purple Haze

Despite the role drug-taking has in demarcating and controlling the borders of reality in *Inherent Vice*, it also provides a block to the epistemological mastery older Pynchon works celebrated in their form, if not wholly in their content. The inferred mind behind the text of *Gravity's Rainbow* and *Against the Day* was undeniably a genius polymath, despite whatever hermeneutic difficulties troubled the characters and readers. In *Inherent Vice*, however, Pynchon seems far more interested in cloudy or even withered mental powers, and creates far less separation between the characters' knowledge and that of the narrator by focalizing the narrative almost entirely through Doc. The narrator never seems to know much more than Doc does; readers never see into the computer-whiz minds of Fritz Drybeam or Sparky. Our understanding always remains restricted to Doc's own, which is haphazard at the best of times. The unsteady nature of his cognition is frequently noted, as when a thought comes to him out of "the permanent smog alert he liked to think of as his memory" (66), or his brain is referred to as an "unkempt barnyard" (267).

Much of the experience the novel offers is due to Doc's cloudy mental powers, his propensity to—like many classic Pynchon characters since Benny Profane—yo-yo through the world. If Doc were a more disciplined investigator with a rigorous commitment to method, half of the leads and clues that he freewheels after would be immediately dismissed as worthless and never investigated. Although Benny's and Slothrop's "yo-yo" lives gave ominous impressions of a controlling hand that pulled their strings in this or that direction, Doc's life is more like a yo-yo broken free of its master, chaotically rolling down the street. Doc's acquaintance Jade describes herself as "a small-diameter pearl of the Orient rolling around on the floor of late capitalism" (136). This fits Doc's existence, too: he's a stone that "just goes a-rollin on" (136).

Although *Gravity's Rainbow* was "good, if strenuous, training in negative capability,"[32] forcing readers through all kinds of confusion and bewilderment, the historical, mathematical, and scientific detail of the text often allowed readers to reclaim a kind of certainty in facticity.[33] In *Inherent Vice*, much less importance is placed on the necessity of intellectual activity and scholarly research in apprehending the problems of its world. Indeed, the Amazon playlist warns us against these habits of "wised-up" readers, and doesn't allow us to escape the novel by focusing on its facts and references. We largely remain mired in its world of insufficiencies and uncertainties, unable to structure our experience of the text along the lines of Liu's triumphant "can-do sufficiency."

Part of the essential experience of the book, then, is being swept up in the pulsating excess of story, plotlines, and characters that form an immersive analog of Doc's "rolling stone" life, but without the possibility of escape through the scholarly exercise of reading detail or parsing ontological slipperiness. In the historical-epic Pynchon novels such as *Against the Day* and *Mason and Dixon*, Doc-like characters are certainly present, but always accompanied by the text's management of the complex details of history, science, and other erudite discourses that provide the novel with the potential for intellectual pursuits not available to those with smog-for-brains—pursuits that would, presumably, go over their heads. In *Inherent Vice*, we are not offered the possibility of much "transcendence" through the reading of detail, and so the potential for turning this text into a source of scholarly labor is deliberately limited. Rather than solving all the problems and mastering the many messy plots of his life, Doc thinks he'll "settle for finding [his] way through this" (295). Such a humble solution seems to be offered to us readers, as well.

In *Inherent Vice*, Pynchon is consciously detaching his writing from the sprawling, information-packed, academic-titillating maximalism that has been considered characteristic of his oeuvre. Fritz's room full of whirring computers is what Doc's mind is pitted against throughout *Inherent Vice*, but the novel is ultimately guided by Doc's mind, not the computer. Even though Doc worries that his kind of story and employment risks becoming redundant in the age of information and knowledge work, Pynchon seems to be suggesting that this tale of mental fog and struggle is much more apt for our age's literature than the story of the triumphant computer. Perhaps Pynchon's other books were guided by fantasies of a processing power similar to that contained within Fritz's network, but *Inherent Vice* certainly isn't. Fantasies of maximalist intelligence do not dominate *Inherent Vice*, nor are they seen as important in its world. The novel is much more interested in the possibilities of a kind of human fogginess: one that certainly obscures much, but also allows other things, relations, and pleasures to come into focus. It's not a high-definition attention to detail that is promoted as a use of maximalism here, but a less anxious engagement with the experience of overloadedness, one that embraces the flow of data and that "surfs" its waves.[34]

And this brings us to the importance of the novel's final scene. After reaching an uneasy conclusion to his investigations, Doc strikes out on the Santa Monica Freeway as the fog begins "its nightly roll inland" (367). Soon enough, the whole place is covered, reducing visibility to a minimum. Rather than fight it, or fret, Doc

> pushed his hair off of his face, turned up the radio volume, lit a Kool, sank back in a cruising slouch, and watched everything slowly disappear, the trees and shrubbery along the median, the yellow school-bus pool at Palms, the lights in the hills, the signs above the freeway that told you where you were, the planes descending to the airport. (367)

Head- and taillights are the only visible objects, and after a while Doc settles in behind another car to trail behind, and then another car in turn falls in behind him, the blind leading the blind out of this fog not by penetrating it, or seeing through it with supernatural, x-ray vision, but by forming "a caravan in a desert of perception." This becomes "one of the few things he'd ever seen anybody in this town, except hippies, do for free" (368). Doc eventually begins to wonder how he'll get off the freeway and out of the fog. He "figured if he missed the Gordita Beach exit he'd take the first one whose sign he could read and work his way back on surface streets. He knew that at Rosecrans the freeway began to dogleg east, and at some point, Hawthorne Boulevard or Artesia, he'd lose the fog" (368). But as soon as he begins to hatch this escape plan based on signs and maps and knowledge, he supposes that "maybe he'd just have to keep driving" until he was outside of the city, across the border to Mexico, into a world cloaked universally in a fog in which "nobody could tell anymore … who was Mexican, who was Anglo, who was anybody" (369). The fog doesn't allow demarcations. The only thing one can do is drive blindly through it and help others on their journey.

Finally, Doc simply fantasizes that he might break down and be left standing at the side of the road, waiting for come what may, going along with whatever ride seems best. This is just Doc's hippie dreaming, of course. But I think Pynchon hopes it isn't. The fog forces us into admitting that, separated from "the morning papers half of [us] read while [we are] driving to work on the freeway" (and from which many of us have tried to deduce the historical accuracy of Pynchon's novels), we aren't so wised-up after all. Like Doc, we are to embrace insufficiency, see where it might lead us.

Notes

This is a revised version of "Mindless Pleasures: Playlists, Unemployment, and Thomas Pynchon's *Inherent Vice.*" *Journal of Modern Literature* 39.3 (Spring 2016). © Indiana University Press, 2016.

1. "Thomas Pynchon – Inherent Vice," YouTube video, 2:43, posted by Penguin Books USA, August 4, 2009, http://youtu.be/RjWKPdDk0_U.
2. "Inherent Vice: A Novel," *Amazon.com*, accessed January 12, 2015, http://www.amazon.com/Inherent-Vice-Novel-Thomas-Pynchon/dp/0143117564.
3. For a brief history of the situation, see Alison Flood, "Amazon-Hachette Fight Deepens as Authors Take Sides," *The Guardian*, July 4, 2014, http://www.theguardian.com/books/2014/jul/04/amazon-hachette-self-published-authors-stephen-king-james-patterson.
4. The following is a small sampling of the peer-reviewed articles and edited books devoted to *Against the Day*: Sascha Pöhlmann, ed., *Against the Grain: Reading Pynchon's Counternarratives* (New York, Rodopi, 2010); Jeffrey Severs and Christopher Leise, eds., *Pynchon's Against the Day: A Corrupted Pilgrim's Guide* (Newark: University of Delaware Press, 2011); Henry Veggian, "Thomas Pynchon Against the Day," *boundary 2* 35, no. 1 (2008); Kathryn Hume, "The Religious and Political Vision of Pynchon's *Against the Day*," *Philological Quarterly* 86, no. 1/2 (2007); Toon Staes, "'Quaternionist Talk': Luddite Yearning and the Colonization of Time in Thomas Pynchon's *Against the Day*," *English Studies* 91, no. 5 (2010); Richard Hardack, "Consciousness without Borders: Narratology in *Against the Day* and the Works of Thomas Pynchon," *Criticism* 52, no. 1 (2010).
5. Excluding, of course, the sort done on ostensibly amateur forums like the Pynchon wikis. For an illuminating discussion of these wikis, see Rowberry, "Pynchon Wiki."
6. Mendelson, "Encyclopedic Narrative," 1274.
7. Ibid., 1274–75.
8. Amy J. Elias, "History," in *The Cambridge Companion to Thomas Pynchon*, ed. Inger H. Dalsgaard et al. (New York: Cambridge University Press, 2012), 134.
9. See David Cowart: "an interest in Pynchon's fiction may seduce readers not scientifically inclined into investigating subjects to which they thought themselves indifferent or hostile." Cowart, *Thomas Pynchon*, 1.
10. Alan Liu, "Local Transcendence: Cultural Criticism, Postmodernism, and the Romanticism of Detail," *Representations* 32 (1990): 93–94.
11. Ibid., 94.
12. Justin St. Clair, "Binocular Disparity and Pynchon's Panoramic Paradigm," in *Pynchon's Against the Day*, 67.
13. Ibid., 85n6.

14. "Real Time and Narrative Time in *Inherent Vice*," *Pynchon Wiki: Inherent Vice*, last modified October 13, 2009, http://inherent-vice.pynchonwiki.com/wiki/index.php?title=Real_Time_and_Narrative_Time_in_Inherent_Vice.

15. Another interesting thing about the playlist is that among the links to real songs are those of Pynchon's invention—"Soul Gidget" by Meatball Flag, for example. You can't listen to these imaginary songs, of course, but they are still listed as if you could.

16. When I originally wrote this chapter, I could find only one peer-reviewed article entirely devoted to *Inherent Vice* (Wilson), as well as part of a book chapter (Schaub). Since then, *Pynchon's California* has been published, which contains two chapters wholly devoted to the novel, as well as others that analyze it productively in tandem with other Pynchon novels. Rob Wilson, "On the Pacific Edge of Catastrophe, or Redemption: California Dreaming in Thomas Pynchon's *Inherent Vice*," *boundary 2* 37, no. 2 (2010). Thomas Hill Schaub, "*The Crying of Lot 49* and other California novels," in *The Cambridge Companion to Thomas Pynchon*. Scott McClintock and John Miller, eds., *Pynchon's California* (Iowa City: University of Iowa Press, 2014).

17. Thomas Pynchon, *Inherent Vice* (London: Jonathan Cape, 2009), 53. In this chapter, all subsequent references to this text will be given in parentheses.

18. Considering that Pynchon's most recent novel, *Bleeding Edge*, did display a thorough knowledge of the topic, it seems as though Doc's thoughts are probably Pynchon's own, the latest novel being the result of his self-education.

19. Pynchon, *The Crying of Lot 49*, 56.

20. Jonathan Franzen, "Ten Rules for Writing Fiction," *The Guardian*, February 20, 2010, http://www.guardian.co.uk/books/2010/feb/20/ten-rules-for-writing-fiction-part-one.

21. Thomas Jones, "Call it Capitalism," *London Review of Books* 31, no. 17 (2009), http://www.lrb.co.uk/v31/n17/thomas-jones/call-it-capitalism.

22. Schaub, "California Novels," 40–41.

23. McHale, *Constructing Postmodernism*, 66.

24. Ibid., 70.

25. Shawn Smith, *Pynchon and History: Metahistorical Rhetoric and Postmodern Narrative Form in the Novels of Thomas Pynchon* (New York: Routledge, 2005), 110.

26. Thomas Pynchon, *Vineland* (London: Vintage, [1990] 2000), 247–248. *Inherent Vice* also narrates the filming of a murder, although this time it is actually captured by the camera in full.

27. Smith, *Pynchon and History*, 117.

28. Ibid., 118.

29. Ibid.

30. Pynchon, *Vineland*, 248.

31. Wallace, "E Unibus Pluram," 180.

32. McHale, *Constructing Postmodernism*, 82.

33. Such is the effect of a work such as Steven Weisenburger's *A Gravity's Rainbow Companion*.

34. The placing of the beach and a computer network in close proximity is perhaps, after all, to be seen as a play on the notion of "surfing" the internet today.

Conclusion
Overflow: The Margins of American Maximalism

Disharmonies

One of the defining features of music from the early twentieth century is the twelve-tone chord, a once "prohibited" aggregate harmony that included every pitch class of the Western tonal system. For Richard Taruskin, it was the epitome of the musical maximalism toward which many modernist composers aspired—initially with caution, as to sound its full range was risky. When at the end of *The Rite of Spring* Igor Stravinsky employed a chord with eight out of the possible twelve pitches, he exemplified "the concept that drove the radical new music of the early twentieth century,"[1] what Taruskin labels the maximalist spirit of "intensification of means."[2] But he still couldn't bring himself to reach the limit. The aggregate chord stood to give a portrait of "complete chromatic saturation," yet at the same time presented a possibility of chromatic exhaustion into which Stravinsky, being at this stage of his career still residually attached to harmony and other ideals of musical form, was not yet willing to proceed.[3]

There are several overlapping ways to listen to an aggregate chord, which is natural considering its density. We can hear it as a singular, immense, unfractured wall of sound, the whole of musicality present at once. It is something like the "view from above" of tonality, the container of all possible music. We can also hear within the chord the victory of detailedness, the rallying together of the disparate parts of tonality. Here is a chord that sounds the world with such precision and acuity that it includes all of Western music's sonic texture; here is a composer so deft of hearing that nothing but the presence of all pitch classes will satisfy the complexity of his aural vision. In the chord's dissonance, one can hear the multitude it triumphantly contains. The composer who notates it puts into practice a utopian ethic of egalitarian inclusion, refusing to exclude anything, no matter how jarring and difficult the resulting sound.

But this chord is also a critique of itself. Alongside its density, the aggregate chord is intended to give an experience of *limitation*, a barrier to what we can assemble, hear, and understand. The whole of music is both everything and nothing, all possible tones and none at the same time, the sound of pure music and its erasure. It stands to mock what readers might want to get from music, giving them too much sound to use in any conventional manner.

This chord's maximalist overtones can certainly be heard in novels such as Thomas Pynchon's *Gravity's Rainbow*, David Foster Wallace's *Infinite Jest*, and Nicholson Baker's *The Mezzanine*. As readers, we have grown increasingly attuned to the usefulness of maximalist statements. When the "rhetoric of inclusion" embodied in the chord is translated into literary form, it valorizes the ability to collect, manage, and communicate information, and encourages readers to be patient or receptive enough to contain the results of unremitting comprehensiveness. The density of the maximalist text frequently hardens into a celebration of an individual's ability to manage so much, to be so maximalist, and offers a commentary on the benefits of paying attention to particulars in the so-called information age.

The multitude of approaches the aggregate chord allows is something that we can also use to unify the varied nature of the maximalism investigated in this book. I have attempted to provide a demonstration of the complexities of maximalist poetics in the work of three American novelists. But I have also aimed to show that these writers appraise and critique their own use of maximalism and their status as maximalist authors. The results have been varied, but I mean to suggest that they probably *should* be, owing to nature of the topic. I have not tried to provide a survey of a particular kind of text, or to produce a neat narrative of literary history, but instead attempted to show how maximalism, an ever-present approach to writing, has recently become prominent in ways that draw attention to how and why we read, write, and value novels in the current cultural environment. I find maximalism an especially useful vehicle for such considerations as it's a style of writing that forces us to reflect on many of the fundamental activities involved in the production and reception of texts, and can thus bring us very close to what is immediately "at stake" in literary experiences. To return to the example with which I began this book, a stubborn description of a banal wall of useless photographs will certainly make us ask why the writer is bothering to provide it, but also why we are taking so much care to read it attentively. In these moments, the writer is, in a sense, speaking directly to us about the activity that is the basis of his employment. He simply seems to *write*, and wants us, in return, to stay with the text in the moment of its unfolding.

Elif Batuman has suggested that a sense of shame haunts all writers in the contemporary world because literary writing is inherently "impractical." Writing "doesn't directly cure disease, combat injustice, or make enough money, usually, to support philanthropic aims."[4] And yet it's still undeniably valuable. As Karen Tei Yamashita writes in her novel *I Hotel*, the desire to write and record the details of the world is often an "obsessive trait," having "nothing to do with talent or giftedness," persisting as an "enigma" to which we attach other values in the hope of explanation:

> You say, I want to be famous; I want to be remembered; I want to speak; I want to communicate; I want to imagine; I want to remember.

But writing itself is a strange way to accomplish any of that stuff, sitting alone for hours with a pen and paper or typewriter.[5]

Whatever else it is, maximalism is certainly an expression of obsessive writing and recording. But, in maximalist works, we also get the sense that a writer is trying to celebrate the activity of writing in something akin to its rawest sense. Stravinsky's aggregate chord beckoned chromatic exhaustion; in its literary form, such weariness is also the birth of new possibilities, but ones that refocus our attention back to what writing is an activity before it becomes a culturally and economically valuable object. Here is a person sitting still, the maximalist novel seems to say, typing at a keyboard or writing on paper in an act so outwardly simple and useless, yet that can capture the brilliance of human ability nonetheless.

Yamashita and the Maximalist Mainstream

The fantasy of complete inclusion provided by the aggregate chord is relevant to this book in another manner—namely, the necessity of exclusions. There has been much that has exceeded the scope of this study, which has not been able to sound anything close to the complete tonal range of maximalist literature, and nor has it tried. To some extent, semblances of coherency only become possible with exclusions, and much of what I have been able to posit throughout this book has relied on the limiting of scope and breadth. Although it would have been possible to devote chapters to the works of William T. Vollmann, Don DeLillo, John Barth, Joseph McElroy, and others, to do so would have not allowed the room to focus on the evolving engagement with maximalist poetics that each of my chosen authors demonstrate. My point here was not just to give a survey, but to show how the maximalist approach to the writing of novels often creates a narrative of its own throughout particular works.

Much of the writing I have looked at in *Maximalism in Contemporary American Literature* has a close relationship with the industry of criticism and the institutionalization of literature in general, so any historical account of maximalism that takes into account more than the current scene would need to be conscious of the way maximalist poetics function in relation to the criticism and institutional values of earlier generations, paying attention to the different meanings and uses of excess throughout intellectual history and across different territories. This is because the history of maximalist writing is inseparable from the history of how critics and readers have thought about the place of detail in the form of the novel. It is only in the post-Pynchon environment that maximalist writing has become an easily valued literary commodity because of there being a more obvious reason than authorial indulgence for the presence of excessive detail in novels. The perceived arrival of the "information age" makes the presence of maximalist amounts of detail seem purposeful rather than superfluous. It's not just that there is a formal homology between a society flooded by data and a detailed novel, but that, most often, the writer of detailed novels offers readers pleasing fantasies of intelligence and ability. Slothrop casting his gigantic shadow across the German landscape—a scene covered in my discussion of *Gravity's Rainbow*—is instructive here. No one needs a novel to tell them that we live in a world overfull with information; they might need a novelist to tell them how to come to grips with this place, however, and few set better examples than Pynchon, Wallace, and Baker. Overdetailed novels have typically been derided by critics as decadent, but contemporary novelists embrace specificity without feeling obliged to make description subordinate to narration. This is largely because readers today recognize that an ability to "humanize" our relationship to information and nonhuman things—something that comes, inevitably, through their treatment as primary objects of consideration in novels—is comforting. A passion for detail is not new in literature, but today's readers tolerate it in a new way.

At the center of the contemporary popularity of maximalism is the return of the figure of the author. That this author often happens to be male, white, and North American is not insignificant. There are examples of nontypical maximalist authors, of course, which we'll look at later, but accounts of maximalism tend to be occupied by men. Is maximalist writing then also *male* writing? I'm not sure what it really means to say a style of writing is connected with a gender because such statements not only depend upon essentialist and stereotyped understandings of gender identity but also quickly enough lead to value judgments. The implied point of saying that there aren't many women maximalists might be that women *can't* write maximalist novels because of some failure of ability. Such a claim is, of course, silly. Could we ask, instead, if male and female novelists are socialized to write differently? Possibly; it's difficult, if not impossible, to prove, but one might expect that women and men are taught to value and express experience differently in a manner that affects how they approach writing novels. Tom LeClair has argued that the works of Pynchon and similar writers are able to express mastery of the contemporary environment because, being male and white, these writers are allowed privileged access to a broader range of knowledge and tools than marginalized authors, or at least don't see clear limits to what is part of "their" culture (having what LeClair calls a "full membership" to American culture).[6] But we might also say that the desire *to appear* polymathic lies at the heart of these novels, rather than a genuine mastery of the full range of cultural discourses, and that this desire to appear supremely knowledgeable is perhaps an effect of occupying a dominant subject position.

This returns us to an idea I suggested at the beginning of this book—that these maximalist novels are perhaps also novels of the "mainstream" North American experience, with all of the problems that this term implies. Mainstream is, of course, a deeply problematic concept in that it performs that which it claims to describe: in "observing" a mainstream one erases individual differences, forcing others into the margins so that one can pretend to see an object which is often not much more than a tendentious articulation of one's own viewpoint. While the notion of a mainstream has obvious problems, it still holds some heuristic value when we use it to assert a knowingly hazy abstraction, or are at least aware of the "positionality" inseparable from the term. Wallace's novels are set in educational institutions and the IRS; Baker's are set in shopping malls and domestic homes; although Pynchon's novels range the globe, ostensibly offering rebuttals to the mainstream of American culture, they have nevertheless found a place in the center of the contemporary literary canon, their subversiveness contained as an effect of a hippy counterculture now understood to be part of mainstream America's social history. So it's fair to say that these settings and themes are familiar to large portions of American society, and they also reveal that these writers occupy subject positions that allow them to be comfortable covering dominant cultural landmarks and institutions. This "mainstream" position perhaps also accounts for the ethic of inclusivity exhibited in their works. The desire for specificity apparent on the sentence level of maximalist writing often extends to a broader desire to articulate marginalized areas of cultural experience, but perhaps only as confirmation that these authors reside comfortably in the center of a culture from which they are able to dabble safely in the experiences of the marginalized without losing themselves in the peripheries for too long. Pynchon's novels are interested in African, African-American, and other "nonwhite" characters; Wallace's *Infinite Jest* contains an awkward and somewhat token monolog from an African-American character; Baker's *Room Temperature* places a man in a typically female domestic environment. This desire to articulate the "full range" of a culture is perhaps where these texts are most mainstream, by which I mean they are written from a position that feels impelled toward the inclusion of diversity as a way of accounting for the felt privileges of being part of the mainstream. To appear inclusive is a luxury available to those from a cultural position who find little need to argue for the legitimacy of their own (already) dominant one. I take this as one way to read the awkward "Wardine" monolog in *Infinite Jest*,[7] in which the fumbled representation of an African-American character might be a parody of white writers' attempts to appear culturally inclusive as much as it seems a failed example of this same imperative.

An example of a maximalist novel written by a female author engages with this gendered nature of maximalist writing, but also demonstrates the difficulty an arguably marginalized writer faces achieving success with the maximalist form. Karen Tei Yamashita's *I Hotel* begins, significantly, in the wake of a polymath father's death. Paul Lin's father has passed away and left behind an apartment full of books, paintings, and clothes. In the bookshelves that cover every wall are works in "Chinese, English, and French," volumes on "Chinese literature, painting, ancient and contemporary Chinese, Western and American history, philosophy, politics and religion:"

> Books are open to selected pages, annotated in the margins, wedged in every cranny of available space in the room. And behind everything else, stacked in the corners are painted canvases. ... Everything is the same as it's always been. He can't remember his mother's feminine touch, her tidy ways. It's all forgotten. He looks back at the torn leather on his dad's old reading chair, and the way the wood floor is worn from the chair to the desk.[8]

In the bedroom are more books, canvasses, and clothes. Yamashita is here describing her position in relation to the gendered past of maximalism. Interestingly, the masculine grappling with polymathy is here seen as leading toward decay and disorder rather than power. But Yamashita's book also intends to transgress the neatness associated with the "feminine touch" of Paul's mother. Instead of the "tidy ways" expected of the female writer, this novel styles itself after the messiness of the father, transgressing into "masculine" disorder.

Rather than a novel of the putative American mainstream, *I Hotel* is a text that tries to reshape the mainstream understanding of American history by inserting the experience of Asian-Americans into the narrative of the civil rights era. To some extent, Yamashita imagines herself in the position of Paul Lin, left sorting through cultural artifacts to piece together a guiding narrative. Early in the novel Paul starts doing editorial work to help republish works of Asian-American writers, and this also seems to mirror the position Yamashita found herself in, bringing the stories of this population to life through her research. The novel remains deliberately fractured, however, and the individual polymath trying to filter a range of sources through his individual perspective—the figure that unites the varied nature of the typical maximalist novel—is replaced in this work by a collective of characters attempting to tell a collective assemblage of stories. Divided into ten relatively separate novellas linked by the landmark of the book's title, *I Hotel* is often dense with detail and contains a vast array of characters, styles, and modes of delivery that refuse to offer a simplified and centered narrative, preferring the disorder and chaos of a detailed multitude.

Yamashita uses maximalism to comment on the political purpose of her novel's content, showing the immense amount of historical information that is left out of mainstream accounts of history. The density of the text and its large cast of characters create the impression that the novelist is here battling between the needs of historical research and the aesthetic form of the novel. Yamashita seems to give voice to this concern in the latter half of *I Hotel*:

> When it's all said and done, you might have a compilation of events, and you might have a story with meaning. Someone says, don't worry

about the details, just get the stories. Someone else says, get the details and the hard facts, and then you can build a case for a story.[9]

There are certainly a lot of details in the text, and the range of styles, forms, and modes of delivery that present them represent Yamashita's search for the most forceful way of telling the many stories that make up the diverse and overlooked culture of its subjects. From a formalist perspective, her use of a range of textual approaches seems to suggest an endless search to find a mode that will allow these stories to gather the force and weight that they deserve. But the variousness also suggests the inevitable failure—or at least endless difficulty—of this act. The disorder of the text is not so much liberatory as pained, a testament to the struggle of these voices to find a solid and settled articulation in the narrative of American history. The unsettledness of the text reminds readers that Yamashita's project is ongoing and can't afford the complacency of having only one approach to storytelling.

But the maximalist style and form is also one of the weaknesses of *I Hotel*. The experimental nature of the novel does tend to estrange and obfuscate what is already an overlooked and unclear historical archive, thus replicating the marginalization of its subject matter in the difficulty of the book's form. The general lack of familiarity with the novel's subject matter—what, on one hand, makes it such a necessary book—means that the fractured and deliberately opaque nature of the text can push readers further away, and thus work against the novel's political purpose, which is, we can assume, to increase familiarity with the marginalized struggles of Asian Americans. The novel's maximalism does enable Yamashita to *perform* the struggle of rewriting the historical consciousness of a nation. This is a difficult and messy book because this is the nature of the task Yamashita has set herself, refusing the fantasy of a simple and simplified narrative. But this perhaps comes at the cost of the text's outward social and political purpose. Marginalized experience is perhaps not well-suited to the maximalist mode of inquiry because maximalism's estranging effects, at least as Yamashita uses them, risk further obfuscating subject matter that already lies outside the mainstream.

Knausgaard, Bolaño, and a Global Maximalism

My focus throughout *Maximalism in Contemporary American Literature* has been on North American writing. This is not because this is the only location in which maximalist novels have been written, but the North American strain of maximalist writing does seem the most prominent, or at least the place in which maximalist novelists have been able to achieve the most success, as seen in the considerable celebrity of Wallace and Pynchon.[10] The renown of these maximalists has also surely emboldened writers and readers from other nations.

We can turn to Karl Ove Knausgaard's *My Struggle* series as an example of the progress of contemporary maximalist fiction outside of North

America, but also to see how non-American maximalism is used for different purposes. Knausgaard is a Norwegian author whose fame has come on the back of a series of putatively autobiographical novels. What makes the novels so fascinating, at least according to reviewers, is Knausgaard's obsession with detail. As Ben Lerner puts it:

> Most critics attempt to demonstrate a novelist's perceptiveness by providing examples of his eye for the significant detail. But part of what makes Knausgaard's writing unusual is that he seems barely to adjudicate significance; he's like a child who has taken Henry James's injunction to novelists—"be one of the people on whom nothing is lost"—literally; he appears to just write down everything he can recall (and he appears to recall everything).[11]

Like Baker and Wallace, Knausgaard is often fascinated with banal details. Descriptions of the weather, house interiors, and traffic proliferate, as do long catalogs of household objects:

> Ten minutes later I put a bucket of steaming water, a bottle of Klorin and a bottle of Jif down on the floor by the bath. I shook the bin bag I had brought with me to open it, then started clearing everything from the bathroom. First of all, the stuff on the floor: dried-up bits of old soap, sticky shampoo bottles, toilet roll tubes, the brown-stained loo brush, medical packaging—silver paper and plastic—a few loose pills, a sock or two, the odd hair curler. After finishing this, I emptied everything out of the wall cupboard apart from two expensive-looking bottles of perfume. Blades, safety razors, hairpins, several bars of soap, desiccated creams and ointments, a hair net, aftershave, deodorants, eyeliners, lipsticks, some small cracked powder puffs—not sure what they were used for, but it must have been something to do with make-up—and hairs, both short curly ones and longer straighter ones, nail scissors, a roll of plasters, dental floss and combs.[12]

Although there is a feeling that such details are trivial and their inclusion arbitrary, they nevertheless invest the works with a quality of necessity. The above scene occurs soon after Knausgaard's narrator (who we take to be Knausgaard himself) learns about the death of his father and sets about cleaning the messy interior of the house in which he lived. The focus on the details of leftover bathroom products mirrors the intention of Knausgaard in this novel to move closer to the interior of an aloof and often difficult father. But there is a double movement in this passage: on the one hand, Knausgaard is removing these objects, yet by recording them in his novel in such a foregrounded manner he is also preserving them. The details offer a gesture of intimacy: this is the detritus of novelistic interest, those objects which ordinarily are kept hidden from sight in bathroom cupboards and that likewise fall beneath the threshold of narrative relevance, but which here occupy it unashamedly.

What seems to make the detailedness of Knausgaard's work so engaging for readers is its involvement in two related effects—one of power and one of intimacy. Here is a writer that can describe in detail what he supposedly had for breakfast thirty years ago, and also one that refuses to filter out those aspects of his private life otherwise seen as unfit for public consumption. The fascination with Knausgaard's work appears motivated by these fantasies of masterly memory and intense intimacy that, when combined, appeal to the desires of today's readers. This twin hope of complete recall and closeness is also what we can observe when Knausgaard himself sorts through his father's bathroom junk in the above scene. The novel records compulsively, and compulsively discloses aspects of life usually hidden from the center of novelistic focus.

In her review of the second book in the *My Struggle* series, Sheila Heti describes a disillusioning conversation she once had with Knausgaard regarding a description of his mother peeling potatoes. Heti asked if "that was a real memory—your mother scrubbing potatoes in the sink that night—or did you make it up?" Knausgaard replied that the detail was invented, and Heti became so disappointed that she was "unable to pick up his books for another year."[13] If *A Man in Love* is not fiction, then it contains an unusually intense focus on those details that need to be invented owing to the limitations of human memory. The level of detail throughout the work goes so far beyond the needs of verisimilitude or the plausibility of recall that the bulk of the book is detailed *invention* rather than anything that is being truly remembered. But because it is offered as a "true" story, the effect of the book is to generate an excessive pleasure in the (fantasized) power of the author's memory nevertheless—one that caused Heti to be so deflated upon learning of its fictitiousness. What is most fictional about Knausgaard's work, perhaps, is this portrait it gives of a writer able to recall with eidetic precision exactly what detritus filled his grandmother's house or how his mother prepared dinner on one particular evening. And Knausgaard is perhaps part of the last generation of writers for whom the return to the past will be an act that relies primarily on the powers of human memory and "analog" archival materials, so the fascination with his supposed recall of detail is probably motivated in part by a feeling that human memory is becoming displaced by technological memory in the digital age. The proliferation of personal records in the age of the internet—photographs, videos, and written artefacts easily stored, searched, and retrieved on hard drives and the "cloud"—can have the effect of fetishizing powers of "analog" memory at the same time as it draws its weaknesses. The close recall of personal events and locations from one's childhood might not be so impressive for those readers of the future who have grown up with an extensive and easily searchable digital-media archive of some sort, and so Knausgaard's performance of superhuman recall is something akin to the curtain call for heroic acts of "pure" remembering.

The impression of intimacy that detail allows is the function that Knausgaard intends most, however. In a recent essay in *The New Yorker* adapted from an acceptance speech for a German literary award, Knausgaard wrote about the "sheer volume of images" that typifies our age, and that has the effect of numbing us to reality, turning people into numbers and statistics rather than human beings with complex emotions and relationships. It's a familiar critique of the postmodern media society, but Knausgaard uses it to mount a defense of the place of detail in the novel. The novel is, for Knausgaard, "an oddly intimate genre: at root, it is always a matter between two individuals, writer and reader."[14] For Knausgaard, news reportage is often in the business of abstracting individuals so that they lose their particularity and become mere numbers, statistics, images, and bits of Big Data, whereas the novel aims to create an idiosyncratic space in which the reader is able to engage with other individuals in all of their particularity and strangeness. There are problems with his argument, not the least in forgetting that the novel, like other media, is involved in the same standardization that "protects us from reality" as much as it reminds us of its presence. But his main point is that by focusing on the particular and peculiar details that make up a person, rather than on the broad strokes of a life painted by Big Data, we encourage an intimacy that is also an ethical engagement with other humans. For it is the lack of focus on the particulars of each individual's life that enables catastrophes of human care like the holocaust to occur:

> But such a perspective, whereby we view human beings as part of a mass rather than as unique individuals, may also be a strategy by which soldiers are trained so as to be able to kill, and it is a prerequisite of all massacres, as it was, for instance, in the Germany of the Second World War, when the Jews were deprived of their identity, first at the national, then the individual level, their names replaced by numbers, each individual scraped into the nameless, faceless mass to be slaughtered like sheep or cattle, gassed or burned as creatures without identity. And of course the same goes for the inhabitants of Dresden or Hiroshima, wiped out by bombs from above, but tiny dots to their executioners, figures in a calculation thereby concluded.[15]

These are novels that use a maximalist mode of inquiry to offer readers a feeling of intimate connection with the particulars of an individual's life. They "zoom in" toward intimate details rather than pull back to appraise the entirety of a culture, as in the encyclopedic fiction of Mendelson's account, but are just as detailed as the works of Joyce, Pynchon, or Wallace.

When Knausgaard writes with a maximalist attention to detail, readers also stand to become aware of his novels as compositional acts. The too-many details draw attention to his novels as *written* objects, the product of one individual's labor. The maximalist book becomes something like a dereified object, reminding readers of the work and effort that has gone into its production, and preserving the traces of its creator. It's not what the details reflect that is important, so much as what their presence reminds us: that there has been someone writing here, engaged in an activity that is giving value to our lives. Through this noticing a different kind of intimacy occurs.

As a Norwegian, Knausgaard comes from a much different literary heritage than Pynchon, Baker, and Wallace (although they surely share some influences; it's naïve to think literary cultures are geographically separate). Knausgaard's use of maximalism to investigate personal history without obvious traces of what McGurl has called "technomodernism"—the cultural capital that comes through exhibiting technological know-how, common to all of the American writers studied here—does prove my point that maximalism is not *only* a reaction to the information age, or at least is not just a style that attempts to map a cultural landscape through mimesis. The maximalist management of detail gains particular cultural value in the information age because of the effect it has of, among other things, aligning writing with postindustrial conceptions of productivity and assuaging doubt about the power of the human mind in the age of the internet, but maximalist writing isn't overdetailed simply because there is an excess of detail and information filling our culture. Knausgaard's relative disinterest in technology and cultures of consumption, compared to Pynchon, Wallace, and Baker, does suggest that these things loom especially large in the American imagination more than the Scandinavian one, and it's notable that in Knausgaard's description of bathroom objects quoted previously that there are no brand names cited, which is an extra layer of information and detail that preoccupies the work of American maximalists. To generalize ambitiously, we could suggest that the American relationship to detail appears inseparable from a critique of American capitalism, whereas the Scandinavian one is more invested in the use of detail to capture the complexities of an individual's life and to promote the public discussion of private experience. In this regard, Knausgaard seems more influenced by the maximalism of Marcel Proust and similar European writers, rather than those from the American tradition.

Roberto Bolaño's towering novel *2666* is another prominent example that comes to mind of a recent maximalist work from outside North America, although this time in a more direct relationship with writers from that nation. *2666*'s length and range certainly bring to mind North American maximalist writers from Melville to Pynchon (Bolaño notes Melville's influence in the novel when one of his characters laments that bookish readers are today "afraid to take on the great, imperfect, torrential works," preferring *Bartleby* over *Moby-Dick*[16]), and its use of detail and specificity align it with the maximalist mode of inquiry described throughout this study. There are plenty of long novels being written, but few that use detail with such deliberate purpose.

2666 is set in the fictionalized Santa Teresa, a city increasingly overwhelmed by the murder of almost innumerable women. The crimes seem unsolvable primarily because of their excessive number: there are so many victims over such a long period, and so many potential murderers, that the crimes appear impossible to unify unless an almost supernaturally gargantuan culprit is found. Some suspects are identified, but they are mostly petty ones, jaded lovers or husbands or drunks, men whose outward circumstances fail to satisfy the vision of grand evil the crimes seem to demand. Of course, it is possible that all the murders *are* performed by others like these men, because the crimes and culprits are so varied that the idea of there being a unifying principle, a single killer or cause, is a fantasy crept into the world from detective fiction. Indeed, the most correct possibility seems the presence of a widespread culture of violence against women. But the other, more seductive suspicion cannot help but persist, that there is a unifying point, "a chaotic center of gravity ... that would shake us to the core if ever we were to experience it" (174). The crimes become enmeshed with the tropes of the sublime and project a "gigantic" figure at their center, not unlike the readers of Pynchon's novel who fantasize about the polymath author controlling all aspects of his texts. Like *Gravity's Rainbow*, this is a novel about the need to temper complexity with the fantasy of a single, gigantic "author."

Although the killer is the desired center of the novel, what really occupies the heart of *2666* is its longest and most confronting section, "The Part About the Crimes." This fourth section of the book is committed to outlining—often in clinical detail—the seemingly innumerable victims of the murders. The section is stubborn in its refusal to overlook, and continues to record and describe the victims in relatively disconnected sections, without providing much in the way of narrative. Stylistically, "The Part About the Crimes" bares more affinities with record-keeping than narrative art.

The section's density and tedium forces its reader to face the ethical quandary at the heart of the murders; that is, Bolaño's maximalist approach to writing performs the challenge of empathy that the crimes present. Readers might want to skip forward to the next section of the novel once they realize that 300 pages or so are going to partake of this repetitive form. But to do so would be to fail the challenge that Bolaño sets for us. To skip forward is to overlook the victims in favor of the other seductions of narrative. By hearing about *all* the murders that occur over a five-year period (indeed, it would require a work of scholarship just to count how many deaths actually are listed in this section of the book), we are forced to elevate these victims to more than incidental matter. We are forced to face them not as details that help create a more appealing narrative center, but *as* the center. The bodies refuse to move out of the novel's focus or allow it to focus on other things. Presenting all the available knowledge of the crimes is seen as a form of justice to the victims, those individuals who ordinarily become nothing more than clues designed to lead readers toward the goal of detective fiction. The victims are overpresent, and in a way that refuses to serve the typical narrative interests of the novel.

In the other maximalist novels studied here, details are most often equated with objects, which fits the historical trajectory of detailed writing outlined in the work of Janell Watson, Cynthia Wall,[17] and others. In such accounts, details invade the novel at the same time as objects of mass consumption invade the spaces of life. Detailed writing that pays attention to objects also challenges, in these accounts, the manner in which information in novels is structured according to the traditional hierarchy between description and narration. Description gets equated with objects and thus the nonhuman, whereas narration is associated with human action and vitality. In Baker's work, the risk of equating "things" with trivial details is shown, as such an equation neglects the importance of the very human interactions we have with objects.

In Bolaño's novel, however, as in the work of Knausgaard, the danger of relegating *people* to the status of details is on display. Both writers seem interested in the holocaust as a watershed moment for the collapsing of humans into details (part 5 of 2666 is set in Europe during World War II and contains a particularly confronting account of a Nazi's management of a trainload of Greek Jews[18]), and see this process as a general trend in the contemporary world. When we only see people as statistics that make up grand narrative arcs, we narrate without humanity. Raising the description of people into the foreground often problematizes the ability to present a typically "moving" narrative, but it does allow us to appreciate the struggles of overlooked individuals. It is, of course, ironic that maximalism is used to achieve such results—a mode of inquiry linked to excess and giganticness employed to give attention to the overlooked and trivial.

Closing Particulars

This book has shown that, when placed alongside each other, the works of Pynchon, Wallace, and Baker respond (or at least provoke a response) to uncertainty about the directions, uses, and techniques of recent literary production and reception. In the work of all three authors, maximalism is employed to encourage readers to reinvest their experience of the contemporary world with an enthusiasm and confidence that seems missing in many other approaches to novel writing in recent decades. If there is a progression to note here, it is toward a less anxious engagement with the contemporary world, or at least the recognition of possibilities other than difficulty and insufficiency that overdetailedness can offer the form of the novel. Wallace perhaps offers the best example of this development. In *Infinite Jest*, much of the text's maximalism expresses weariness with literary interpretation, taking pleasure in presenting details that will not be transformed into usable matter. Like the AA attendees in the novel who are asked to accept the surface value of clichés, we are often asked to read in a manner that views the text only as a surface—a dense collection of signs rather than an invitation for "professional" work. But while this novel's maximalist descriptions are sometimes employed to frustrate literary value and express ambivalence with the process of textual "interviews," in *The Pale King,* Wallace comes to see a more positive application for detailedness. The activity of writing, of noticing and paying attention to the specifics, is now to be seen as something of a therapeutic process, and one that doesn't need to be translated into the terms of a parallel cultural discourse (science, psychology, etc.) for it to have an effect. In *The Pale King,* what writing represents is not terribly important (as shown by Wallace's choice of the most unmoving and deliberately dull subject matter). Instead, readers are asked to appreciate the experiences implied by the writing and enforced on those engaged with it. Here the novelist is asking for the basic activity of writing to be seen as worthwhile and socially useful. The activities it encourages—paying attention, working slowly and patiently—can be valuable enough without having to connect the writing to "important" social and cultural issues, something the "shame" Batuman noted previously often motivates us to do. In this respect, the maximalist novel attempts to redefine the way texts connect to the world. It's not Lukácsian "reflection" that matters for these artworks so much as the example their maximalist mode of inquiry sets for negotiating a complex reality in which a lack of interest, engagement, depth, and transparency are felt to be problems.

In the two Pynchon novels studied here we can discern a similar progression. In *Gravity's Rainbow,* Pynchon's maximalism is probably best described as anxious. It is used to portray the feelings of insufficiency permeating the diegetic world of the text. But it also, inevitably, stands to offer a somewhat dubious route to safety, a way out of all the chaos the novel dramatizes and enforces on its readers. Although the text is careful to frustrate all hermeneutic avenues of escape, the implied knowledge held by its author, who is seen as being able to conquer the "modern diversity," offers a fantasy of intellect that runs contrary to what is otherwise the text's slipperiness. As a result, *Gravity's Rainbow* becomes a textual field in which various readerly fantasies and competitive maneuvers are allowed to operate.

By the time of *Inherent Vice,* Pynchon seems far less anxious about the directions and possibilities of literary interpretation. Focalizing the novel through Doc Sportello, Pynchon encourages readers to embrace insufficiency because there are no other "minds" guiding the text beside Doc's own. The novel promotes a sense of calm, an encouragement to "surf" the complexities of contemporary life, rather than escape them. *Inherent Vice* also refuses many of the uses of detail with which Pynchon's readers have become familiar.

Baker's work is slightly more difficult to situate in this developmental narrative because it seems, from the outset, to already encourage a positive embrace of the maximalist mode of inquiry. We get the sense from these works that Baker's narrators approach the construction of their texts in largely the same way Baker would have us approach our lives. Again, here the use value of the literary object is very close to the method of its construction. Although the two novels studied here seem outwardly similar, there is an important progression between them, one that aims to intensify maximalism, employing its mode of inquiry to tackle ineffability and aspects of experience often fetishized for their indeterminacy. In *Room Temperature*, maximalism is shown to have the power not just to scrutinize objects, but to tackle aspects of thought and feeling felt to lie in excess of "discourse."[19]

If we wanted to reach for a broader contextualization of this development of maximalism away from discomfort and insufficiency, we could suggest that it points toward a redrawing of the use value of literary objects in today's cultural economy. Although David Letzler has argued that novels such as *Infinite Jest* require us to "develop our abilities to filter information to their maximum capacities," forcing us to "navigate around their junk text to the text that is more important,"[20] much of the maximalism we've studied here encourages an appreciation of the overlooked, this "junk text." The point of *The Pale King* and Baker's work, for instance, is to discover the way important information often disguises itself as what Letzler calls "cruft." These texts overlook (or look too much) to encourage us *not* to overlook any of their particulars and to find worth in what might otherwise be flagged for deletion. To frame the situation in Barthes' terms, these are textual objects that force us to consider that the catalyses of life can have *cardinal* importance.[21]

The repeated push in these novels to have the work of the writer appreciated more for what it is—a record of a person sitting and writing, exercising his or her concentration and organizational skills—than for what it "reflects," relates to this attempt to reconfigure the use-value of the literary object. To understand maximalism in the contemporary literary environment is to refocus our view of the role of the writer and his work. We shift away from the notion of writers who reflect a world in a meaningful or masterly way, toward the significance and usefulness of the mode of inquiry their texts model. Despite my initial weariness of linking contemporary American maximalism too strongly with social context, then, what we've arrived at here is an understanding of how the style offers approaches to detail that we might use to overcome some of the difficulties of living in the putative information age. In one way or another, all of these novels encourage methods of coping, which is perhaps an area in which the literature of a postindustrial society can find a clear purpose again, overcoming anxiety about the novel's marginalization.

Notes

1. Taruskin, *Western Music*, 192.
2. Ibid., 5.
3. Ibid., 192.
4. Elif Batuman, "Get a Real Degree," *London Review of Books* 32, no. 8 (2010), http://www.lrb.co.uk/v32/n18/elif-batuman/get-a-real-degree.

5. Yamashita, *I Hotel*, 95.

6. LeClair, *The Art of Excess*, 29.

7. Wallace, *Infinite Jest*, 37–38.

8. Yamashita, *I Hotel*, 3–4.

9. Yamashita, *I Hotel*, 414.

10. This is, of course, not to say that all or even most North-American maximalist novels achieve or desire mainstream literary success. The "uncreative writing" of Kenneth Goldsmith, including *Soliloquy* and the *Weather, Traffic,* and *Sports* books, are certainly maximalist in their approach to detail, yet have little interest in conventional literary success. Goldsmith claims, for instance, that he doesn't have a "readership," only a "thinkership" interested in the conceptual underpinnings of his work. Quoted in Alec Wilkinson, "Something Borrowed," *The New Yorker*, October 5, 2015, http://www.newyorker.com/magazine/2015/10/05/something-borrowed-wilkinson.

11. Ben Lerner, "Each Cornflake," *London Review of Books* 36, no. 10 (2014), http://www.lrb.co.uk/v36/n10/ben-lerner/each-cornflake.

12. Karl Ove Knausgaard, *A Death in the Family*, trans. Don Bartlett (London: Vintage Books, 2013), 283–84.

13. Sheila Heti, "So Frank," *London Review of Books* 36, no. 1 (2014), http://www.lrb.co.uk/v36/n01/sheila-heti/so-frank.

14. Karl Ove Knausgaard, "Vanishing Point," *The New Yorker*, November 17, 2015, http://www.newyorker.com/books/page-turner/vanishing-point.

15. Knausgaard, "Vanishing Point."

16. Roberto Bolaño, *2666*, tr. Natasha Wimmer (London: Picador, 2009), 227.

17. Watson, *Literature and Material Culture*. Cynthia Wall, *The Prose of Things: Transformations of Description in the Eighteenth Century* (Chicago: University of Chicago Press, 2006).

18. Bolaño, *2666*, 752–66.

19. Baker's oeuvre is far from settled, and a disappointing omission from this book has been his later foray into erotica. Such works, the most interesting and confronting of which is *The Fermata* (1994), in which a man discovers that he can freeze time and thus embarks upon various sexual adventures, take the maximalist mode of inquiry outlined in Baker's first two novels into the domain of sexuality. These novels largely refuse to omit "unspeakable" details or censor themselves in any way, expressing the joy of writing openly about sexual experience. Reading them in relation to maximalism is a task for further study.

20. Letzler, "Cruft of Fiction," 321.

21. See Barthes, "Structural Analysis of Narrative," 247–48.

Bibliography

Allington, Daniel, Sarah Brouillette, and David Golumbia. "Neoliberal Tools (and Archives): A Political History of Digital Humanities." *Los Angeles Review of Books*, May 1, 2016, https://lareviewofbooks.org/article/neoliberal-tools-archives-political-history-digital-humanities/.

Alpers, Svetlana. *The Art of Describing: Dutch Art in the Seventeenth Century.* London: John Murray, 1983.

Anderson, Tore Rye. "Pay Attention! David Foster Wallace and his Real Enemies." *English Studies 95*, no. 1 (2014): 7–24.

Auster, Paul. *The New York Trilogy.* London: Faber and Faber, 1987.

Bacon, Francis. *The Advancement of Learning.* New York: Modern Library, 2010.

Baker, Nicholson. *The Mezzanine.* London: Granta, 1988.

———. *Room Temperature.* London: Granta, 1990.

———. *U and I: A True Story.* New York: Random House, 1991.

———. *The Fermata.* New York: Vintage Contemporaries, 1994.

———. *Double Fold: Libraries and the Assault on Paper.* New York: Random House, 2001.

———. *The Way the World Works: Essays.* New York: Simon & Schuster, 2012.

Barker-Nunn, Jeanne, and Gary Alan Fine. "The Vortex of Creation: Literary Politics and The Demise of Herman Melville's Reputation." *Poetics 26* (1998), 81–98.

Barth, John. "A Few Words About Minimalism." *The New York Times.* December 28, 1986.

Barthes, Roland. "Introduction to the Structural Analysis of Narrative." *New Literary History 6*, no. 2 (1975): 237–72.

———. *Image-Music-Text.* Translated by Stephen Heath. London: Fontana, 1977.

Beer, John. "William Gaddis." *Review of Contemporary Fiction 21*, no. 3 (2001): 69–110.

Bell, Daniel. *The Coming of Post-Industrial Society: A Venture in Social Forecasting.* London: Heinemann Educational, 1974.

Bewes, Timothy. *Reification, or The Anxiety of Late Capitalism.* London: Verso, 2002.

Bolaño, Roberto. *2666.* Translated by Natasha Wimmer. London: Picador, 2009.

Boswell, Marshall. "Trickle-Down Citizenship: Taxes and Civic Responsibility in David Foster Wallace's *The Pale King*." *Studies in the Novel 44*, no. 4 (2012): 464–79.

———. *Understanding David Foster Wallace.* Columbia, SC: University of South Carolina Press, 2003.

Brannon, Julie Sloan. *Who Reads Ulysses? The Common Reader and the Rhetoric of the Joyce Wars.* New York: Routledge, 2003.

Brown, Bill. "Thing Theory." *Critical Inquiry* 28, no. 1 (2001): 1–22.

Bruni, Frank. "The Grunge American Novel." *The New York Times Magazine*, March 24, 1996. https://www.nytimes.com/books/97/03/16/reviews/wallace-v-profile.html.

Burnham, Michelle. "Merchants, Money, and the Economics of 'Plain Style' in William Bradford's *Of Plymouth Plantation*." *American Literature* 72, no. 4 (2000): 695–720.

Carver, Raymond. *Cathedral: Stories*. New York: Vintage Books, 1984.

Chambers, Ross. "Meditation and the Escalator Principle: On Nicholson Baker's *The Mezzanine*." *Modern Fiction Studies* 40, no. 4 (1994): 765–806.

Clare, Ralph. "The Politics of Boredom and the Boredom of Politics in David Foster Wallace's *The Pale King*." *Studies in the Novel* 44, no. 4 (2012): 428–446.

Clinton, Alan. "Conspiracy of Commodities: Postmodern Encyclopedic Narrative and Crowdedness." *Rhizomes* 5 (2002). http://www.rhizomes.net/issue5/clinton.html.

Cohen, Samuel. "To Wish to Try to Sing to the Next Generation: *Infinite Jest's* History." In *The Legacy of David Foster Wallace*, edited by Samuel Cohen and Lee Konstantinou, 59–79. Iowa City: University of Iowa Press, 2012.

Cowart, David. *Thomas Pynchon: The Art of Allusion*. Carbondale: Southern Illinois University Press, 1980.

Culler, Jonathan. "The Hertzian Sublime." *MLN* 120, no. 5 (2005): 969–985.

Cunningham, Michael. "Letter from the Pulitzer Fiction Jury: What Really Happened This Year." *The New Yorker Online*, July 9, 2012. http://www.newyorker.com/online/blogs/books/2012/07/letter-from-the-pulitzer-fiction-jury-what-really-happened-this-year.html#ixzz2HWuTrDVu.

De Certeau, Michel. *The Practice of Everyday Life*. Translated by Steven Rendall. Berkeley: University of California Press, 1984.

DeLillo, Don. *White Noise*. London: Picador, 1984.

Delville, Michel, and Andrew Norris. "Frank Zappa, Captain Beefheart, and the Secret History of Maximalism." In *Contemporary Poetics*, edited by Louis Armand, 126–149. Evanston, IL: Northwestern University Press, 2007.

Duffin, Ross W. *How Equal Temperament Ruined Harmony (And Why You Should Care)*. New York: W.W. Norton & Co., 2007.

Eagleton, Terry. *The Ideology of the Aesthetic*. Oxford: Basil Blackwell, 1990.

Eggers, Dave. "America in 2010: Everyone's Hooked on Something." *The San Francisco Chronicle*, February 11, 1996.

Elias, Amy J. "History." In *The Cambridge Companion to Thomas Pynchon*, edited by Inger H. Dalsgaard, Luc Herman, and Brian McHale, 123–35. New York: Cambridge University Press, 2012.

Ercolino, Stefano. "The Maximalist Novel." *Comparative Literature* 64, no. 3 (2012): 241–256.

———. *The Maximalist Novel: From Thomas Pynchon's Gravity's Rainbow to Roberto Bolaño's 2666*. London: Bloomsbury Publishing, 2014.

Finn, Ed. "Becoming Yourself: The Afterlife of Reception." In *The Legacy of David Foster Wallace*, 151–176.

Fiske, John. *Understanding Popular Culture*. Boston: Unwin Hyman, 1989.

———. *Reading the Popular*. 2nd edition. Hoboken: Taylor & Francis, 2010.

Fitzpatrick, Kathleen. *The Anxiety of Obsolescence: The American Novel in the Age of Television*. Nashville, Vanderbilt University Press, 2006.

———. "Infinite Summer: Reading, Empathy, and the Social Network." In *The Legacy of David Foster Wallace*, 182–207.

Flaubert, Gustave. *Madame Bovary*. Translated by Gerard Hopkins. Oxford: Oxford University Press, 1981.

Franzen, Jonathan. "Ten Rules for Writing Fiction." *The Guardian*, February 20, 2010. http://www.guardian.co.uk/books/2010/feb/20/ten-rules-for-writing-fiction-part-one.

Gaddis, William. *The Recognitions*. London: Atlantic Books, 2003.

Gogarty, Oliver. "They Think They Know Joyce." In *James Joyce: The Critical Heritage*, edited Robert H. Deming, vol. 2. London: Routledge, 1970. 764–65.

Golumbia, David. *The Cultural Logic of Computation*. Cambridge, MA: Harvard University Press, 2009.

Gorz, André. *Critique of Economic Reason*. Translated by Gillian Handyside and Chris Turner. London: Verso, 1989.

Green, Jeremy. *Late Postmodernism: American Fiction at the Millennium*. New York: Palgrave Macmillan, 2005.

Greif, Mark. "'The Death of the Novel' and Its Afterlives: Toward a History of the 'Big, Ambitious Novel,'" *boundary 2* 36, no. 2 (2009): 11–30.

Grossman, Allen. "The Poetics of Union in Whitman and Lincoln: An Inquiry toward the Relationship of Art and Policy." In *The American Renaissance Reconsidered: Selected Papers from the English Institute, 1982–83*, edited by Walter Benn Michaels and Donald E. Pease, 183–208. Baltimore: The John Hopkins University Press, 1985.

Guetti, James. *The Limits of Metaphor: A Study of Melville, Conrad, and Faulkner*. Ithaca: Cornell University Press, 1967.

Hardack, Richard. "Consciousness without Borders: Narratology in *Against the Day* and the Works of Thomas Pynchon." *Criticism* 52, no. 1 (2010): 91–128.

Harman, Graham. *Tool-Being: Heidegger and the Metaphysics of Objects*. Peru, IL: Open Court Publishing, 2002.

Heidegger, Martin. *Being and Time*. Translated by John Macquarrie & Edward Robinson. Malden, MA: Blackwell Publishing, 1962.

———. *The Fundamental Concepts of Metaphysics: World, Finitude, Solitude*. Translated by William McNeill and Nicholas Walker. Bloomington: Indiana University Press, 1995.

Hertz, Neil. *The End of the Line: Essays on Psychoanalysis and the Sublime*. New York: Columbia University Press, 1985.

Heti, Sheila. "So Frank." *London Review of Books* 36, no. 1 (2014). http://www.lrb.co.uk/v36/n01/sheila-heti/so-frank.

Holland, Mary K. "'The Art's Heart's Purpose': Braving the Narcissistic Loop of David Foster Wallace's *Infinite Jest*." *Critique: Studies in Contemporary Fiction* 47, no. 3 (2006): 218–242.

House, Richard. "The Encyclopedia Complex: Contemporary Narratives of Information." *Substance* 29, no. 2 (2000): 25–46.

Hume, Kathryn. "The Religious and Political Vision of Pynchon's *Against the Day*." *Philological Quarterly* 86, no. 1/2 (2007): 163–87.

James, Henry. *The Art of the Novel: Critical Prefaces*. Chicago: University of Chicago Press, [1934] 2011.

Jameson, Fredric. *The Cultural Turn: Selected Writings on the Postmodern 1983–1998*. London: Verso, 1998.

———. *Jameson on Jameson: Conversations on Cultural Marxism*, edited by Ian Buchanan. Durham: Duke University Press, 2007.

———. "New Literary History after the End of the New." *New Literary History* 39, no. 3 (2008): 375–387.

———. *The Political Unconscious: Narrative as a Socially Symbolic Act*. London: Routledge, 1983.

———. *Postmodernism, or, The Cultural Logic of Late Capitalism*. Durham: Duke University Press, 1991.

Jay, Martin. *Marxism and Totality: The Adventures of a Concept from Lukács to Habermas*. Cambridge: Polity Press, 1984.

Johnson, Pauline. *Marxist Aesthetics*. Hoboken: Taylor and Francis, 2013.

Jones, Thomas. "Call it Capitalism." *London Review of Books* 31, no. 17 (2009). http://www.lrb.co.uk/v31/n17/thomas-jones/call-it-capitalism.

Kafka, Ben. *The Demon of Writing: Powers and Failures of Paperwork*. New York: Zone Books, 2012.

Kames, Lord. *Elements of Criticism*. New York: Johnson Reprint Corporation, 1967, 3 volumes.

Kant, Immanuel. *Critique of Judgment*. Translated by James Creed Meredith, edited and revised by Nicholas Walker. Oxford: Oxford University Press, 2007.

Karl, Frederick R. *American Fictions: 1980–2000: Whose America is it Anyway?* Bloomington: Xlibris, 2001.

Karnicky, Jeffrey. *Contemporary Fiction and the Ethics of Modern Culture*. New York: Palgrave Macmillan, 2007.

Katz, Steve. "Post Hoc Maximalism." *Guest Editor* 1 (1984).

Kelly, Adam. "David Foster Wallace: the Death of the Author and the Birth of a Discipline." *Irish Journal of American Studies Online* 2 (2010). http://www. ijasonline.com/Adam-Kelly.html.

Knausgaard, Karl Ove. *A Death in the Family*. Translated by Don Bartlett. London: Vintage Books, 2013.

———. "Vanishing Point." *The New Yorker*, November 17, 2015, http://www. newyorker.com/books/page-turner/vanishing-point.

Kuehl, John. *Alternate Worlds: A Study of Postmodern Antirealistic American Fiction*. New York: New York University Press, 1989.

Lacan, Jacques. *Écrits: A Selection*. Translated by Alan Sheridan. London: Routledge, 2001.

Lanham, Richard A. *The Economics of Attention: Style and Substance in the Age of Information*. Chicago: The University of Chicago Press, 2006.

Larsson, Don. "A *Companion's* Companion: Illustrated Additions and Corrections to Steven Weisenburger's *A Gravity's Rainbow Companion*." Accessed June 2, 2011. http://english2.mnsu.edu/larsson/grnotes.html.

LeClair, Tom. *The Art of Excess: Mastery in Contemporary American Fiction*. Urbana: University of Illinois Press, 1989.

Lerner, Ben. "Each Cornflake." *London Review of Books* 36, no. 10 (2014). http:// www.lrb.co.uk/v36/n10/ben-lerner/each-cornflake.

Letzler, David. "Encyclopedic Novels and the Cruft of Fiction: *Infinite Jest*'s Endnotes." *Studies in the Novel* 44, no. 3 (2012): 304–365.

Lipsky, David. *Although of Course You End Up Becoming Yourself: A Road Trip With David Foster Wallace*. New York: Broadway Books, 2010.

Liu, Alan. *The Laws of Cool: Knowledge Work and the Culture of Information*. Chicago: University of Chicago Press, 2004.

———. "Local Transcendence: Cultural Criticism, Postmodernism, and the Romanticism of Detail." *Representations* 32 (1990): 75–113.

Lukács, Georg. *History and Class Consciousness: Studies in Marxist Dialectics.* Translated by Rodney Livingstone. London: Merlin Press, 1971.

———. *The Meaning of Contemporary Realism.* Translated by John Mander and Necke Mander. London: Merlin Press, 1963.

———. *Writer and Critic, and Other Essays.* Translated and edited by Arthur Kahn. London: Merlin Press, 1978.

McCaffery, Larry. "An Expanded Interview with David Foster Wallace." In *Conversations with David Foster Wallace*, edited by Stephen J. Burn, 21–52. Jackson: University Press of Mississippi, 2012.

———. "An Interview with David Foster Wallace." *Review of Contemporary Fiction* 13, no. 2 (1993): 127–50.

McCarthy, Cormac. *Suttree.* London: Picador, [1979] 2010.

McCourt, John. *James Joyce in Context.* Cambridge: Cambridge University Press, 2009.

McGrath, Charles. "The Souped-Up, Knock-Out, Total Fiction Experience." *The New York Times*, April 17, 2005, C16.

McGurl, Mark. "The Institution of Nothing: David Foster Wallace in the Program." *boundary 2* 41, no. 3 (2014): 27–54.

———. *The Program Era: Postwar Fiction and the Rise of Creative Writing.* Cambridge, MA: Harvard University Press, 2009.

McHale, Brian. *Constructing Postmodernism.* London: Routledge, 1992.

Malewitz, Raymond. "Regeneration through Misuse: Rugged Consumerism in Contemporary American Culture." *PMLA* 127, no. 3 (2012): 526–41.

Mandel, Ernst. *Late Capitalism.* Translated by Joris De Bres. London: NLB, 1975.

Massumi, Brian. *Parables for the Virtual: Movement, Affect, Sensation.* Durham: Duke University Press, 2002.

Max, D.T. *Every Love Story is a Ghost Story: A Life of David Foster Wallace.* London: Granta, 2012.

Melley, Timothy. *Empire of Conspiracy: The Culture of Paranoia in Postwar America.* Ithaca: Cornell University Press, 2000.

Melville, Herman. "Letter to Lemuel Shaw," October 6, 1849. In *Correspondence: The Writings of Herman Melville*, edited by Lynn Horth, 139. Evanston and Chicago: Northwestern University and The Newberry Library, 1993.

Mendelson, Edward. "Encyclopedic Narrative: From Dante to Pynchon." *MLN* 91, no. 6 (1976): 1276–75.

Miller, D.A. *Narrative and Its Discontents: Problems of Closure in the Traditional Novel.* Princeton: Princeton University Press, 1981.

Moretti, Franco. *Graphs, Maps, Trees: Abstract Models for a Literary History.* London: Verso, 2005.

———. *Modern Epic: The World System from Goethe to Garcia Marquez.* Translated by Quintin Hoare. London: Verso, 1996.

Olsen, Lance. "Notes Toward the Musicality of Creative Disjunction, or: Fiction by Collage." *Symplokē* 12, no. 1/2 (2004): 130–35.

Paige, Nicholas D. *Before Fiction: The Ancien Régime of the Novel.* Philadelphia: University of Pennsylvania Press, 2011.

Paulson, William R. *The Noise of Culture: Literary Texts in a World of Information.* Ithaca: Cornell University Press, 1988.

Pöhlmann, Sascha, ed. *Against the Grain: Reading Pynchon's Counternarratives.* New York: Rodopi, 2010.

Potts, Robert. "In a Hall of Mirrors: David Foster Wallace's Less-Than-Final Text." *Times Literary Supplement*, Apr 15, 2011, 19–20.

Puttenham, George. *The Art of English Poesy: A Critical Edition*, edited by Frank Whigham and Wayne A. Rebhorn. Ithaca: Cornell University Press, [1589] 2007.

Pynchon, Thomas. *Against the Day*. London: Vintage Books, 2006.

———. *The Crying of Lot 49*. London: Vintage Books, [1965] 2000.

———. *Gravity's Rainbow*. New York: The Viking Press, 1973.

———. *Inherent Vice*. London: Jonathan Cape, 2009.

———. *Vineland*. London: Vintage Books, [1990] 2000.

Raban, Jonathan. "Divine Drudgery." *The New York Review of Books* 58, no. 8 (2011): 8–12.

Robinson, Marilynne. *Housekeeping*. London: Faber, 1981.

Rowberry, Simon Peter. "Reassessing the *Gravity's Rainbow* Pynchon Wiki: A New Research Paradigm?." *Orbit: Writing Around Pynchon* 1, no. 1 (2012): 1–25. DOI: http://doi.org/10.7766/orbit.v1.1.24.

Ruland, Richard, and Malcolm Bradbury. *From Puritanism to Postmodernism: A History of American Literature*. New York: Routledge, 1991.

Saltzman, Arthur M. "To See a World in a Grain of Sand: Expanding Literary Minimalism." *Contemporary Literature* 31, no. 4 (1990): 423–33.

———. *Understanding Nicholson Baker*. Columbia, SC: University of South Carolina Press, 1999.

Schaub, Thomas Hill. "*The Crying of Lot 49* and other California novels." In *The Cambridge Companion to Thomas Pynchon*. New York: Cambridge University Press, 2012. 30–43.

Schor, Naomi. *Reading in Detail: Aesthetics and the Feminine*. New York: Methuen, 1987.

Schryer, Stephen. *Fantasies of the New Class: Ideologies of Professionalism in Post-World War II American Fiction*. New York: Columbia University Press, 2011.

Sebald, W.G. *The Emigrants*. Translated by Michael Hulse. London: Vintage Books, 1996.

Severs, Jeffrey, and Christopher Leise, eds. *Pynchon's "Against the Day": A Corrupted Pilgrim's Guide*. Newark: University of Delaware Press, 2011.

Smith, Shawn. *Pynchon and History: Metahistorical Rhetoric and Postmodern Narrative Form in the novels of Thomas Pynchon*. New York: Routledge, 2005.

Spacks, Patricia Meyer. *Boredom: The Literary History of a State of Mind*. Chicago: The University of Chicago Press, 1995.

Spalding, William. *The History of English Literature: With an Outline of the Origin and Growth of the English Language. Illustrated by Extracts. For the Use of Schools and of Private Students*. Edinburgh: Oliver and Boyd, 1853.

Staes, Toon. "'Quaternionist Talk': Luddite Yearning and the Colonization of Time in Thomas Pynchon's *Against the Day*." *English Studies* 91, no. 5 (2010): 531–47.

St. Clair, Justin. "Binocular Disparity and Pynchon's Panoramic Paradigm." In *Pynchon's Against the Day: A Corrupted Pilgrim's Guide*, 119–55.

Tabbi, Joseph. *Postmodern Sublime: Technology and American Writing from Mailer to Cyberpunk*. Ithaca: Cornell University Press, 1995.

Tanner, Tony. *Thomas Pynchon*. London: Methuen, 1982.

Taruskin, Richard. *The Oxford History of Western Music*, volume 4, *Music in the Early Twentieth Century*. Oxford: Oxford University Press, 2005.

Teague, Ben. *A "Gravity's Rainbow Companion" Companion: Notes and Rebuttals to "A Gravity's Rainbow Companion."* Accessed June 1, 2011. http://www.benteague.com/books/titles/gravitys.html.

Twain, Mark. *The Adventures of Huckleberry Finn.* London: Vintage Books, 2007.

Veggian, Henry. "Anachronisms of Authority: Authorship, Exchange Value, and David Foster Wallace's *The Pale King.*" *boundary 2* 39, no. 3 (2012): 97–124.

———. "Thomas Pynchon *Against the Day.*" *boundary 2* 35, no. 1 (2008): 197–215.

———. *Understanding Don DeLillo.* Columbia, SC: University of South Carolina Press, 2015.

Wall, Cynthia. *The Prose of Things: Transformations of Description in the Eighteenth Century.* Chicago: University of Chicago Press, 2006.

Wallace, David Foster. *Brief Interviews with Hideous Men.* London: Abacus, 1999.

———. *The Broom of the System.* London: Abacus, 1987.

———. "E Unibus Pluram: Television and U.S. Fiction." *Review of Contemporary Fiction* 13, no. 2 (1993): 151–94.

———. *Girl with Curious Hair.* London: Abacus, 1989.

———. *Infinite Jest: A Novel.* New York: Back Bay Books, 1996.

———. *Oblivion: Stories.* London: Abacus, 2004.

———. *The Pale King: An Unfinished Novel.* London: Hamish Hamilton, 2011.

Watson, Janell. *Literature and Material Culture from Balzac to Proust: The Collection and Consumption of Curiosities.* Cambridge: Cambridge University Press, 1999.

Weisenburger, Stephen. *A "Gravity's Rainbow" Companion: Sources and Context's for Pynchon's Novel.* 2nd edition. Athens, GA: The University of Georgia Press, 2006.

Wilkinson, Alec. "Something Borrowed." *The New Yorker*, October 5, 2015, http://www.newyorker.com/magazine/2015/10/05/something-borrowed-wilkinson.

Willis, Susan. *A Primer for Daily Life.* London: Routledge, 1991.

Wilson, Rob. "On the Pacific Edge of Catastrophe, or Redemption: California Dreaming in Thomas Pynchon's *Inherent Vice.*" *boundary 2* 37, no. 2 (2010): 217–225.

Wood, James. "The Digressionist." *The New Republic*, Aug 9, 2004, 26–31.

———. *How Fiction Works.* London: Vintage, 2009.

———. "Human, All Too Inhuman: The Smallness of the 'Big' Novel." *The New Republic*, July 24, 2000, 41–45.

Yamashita, Karen Tei. *I Hotel.* Minneapolis: Coffee House Press, 2010.

Zelenak, Lawrence. "The Great American Tax Novel." *Michigan Law Review* 110, no. 6 (2012): 969–84.

Index

Amazon 132
Asian-American literature 28–9; 154–5
attention: and autonomy 105–6; economics of 85; and political agency 85, 91; and *The Pale King* 85–6, 88
authors: death of 24–5; and fantasies of ability 23–4, *see also* intelligence; return of 25, 152

Baker, Nicholson 7, 9, 13, 26, 27, 31; and description 105; and libraries 101–3; as maximalist 7, 9, 99–100, 103; *The Mezzanine* 91–101, 106, 108–14; and miniaturism 104; and optimism 5, 100, 114; *Room Temperature* 117–30; and Wikipedia 101
Barth, John 10
Barthes, Roland 62, 64, 66, 163
Bewes, Timothy 108
Bolaño, Roberto: *2666* 159–61
books: preservation of 101–3
boredom 77–9, 81–2, 85–6
Bradford, William 15–16

Carver, Raymond 15, 29; "Cathedral" 117, 121
class: in *The Pale King* 90, 92–4
commodities 106–8, 113–14; books as 25
creative writing programs 58; minimalism vs maximalism in 11–12. *See also* Program Era

DeLillo, Don 59, 84; *White Noise* 100
description 25, 105; and capitalism 66–7; and detail 84–90, 151–2; in *Infinite Jest* 62–4, 67, 68; Lukács'

critique of 13–14, 64–6; in *The Mezzanine* 105, 109; as skill 22
detail: and the feminine 13; and information age 80; and intimacy 158; and material culture 14–15; and memory 157; and mimesis 19; preference for 48–9; and reading 21, 91, 134; and things 19; uses of in fiction 23
domesticity: in recent fiction 118–19; and writing 116

eBooks 137
encyclopedic fiction 5, 8–9

failure: in *Infinite Jest* 56–7
Ferrante, Elena 118
Fiske, John 108, 111–12
Flaubert, Gustave: *Madame Bovary* 1–2
Franzen, Jonathan 118, 137

Gaddis, William 18
gender: and domesticity 117, 119; of maximalist authors 28–9, 152
Gorz, André 92
Gravity's Rainbow (Pynchon) 9, 23–4, 27, 30; and anti-paranoia 45–6; and detail 19, 38–41, 45–8; and difficulty 37–9, 40; and giants 39–40; compared to *Inherent Vice* 139–40; paranoia 43–4; importance in postwar literary field 51–2; and readers 37–9, 50–2; and the sublime 44–5

Heidegger, Martin 79, 97–98
Hertz, Neil 44–5
human ability: vs. technology 20–1, 50, 136–8, 157; writing as record of 20–1

Infinite Jest (Wallace) 5, 6, 26–7, 29, 30, 76, 77, 78, 79, 80, 81, 82, 86, 90, 91, 121, 153; description in 2–3, 62–4, 66–7, 68–70, 71–2; difficulty of 55, 61; and fatigue 56–7, 69–70, 72, 161–2; and school culture 61–2
information age 19–21, 25–6, 151–2; class in 92–4; and maximalism 45, 79–80
Inherent Vice (Pynchon) 6, 27, 31, 118, 133, 162; compared to *Against the Day* 135; critical disinterest in 135–6; compared to *Gravity's Rainbow* 145; and the internet 136–8; and postmodernism 139–44
intelligence: maximalism and fantasies of 24–6, 38–9, 49, 52, 134–5, 137–8, 157
Internet 136–8

James, Henry 24
Jameson, Fredric 64–7
Joyce, James 17–18

Kant, Immanuel 44
Katz, Steve 3–4
Knausgaard, Karl Ove: *My Struggle* 118, 156–9
knowledge work 103; comparison to writing and reading 87–9; and maximalism 80, 84; physical aspects of 87

libraries, 101–3
literature: and anxiety of obsolescence 77; marginalization of 22–3, 163
Lukács, Georg: critique of description 19, 64–6; critique of detailed writing 13–14; on commodities 106–7; on totalization 43, 113

McCarthy, Cormac 77
McGurl, Mark 11, 22, 29, 58, 104
Mandel, Ernst 111
Marxism: and commodity form 106–8; and reification 108
masculinity 116, 119; and maximalism 28, 152, 154
material culture 14–15, 19
maximalism: and ambitiousness 23–5; as comforting 25–7, 45; contemporary popularity of 21–2; and fantasies of ability / intelligence 20–1, 52–4, 71–2, 157–8; and gender 28–9, 152–3;

historical bias against 10–14; and the information age 19–21, 25–6, 45, 79–80, 159; and knowledge work 80, 84; and literary labor 5, 25–6, 61–2, 133–4; and the mainstream 29–30, 151–5; and mastery 20–1, 23–6, 45, 104, 152; and mimesis 2–3, 5, 21, 23–4, 27, 79–80, 99, 113–14, 128, 159; in music 7–8, 149–50; and optimism 100, 113–14; and return of the author figure 25, 152; and whiteness 28–30, 153
Melville, Herman 18, 57
memory 157
mimesis: and capitalism 13–14, 64–7; limits of 126–8, 130; maximalism and 2–3, 5, 21, 23–4, 27, 79–80, 99, 113–14, 128, 159
miniaturism 104
minimalism 7, 11–12, 22, 29–30
modernism 82–3; vs postmodernism 66
Moretti, Franco 15, 16–17
music: maximalism in 7–8, 149–50

narrative form 120–1
naturalism 2, 13–14, 19, 64
New Criticism 88

Pale King, The (Wallace) 22, 30–1, 162; and attention 16, 85–7, 91–2; and boredom 5, 16, 22, 25, 76–9, 81–4, 91–2; class in 88–9, 90, 92–4; and Puritan aesthetics 16
paranoia: as hermeneutic practice 43–4; and puritanism 15–16
Paulson, William 22
plain style 15–16
polymathy 20, 23–4, 137, 152, 154; and Pynchon 23–4, 38, 45, 49, 144
postindustrialism 76, 79–80, 84–5, 87, 93–5; class in 90
postmodernism 9, 66, 91, 139–42
Program Era, the 11–12, 57–8
Proust, Marcel 120, 159
puritans: literary style of 15–16; and paranoia 15
Pynchon, Thomas 5–6, 17, 23–5, 27, 132–3; *Against the Day*, 133–5, 138, 139, 144, 145; *Bleeding Edge* 118, 137; *Crying of Lot 49, the* 9, 39, 49, 121, 135, 139; and fantasies of intelligence 38–9; *Mason & Dixon* 134, 145; and polymathism 23–4,

38, 45, 49, 144; and postmodernism 139, 140–2, 143–4; *Vineland* 135, 138, 140–2. See also *Gravity's Rainbow*; *Inherent Vice*

race: and maximalism 28–30, 152–5
reading: as profession 21, 88–9; as work 89, 133–4, 137

Saltzman, Arthur 6, 7, 117
Sebald, W.G. 122–3
Schor, Naomi 13, 28
Schryer, Stephen 88
Stravinsky, Igor 149–50
sublime, the 44–5

technology 20–1; and libraries 102–3; and reading 136–8; and writing 20, 50
television 144
things 14–15, 19, 106–13, 161
Thing Theory 98, 106
totalization 13–14, 17, 44–4
triviality 105–6, 161

Wallace, David Foster 2–3, 6, 9, 17, 20, 22, 26, 27, 29, 30–1; and fatigue with evaluation 26, 60, 62, 69–70, 72; Impact on literary culture 59–60; Influence on interpretation 59–60, 77; on irony 143–4; and the Program Era 12, 56–7, 60, 61–2. See also *Infinite Jest*; *The Pale King*
Weisenburger, Stephen 46–52
Whitman, Walt 16–17
Wikipedia 101
work 90, 92–3. *See also* knowledge work; reading; writing
writing: and domesticity 116; as intellectual practice 23–4; as physical practice 26–7, 87–8, 151; as work 22, 25–7, 151

Yamashita, Karen Tei: *I Hotel* 28–9, 150, 153–5

Zola, Émile 14, 19, 64–5